The Fiction of Doris Lessing

The Fiction of Doris Lessing

Re-envisioning Feminism

Ratna Raman

BLOOMSBURY
NEW DELHI • LONDON • OXFORD • NEW YORK • SYDNEY

BLOOMSBURY INDIA
Bloomsbury Publishing India Pvt. Ltd
Second Floor, LSC Building No. 4, DDA Complex, Pocket C – 6 & 7,
Vasant Kunj, New Delhi, 110070

BLOOMSBURY, BLOOMSBURY INDIA and the Diana logo
are trademarks of Bloomsbury Publishing Plc

First published in India 2021
This edition published 2021

ISBN: HB: 978-93-90176-90-8; eBook: 978-93-90176-92-2
2 4 6 8 10 9 7 5 3 1

Typeset in Manipal Technologies Limited
Printed and bound in India by Replika Press Pvt. Ltd.

Contents

Acknowledgements

This book on Doris Lessing's fiction has finally taken shape around her centenary year. Lessing's work is a tour de force, easily among the most significant writing of our times. My life-long affair with Lessing's work began with a reading of *The Golden Notebook* as part of the MPhil programme at Delhi University. While I inverted an academic sand clock by registering for a doctoral dissertation, there was also a programmed biological, cultural and social clock that was being wound down simultaneously, requiring me to keep pace and work in tandem with the modern requirement of juggling multiple lives. I finished the fleshing out of my research in the interstices of times, often putting all writing on the back burner due to the insistent demands of the quotidian. This work was fuelled entirely by the hope, faith and support that family and friends invested in me.

To Subramaniam Iyer, one of the genuinely feminist men I know, I owe years of emotional and tactical support, endless rounds of tea, photocopying and more than his fair share of domesticity and parenting.

To my mother and father, for allowing me to believe that thought and writing constitute the most precious human achievement that individuals can aspire to. How I wish dad could have seen this book in print.

To Nataraj and Sandhya, my siblings, for material help and emotional bonding.

To Susan Visvanathan, for years of handholding, long conversations, reading and commenting on innumerable written drafts, unstinting support and a mellow friendship.

To Smriti and Siddhartha, my daughter and son, from whose childhoods I stole innumerable hours to read, research and write.

To Rajeswari Sunder Rajan, for an expansive and nurturing friendship and valuable advice about the dangers of going against the grain in writing a tome on a single author in postcolonial, multicultural times.

To the memory of Professor G.K. Das, who steered Lessing's fiction in my direction and was also my PhD guide briefly. I am so sorry that he is no longer around to share this moment with me.

To Malashri Lal, my supervisor, whose carefully timed motivation went a long way in furthering my research.

To the memory of my grandfathers, maternal and paternal, who did not live to see me embark on this project.

For Manni Paati and Madras Paati, my late grandmothers, and their long and incredibly demanding lives to which they gave themselves selflessly.

To Natesan, Jambunathan and Tyageshwaran, my late Chittappas, who would have been delighted to see this finished book.

To Tripta Wahi for rallying around and helping me believe in myself and my work when the going got rough.

To the British Council and the Charles Wallace Trust, a delightful six weeks at The Scottish Universities' International Summer School, Edinburgh and the pleasure of being in England, first hand. I would also like to thank the University Grants Commission for a Minor Research Grant.

I am indebted to the libraries of Delhi University in the North and South Campus, the CWDS library in Central Delhi and the Nehru Memorial Library at Teen Murti where the abundance of materials is offset by the helpfulness extended by library staff to nondescript scholars who are part of a free-floating, reading universe.

Some of the chapters in this book were developed from preliminary arguments presented at international conferences held in places like New Delhi, New Orleans and Plymouth. Duke University, North Carolina, made it possible for me to attend a week-long workshop on discussions around *The Golden Notebook*. Being on a sabbatical, away from teaching responsibilities at Sri Venkateswara College, gave me sufficient leeway to hone my writing.

To Shiv Visvanathan, Leela Gandhi, Lalitha Subbu, Kumkum Roy, Kanchana Natarajan, Bharati Sud, Anshu Malhotra and Jaya Sinha Tyagi for their interest in my work.

To my father-in-law, for a useful reader in feminist theory, and to Ahmer Anwer, Tapan Basu, Badri Raina, Sunil Charnalia,

Nita Aggarwal, Rita Sahai, Rajaram Iyer and Deepa Vasudevan for helping me expand my collection of Lessing's books by bringing me one book at a time from diverse parts of the world.

To Rajeev Agrawal, Veronica Rot, P.C. Jain and Anuj Prasad, for tech support and for deepening and widening my learning curve in computer literacy in my early dinosaur years.

The penultimate shout-out is for generations of students who have enabled me to hone my learning and teaching skills through long discussions around philosophy, ideas, ideologies, fiction, poetry, literature and feminism.

I end with deeply felt thanks to Chandrasekhar of Bloomsbury Publishing for evincing keen interest in my manuscript. I remain very admiring of his commitment to his metier and the energetic and professional manner in which he sets deadlines and delivers.

Thank you.

Introduction

The year 2020—about a hundred years after her birth in 1919—echoes some of the salient features of the year Lessing was born in. The First World War had ended and Lessing would later recall her childhood years as those in which the Great War had squatted upon her. In 2020, over a century later, the terrain continues to be that of a world at war—only the war seems to have extended itself all over the world in the form of multiple hostilities in peacetime. How do we engage with Lessing's work in the years after her centenary and what are the insights that a reading of her voluminous writing, fictional and non-fictional, provide to us as curious lay readers?

This book discusses Doris Lessing's fiction from the middle of the twentieth century to the first decade of the twenty-first century. It engages with the significance of feminism as an idea and its growth into theoretical formulations from movements that initially engaged with women's freedom, spaces and rights, to its current avatar today as a protean world view allowing for plurality and differences. The book also explores Lessing's articulation of this idea of feminism in the lived realities of women's lives, through newer constructions and representations of women's identities in the fiction that she wrote as she created new personas and new contexts for modern women.

The term 'feminism,' as Sarah Gamble points out, 'can very generally be categorised as the struggle to increase women's access to equality in a male-dominated culture'.[1] The equality that women have demanded in 'male-dominated culture' has meant asking for equal opportunities with regard to education, economic freedom, and personal and political rights in patriarchal worlds where occasionally women were sheltered and cossetted, but continued to remain second-class citizens. Women's access to learning, property and legal, political and personal rights devolved far more slowly in comparison to men's rights and were less self-evident. This involved a long struggle, and it was around such issues that women's struggles in nineteenth-century England were structured. While the earliest protests for equal rights in the modern period could be traced back to the demand for the incorporation of women in the newly formed French Constitution of 1790, the origin of the term feminism was a later development, emerging in the nineteenth century. The first usage of the word 'feminist' is now attributed to Charles Fourier.[2]

Feminism in France and England has travelled a long distance from its origins a little over 200 years ago. The second half of the nineteenth century saw an increase in women's agitations for access to education and employment and the beginnings of the suffrage movements. However, it was in the latter half of the twentieth century that there was a considerable opening up of boundaries and possibilities, particularly in terms of women's sustained participation outside of their domestic worlds.[3]

The twentieth century has recorded several legal, political and social advances in the lives of women and these have been hard-won triumphs of legislation.[4] It was in the twentieth century that women claimed for themselves political rights as citizens of the modern state, by obtaining the right to vote, thus achieving a victory—both actual and symbolic. The incorporation of legal, political and personal rights for women in England—such as the limited right to vote (1918) and the right to employment (1919), and the subsequent availability of similar rights for women in different parts of the world over some time—introduced a dramatic change in women's everyday lives, providing transformative possibilities. Women, alongside men, also witnessed two world wars—decolonisation struggles and the rise of Third World nationalisms—events that dominated the larger historical framework wherein women's victories were won.

Today, feminism is no longer spoken of as a monolithic construct but is seen as embodying multiple feminisms, rich and diverse. Women's groups and women's movements are now localised in almost every part of the world. Currently, *feminisms* is the expression used to describe movements around the globe that determine equal rights for women and demand women's access to social and political processes. The impact of feminism can be felt at the global level, and this is a feature unique to the twentieth century. It is necessary to stress that this global awareness of women's rights has been enabled, largely, by women's activism and engagement with social, political and cultural milieus—through participation, theorising, writing and praxis. This has resulted in greater dissemination of ideas and self-awareness among women, both in their individual capacities and as part of a larger group.

Writings by women, both theoretical and fictional, have also played a significant role in the spread of this consciousness. Alongside historical records, the literary text itself is a primary marker of the new dimensions that feminism incorporates, and this holds for a great deal of writing done by women—particularly in the second half of the twentieth century. Terry Eagleton, whose observations I will now draw upon, speaks of the vital role literature plays in providing symbolic forms through which new modes of subjectivity can be negotiated. Eagleton sees literature as mediating between the intimate sphere and the public sphere 'intervening to re-organize the arena of intimacy into subjective forms appropriate to the social and political goals of early capitalism.'[5] Eagleton points out that as bourgeois society develops into the modern epoch, the intimate sphere's area of influence diminishes due to the substitution of its actual functions by state education and social policy. It is at this juncture—at the blurring of distinctions between the perceived roles of the intimate sphere and public sphere—that Eagleton posits the emergence of the women's movement, which he sees as arising out of these changed conditions. Locating the conflict between the women's movements and domestic ideologies as a historic move that leads to the reformulation of the relationship between both spheres, Eagleton makes out a case for a 'fresh resurgence' of the intimate sphere in the form of feminist discourse and practice which equalises all participants because of the shared circumstance of gender.

Eagleton, of course, locates the resurgence of feminist discourse and practice in the eighteenth century. However, its most spectacular efflorescence, I would submit, took place in the latter part of the twentieth century where—due to a further blurring of the intimate and public spheres and an opening up of the world—women gained more visibility than ever before.

The end of the first half of the twentieth century ushered in a changed geopolitical scenario. The end of two world wars marked the shift from a Eurocentric focus on the world to a headcount of newly formed Third World identities. In this brave new world, the recognition of plural identities provided exciting possibilities, particularly in the context of women's lives. Both in terms of the possibilities in everyday lives and of experience voiced through fiction, women's writing recorded a quantitative and qualitative increase. Fiction and poetry writing by women, in this new environment, achieved new levels of self-articulation and expression. This articulation—while it originated from the point of women's lived experience—has grown and expanded enormously. This is reflected subsequently in feminist discourse and practice, which has gone from strength to strength in the last three decades of the twentieth century. From accounts of self-articulation and self-expression, women's writing has engaged in theoretical and polemical debates—throwing open all manner of possibilities for all participants, irrespective of gender, race and class. This aspect of feminism provides new inputs and fresh insights for the future course of civilisation.

This book interweaves some representative fictional works by Doris Lessing (1919–2013) and her engagement with feminism in the twentieth and the twenty-first century. It explores Lessing's articulation of feminism through a study of her characters—predominantly women. The year 2019 marked one hundred years of Doris Lessing's life, a woman with a writing career that stretched well over six long decades. Lessing lived out over ninety-two extraordinary years and creatively chronicled women's lives, mapping dilemmas at the personal, cultural and ideological levels.

This book also examines how Lessing's prescient writing draws the reader's attention to the shifts within feminism—from a predominantly white middle-class movement in the first half of the twentieth century to a far more widespread and diffuse global movement. Writing prolifically since the 1940s, Doris Lessing's repertoire of novels, poems, non-fiction, plays, short stories, and two full-length autobiographies is extensive. Lessing draws attention to the white woman, both patriarchal victim and oppressor, in her very first book. Arguably, Lessing is the first modern woman writer of the twentieth century who shifts the gaze from the white male protagonist to the white female and allows us to engage critically with their perspective.

The tensions in white middle-class feminism when it encounters the differences of race, sexuality and culture continue to be reflected in Lessing's work. As a white colonial who grew up in Southern Rhodesia—now Zimbabwe—and as a woman writer, Lessing's writing from its inception was located in the interstices of race and culture. Her move back to England in 1949, early on in her literary career, and her decision to live in cosmopolitan London subsequently allowed her a ringside view of developments related to women's issues in the Western world.

Her reading of two very different geographical and cultural spaces—namely, the Third World and the First World—serves as a sensitive barometer for feminism in the twentieth century. Although her fiction draws upon various issues that the English novel has engaged with over the last two hundred years or so, Lessing's depiction of women has broken new ground. Lessing has shared an uneasy relationship with the insular, white middle-class world that she was thrust into upon her return to England and her work has engaged with rewritings and reorientations. Although Lessing has sometimes anticipated and prophesied events well before their occurrence, there have been occasional skirmishes and fracas between her perception of women's rights and the opinion of the contemporary world. Despite an extensive detailing of women's lives in her fiction, Lessing has often directed uncharitable remarks at women's movements in interviews and public pronouncements.[6]

One controversy between Lessing and other feminists was triggered by Lessing's alleged observations at the Edinburgh International Book Festival in August 2001 where she was accused of lamenting 'the end of feminism'. This is not the exact phrase that Lessing herself used, but Jeanette Winterson attributes this viewpoint to Lessing. Given the widespread nature of feminist studies and the influential set of Lessing aficionados, the literary exchange and the subsequent rebuttals found adequate coverage in Indian papers too.[7]

A few internet searches made available both the newspaper item reporting Lessing's statements and Winterson's rebuttal. To briefly recapitulate: Lessing's unhappiness seems to have been set off by a public visit she made to a school where a teacher, hoping to make a good impression on Lessing, told a class of nine- and ten-year-old children that 'the reason for wars was the innately violent nature of men.' Seizing on this generalisation as an instance of a 'lazy and insidious culture' within feminism, Lessing launched off into an attack on 'the unthinking and automatic rubbishing of men' that 'the most stupid, ill-educated and nasty woman' could indulge in without evoking any protest whatsoever.[8] One feels a little sorry for the unfortunate teacher who could have been using the term 'men' generically. Terms such as 'men' and 'mankind'—the disapproval of feminist linguists notwithstanding—continue to be used as indicative of both men and women.

Lessing's outburst, which was reported in the press, triggered off accusations of both betrayal and senility. Winterson—one of the earliest respondents to Lessing's reported observations—roundly trounced the notion that men were 'continually demeaned and insulted' by women, by drawing attention to the anomalies between men and women in every sphere of public life. She upbraided Lessing for refusing to recognise that '[a]s far as the power struggle goes, men are still on top'.[9] It is difficult, on the face of it, to fault Jeanette Winterson's response. More men are holding remunerative positions in comparison to women and they will continue to be there for a long time in almost every part of the world. In terms of numerical statistics, Winterson will continue to be right.

Yet, is this numerical headcount the only way of evaluating the significance of feminism? Today, one of the claims that can be made for feminism is its more holistic perspective, and its ability to visualise a happier and more equitable world based on possibilities that are not reducible to female heads outnumbering men in every sphere. Although biologically this is the process prescribed by Mother Nature, and the girl child is certainly considered to be better equipped to survive in nature, to propagate such a viewpoint culturally would be to merely replicate an inverted form of sexism—although the demographics in patriarchal societies have seen a drastic reduction in the numbers of women when compared to the number of men, Lessing herself has remained wary of and distanced from projecting such patterns through her work.

I would like to suggest that Lessing's earlier confrontations with feminism had also been based on her unwillingness to identify with any kind of essentialism in reading the lives of either women or men. In the late 1960s, women's groups appropriated Lessing's *The Golden Notebook* as their 'bible'. In response to this appropriation, Lessing wrote a preface to the novel in 1971; this has subsequently been a part of all further editions. Here, Lessing first announced her support for women's liberation, but hastened to point out that the entire world was 'being shaken into a new pattern by the cataclysms we are living through: probably by the time we are through, if we do get through at all, the aims of Women's Liberation will look very small and quaint.'[10] Lessing's words at this juncture were directed at the women's rights groups formed in Hull in 1968, whose agitations were primarily structured around four non-negotiable requirements—namely, equal pay, equal education and opportunity, twenty-four-hour nurseries and free contraception and abortion on demand.[11] These were also predominantly white middle-class gatherings that were subsequently challenged for their limited perspectives by feminists of colour a decade later.[12]

Lessing's remarks at the book festival in 2001 do not seem to be cognizant of the tremendous inroads made by two decades or more of pluralistic feminism. Her blanking out on these changes—either inadvertently or as deliberate provocation—seems reductive in the context of the increasing rise of women's solidarity. It needs to be stated at the outset that although the women's 'libbers' of the 1960s were predominantly white, from England and heterosexual, it was their initial questioning of the *status quo* that provided the impetus for subsequent disquiet, awareness and protest amongst women with differing cultural, political and separatist ideologies. Yet, to dismiss Lessing as anti-feminist based on this particular outburst would be tantamount to throwing out the proverbial baby with the bathwater.

Lessing's position on feminism, one feels compelled to stress, is markedly different from the one that Winterson's remarks attribute to her. Elsewhere in the article, Winterson targets Lessing's generation—placing Lessing among the feminists of 'the 70s, the golden age of the women's movement, that gave us the really damaging, batty stuff; all men are rapists, all sex is power, pornography is abuse, marriage is a crime. And what about separatism and political lesbians? Thank God those days are gone.'[13] Winterson's location of Lessing's oeuvre within the parameters of feminism in the 1970s is inaccurate not only in terms of actual dates but is also a complete misrepresentation of the spirit of Lessing's work.

Lessing, it must be reiterated, was writing and publishing in the 1940s, and her first full-length novel *The Grass is Singing* was published in 1950. As a writer of feminist fiction, Lessing's novels predate the movements of the 1970s by well over two decades. As my subsequent analysis of Lessing's key narratives will show, she has seldom concurred with any of the readings that Winterson identifies as the contribution of 1970s feminism. Lessing's fiction is the best evidence that can be offered of Lessing's ideological distance from the feminists of the 'golden age' of the 1970s when 'separatism' and 'political lesbians' were rampant.

Lessing's sensitivity to women's lives and alertness to the dangers of blinkered thinking go hand in hand. Lessing's ire is directed towards a particular kind of entitled feminist politics, which she has consistently disavowed. She makes it very clear from her earliest novel that her understanding of inequality and unfairness is located beyond and outside essentialist descriptions of gender, wherein notions of the masculine and the feminine are confined within biological male and female bodies respectively.[14] Lessing's work thereby opens up the possibilities of investigating feminism not merely as a politically expedient formula or as a fad but as a larger, philosophical world view that is still in the process of consolidating itself.

This book hopes to place Lessing as a feminist writer who dealt with women's issues and lives as women experienced them—long before what Winterson terms 'the golden age of the women's movement' came into existence. Lessing, as I will show, writes from the 'margins of empire'[15] and provides meaningful insight into the politics of race, class and gender, particularly in the contemporary context. Lessing's criticism of male-bashing by women is in keeping with her refusal to entertain any form of essentialism in her treatment of male or female characters. Her fiction is sensitive to the predicament of women characters and has invariably focused on what could be called a woman's point of view, from which standpoint, she has consistently spoken for the freedom and self-expression of the small, private individual.[16]

Yet, at no point in her fiction does Lessing overlook the larger systems that provide agency to her characters. She has also been responsive to the social and cultural processes through which women continue to be silenced. Lessing's articulation of the lived reality of women's lives is a conscious attempt to give voice to the hitherto silenced and suppressed dimensions of women's identities. This can be seen from the other observations that she made at the same book festival which, unfortunately, have been overlooked. As she points out: 'Great things have been achieved through feminism. We now have pretty much equality at least on the pay and opportunities front, though almost nothing has been done on child care, the real liberation'.[17]

Lessing's observation that women's leadership has been unable to alter or modify the cultural structuring of childcare—which is still viewed as women's work—shows her shrewd understanding of the ground realities of women's lives even today. This is completely overlooked by Winterson. Her essay refers to articulate and economically savvy men and women, who are required to merely redistribute ironing and cooking duties between them. They are part of an elite, urban world where stagnant and decimating population statistics are the order of the day:

> My taxi driver told me that he thinks of himself as boss in his marriage, but he understands why his wife won't do his ironing. He doesn't care—he was one of the first to buy a Power Iron. Him and his mates do it together trying to get the fastest time while they watch the football.[18]

This is not true of many developing societies where the rearing of children consumes the prime years of a woman's life and continues to be culturally ratified as part of a woman's responsibilities. Childcare facilities are yet to be seen as part of shared, community investment. Both the state and the community view child-rearing as the domestic responsibility of women within nuclear households, wherein women live the life of second-class citizens.

Ironically, the identification of childcare as domestic work and women's work is almost universal—whether we speak of children in maximum infrastructure-based countries such as Sweden and Scandinavia, or in places that George Bush repeatedly describes as the 'civilized world'.[19] Although paternity leave facilities have been introduced as a limited option in some countries, maternity benefits remain meagre. A maximum of twenty-eight weeks of maternity leave is provided by the Czech Republic, twenty-four weeks by Hungary, five months by Italy and eighteen weeks by Norway and Denmark, while the ILO Standard for maternity leave is twelve weeks.[20]

In the developing world—despite the cushioning provided by the extended family—childcare facilities are not available to women equitably and are invariably subject to all kinds of vagaries. This holds, with little variation, across the class and caste divide. The absence of childcare facilities on one hand and its relegation as an essentially female responsibility within the domestic sphere on the other is further aggravated by constricting and meagre allowances provided by the state for working mothers. In India, for instance, paid maternity leave for a maximum period of sixteen weeks was subsequently revised for a period of up to twenty-four weeks—a benefit that is now available primarily to central and state government employees.

Yet, one only has to look at a central university—such as Delhi University with its attendant eighty-odd colleges—to understand how these long-fought rights and provisions can be overridden or given short shrift. For the last thirteen years, there have been no permanent appointments in undergraduate colleges which employ young men and women. The duration of their jobs is now four months, and these ad-hoc appointments—on lines similar to that of adjunct professors in universities in the United States—provide little job security and even less sustenance. In these new circumstances, highly qualified young women with MPhils and PhDs, who are also in their childbearing years, cannot avail maternity leave or medical reimbursement. Terrified of being expendable, they take unpaid leave for a month or less and return speedily to work—leaving two-week or month-old infants at home with family and desultory help. While this is a terrible situation for families and infants, paid maternity leave, childcare facilities and medical allowances continue to be arbitrary in the private sector and do not even exist on paper for women who work in the unorganised sector.

Childbearing and nurture, despite feminist intervention, continue to be seen as private activity—*for, by* and *of* the domestic sphere. Maternity leave, it must be noted, also reinforces the role of women as primarily that of caregivers and allows men to transfer responsibility for childrearing to women. This remains an issue for women's groups to engage with to redress the imbalance in the distribution of freedoms and opportunities. Lessing's emphasis on the devolving of child nurture from women's primary responsibility towards an activity collectively shared by both sexes and the community needs to be addressed rigorously. The rights of children and the freedoms of innumerable mothers across the class divide also require articulation and redressal.

Modern fiction that seeks to understand the material realities of women's lives in different cultures and address their concerns has been the context from which my work on Lessing began. In this book, I will also engage with the history of ideas that shaped Lessing's work, the traditions that she is heir to and the interventions she makes through her fiction.

Lessing's Feminism and Feminism's Lessing

Doris Lessing, born in 1919, is located at a very tumultuous point in history—towards the end of the first phase of the feminist movement and well before the revival of the women's movements in the 1960s. Lessing's work interconnects with ideas that are of prime importance to feminism, particularly in the second half of the twentieth century. Lessing grew up in the years after the First World War, when the first phase of the feminist movement was fading out and the right to suffrage was slowly being extended to more and more women in Europe and around the world.[21]

Despite women's increased access to political and civil rights, the centrality of their existence and its relevance to life and society was yet to be affirmed. As Sheila Rowbotham points out, 'by applying a gender lens to a whole range of issues, from social policy to industrial relations, from religion to the forms of protest in social movements, new historical perspectives have emerged',[22] providing us with fresh insights. Stressing the fact that even as late as 1969 the assumption 'that women's lives mattered or that what women had done had shaped this century was not self-evident,'[23] Rowbotham emphasises the need for highlighting, refocusing and retrieving women's experience. Lessing's fiction, through its close focus on women's lives and histories, provides valuable cultural studies of women.

Lessing's novels show the residual traces of important political, social and historical events in the lives of her female protagonists. Women at the beginning of the twentieth century drew their strength from major ideas and debates originating in the Victorian period, and Lessing's fictionalised and actual accounts of her mother Maud McVeagh's life demonstrate this. Lessing's impressionable years were spent in absorbing the atmosphere of her mother's times while simultaneously charting her own differences. Lessing's writing demonstrates the shifts in perspective from her mother's generation to her own, thereby providing an important record of women in the twentieth century. Her eclectic reading—as well as her exposure to ideas and literature from England—is reflected in her narratives which provide linkages between earlier literary texts and the new contexts in which her protagonists and readers find themselves.

Lessing's early experience away from England, her largely solitary childhood and her voracious reading in her years of growing up—encouraged by books and journals ordered by her mother from England—contributed a great deal towards her gifts as a novelist. Born between two wars, coming of age in the years of imperialism, racism and left-inspired political struggle and wending her way through personal and political crises as a woman contributed enormously to Lessing's recognition of the complexities of the world she inhabited. This was a period when political structures were reshuffled as a result of the demand for both individual and national rights. Lessing's writing began at a time when the stranglehold of imperialism was beginning to loosen its grip, and the voices of nationalism were asserting themselves.

Lessing's exposure to cultures outside of British life in her formative years is significant. Lessing could have very easily been a competent, conventional writer writing about the English middle class, had her parents stayed on in England. Instead, their decision to seek fortunes in maize in Southern Rhodesia in 1924 unalterably pushed her outside of the routinely prescribed life which might have been hers in suburban, insular England. Her growing up within new geographical boundaries where the long arm of British commerce and imperialism extended is responsible for how she views a whole range of issues. Lessing's exposure to Persia and, to a much greater extent, Southern Rhodesia gave her an altogether different perspective. An exposure to landscapes, ideas, experience and education outside of England, it needs to be stressed, gave Lessing a unique positioning as a narrator, commentator, critic and chronicler of events. It allowed her, on the one hand, to engage with the central debates of the twentieth century, and on the other, to provide a new dimension sharply at variance with Eurocentric viewpoints. Lessing remains an eclectic writer who—while engaging with the *zeitgeist* of her times in her work and her thinking—articulates a markedly different sensibility. This critical distancing is Lessing's most distinguishing feature as a writer.

Lessing's fictional writing focuses on women and their intersection around the questions of race, gender and positionality, locating them within a long tradition of women's histories. Lessing's later narratives engage with the location of value in women's lives and roles. Her fiction shares the concern of recent feminist literature in its attempts to restructure both language and thinking. It is very seldom that the Lessing text takes anything for granted. There is an insistent re-examination of ideas, precepts, theories, relationships and active engagement with emerging possibilities such as feminist ethics. Lessing's creation of memorable women characters is only one half of the story. In her fiction after *The Golden Notebook*—often seen as her *magnum opus*—Lessing continues to engage with the restructuring of language and thought that is central to recent feminist literature, criticism and critical theory.[24]

Doris Lessing has authored over forty texts, both fictional and non-fictional, in forms varying from the short essay to poems, plays, novellas, serialised fiction and science fiction, to say nothing of experimental writing in the form of notebooks, diaries and memoirs between 1945 and 2005. This prolific output is accompanied by a formidable corpus of criticism that has engaged with her work over the last four decades. It is beyond the scope of any single book on Doris Lessing to discuss all her writings, and the sheer volume of secondary reading material makes reading every single piece on her work a daunting task. In my discussion of Lessing's work over the last six decades, I discuss each decade through one major text and make connections with other interlinked narratives written in the same decade. This book examines Lessing's creation of new spaces for women in fiction over seven chapters and analyses her reworking of older images of women and rewriting them back into history.

I would like to close this introduction to Lessing's fiction by drawing attention to the important themes raised in two of her recent books—namely, *The Cleft* (2007) and *Alfred and Emily* (2008).

The Cleft operates on the level of myth and allegory. Part of the female anatomy itself, the Cleft is also geographical territory designed by mounds, crevices and water in a magical land wherein women lead hermaphrodite lives with great ease and reproduce by giving birth to other female children. Yet a dark mystery surrounds them, which the text uncovers at leisure. The women also give birth to male children called Squirts, whom they find repugnant and offer up as sacrifices to the great eagles that take away the abandoned children. Lessing may be redressing the almost banal destruction of the female child in cultures across the world through her narrative in which the male of the species comes to harm; also, the nomenclature of women and men as Clefts and Squirts—based entirely on their reproductive paraphernalia—is delightfully comic.

The majestic eagles do not devour the discarded male babies but set them up on another island, where female deer suckle the infants and enable them to survive as fully fledged adults. Tensions and explorations in the narrative are set up around these two singular communities and their eventual points of interaction that progress from rejection and mutilation of the Squirts to curiosity, rape and murder of the Clefts, and then, some sort of uneasy truce that leads to a shift from lives as hermaphrodite women to women who need to mate with men to produce children.

The Cleft pokes fun at male hegemonic structures by showing us how women can construct similar hierarchies. It engages closely with the problems that originate from a space of insularity and control. It also explores the growth of violence and fear that is generated in the absence of any real understanding or empathy, thereby providing important life lessons.

Alfred and Emily, written after *The Cleft*, is a short novella followed with excerpts from Lessing's previously published writing. In *Alfred and Emily*, Lessing rewrites the lives of her parents—giving them fictional lives that both of them aspired to before the war threw them together and pushed them away to a new continent, where they struggled in strange unfamiliar landscapes.

Alfred and Emily come of age in England, in the manner of many ordinary men and women impacted by the world wars who did not leave familiar England for an unknown land. Lessing outlines for the reader a story of imagined life set in suburban England where Alfred does not marry Emily but lives a comfortable rustic life—playing cricket at Colchester and raising a family between the wars. Emily's story, on the other hand, takes into account the life of the new woman of the twentieth century who chooses to carve out a different life and finds for the first time in her life, a historical time willing to aid her in her search. Resisting a father and stepmother who want her to choose differently, Emily leaves home to train as a nurse and serves as one during the war—eventually marrying her beau, a successful doctor. She gives up her job later and lives in London, partaking of its rich cultural life. Her husband dies—leaving her with considerable means which she uses to set up libraries and empower poor children in many villages all over England, establishing a model teaching school. Emily's school is shut down because of a hostile response from the local community, echoing for us paradigms that continue to date. Emily lives into her seventies and dies as a result of injuries sustained while trying to save stray dogs from unknown young men at a Tube station. With Emily's death, the impersonal malevolence of the twenty-first century announces itself.

In a sense, this novella is a tidier rendering of the lives of her parents, which were difficult in reality. At another level, the fact that the conditions of war prevail over the lives of the protagonists—despite it being a time of peace—is a sobering reminder of the belligerent world we inhabit. Following the novella is a memoir and autobiographical bits and a detailed history of the hospital where Maud McVeagh—Lessing's mother—worked, making us recall the privilege of medical facilities and the lack of access to it for a large majority; also, reminding us how a lot of things continue to remain the same. Although the modern hospital has rewritten the mysteries of life and health, it continues to limit access to its facilities and sets up hierarchies. Lessing's twenty-first-century narratives push us towards a careful examination of the new structures of power in play in our times.

Chapter I, an introductory frame, locates Lessing's life and work amidst women's movements and feminist theories over half a century. It spells out briefly some central aspects of the feminist movements in the twentieth century. Three of Lessing's short stories, eloquent chronicles on women's lives, will be taken up for discussion. Though 'The Trinket Box' (1964) and 'One off the Short List' (1963) are separated from 'Debbie and Julie' (1989) by a distance of over twenty-five years in Lessing's literary career, they provide a broad overview of the range and scope of her work.

Chapter II looks closely at Lessing's first novel *The Grass is Singing* (1950) and discusses Mary Turner's life as a white woman in South Africa. Although sharing several similarities with the 'New Woman',[25] Mary's personal story is enmeshed within the larger history of colonialism and race. Lessing's narrative, by shifting geographical space, provides a shift in the reader's focus; we are made to engage not only with Mary's dilemma as an independent woman caught in a bad marriage but also with the power she wields in a racial society. We are forced to look closely at the issues raised by Mary's racial privileges—namely, the marginalising of the Black man and the systematic denial of his rights. *The Grass is Singing* is a post-Second World War narrative that shows how in a racial context where larger human rights are vested in a small minority of women—who traditionally form part of the group whose interests are overlooked—they can be co-opted and thus may often collude with the minority elite in acts of oppression.

Mary Turner's story—had it not been enmeshed in racial politics—could have been seen as following the trajectory of the New Woman heroines of the Edwardian period. Lessing, however, writes from a very different location—one in which she looks askance at the enterprise of empire. What Lessing records in this novel through the failure of Mary Turner is the limited vision of white middle-class feminism. As readers, we are prodded towards redefining both the boundaries of women's identities and the socio-political imperatives they spring from.

The Grass is Singing analyses how the formation of female subjectivity is a culturally orchestrated phenomenon. By locating Mary Turner's story within the matrix of racial domination, the text makes explicit the ways in which control is exercised over women. Lessing, in showing how the system operates, is sharply critical of the upholders of civic institutions—ranging from the lawmakers of racial society, the successful white farmer and his urban counterpart, consenting rural and urban wives, the complacent and rootless poor whites and the police. Highlighting the basis of the very system that perpetuates inequalities, Lessing's novel questions the arbitrarily structured schism between public and private worlds and signals its rupture.

Chapter III will discuss *The Golden Notebook* (1962), briefly referring to *Martha Quest* (1952) and *A Proper Marriage* (1954), its sequel, thereby tracing Lessing's rewriting of the twentieth-century *bildungsroman*. It locates *The Golden Notebook* as Lessing's earliest novel that documents her radical shift from the linear, realist novel tradition that she had so far espoused. Lessing continued to experiment with newer fictional formats and, in *The Golden Notebook*, laid the groundwork for the innovations in narrative structures that she would work with subsequently. This novel's relevance cannot merely be limited to its being at the vanguard of the first phase of the women's movement in the late 1960s. It is a seminal text through which Lessing examines—as a writer, an artist and a woman—new ways of seeing and reconstructing women's experiences, imaginatively dredged from literary and political histories dating back to the French Revolution.

The 1960s mark Lessing's break with extant narrative traditions while reworking important debates that broaden the purview of feminism. Chapter III seeks to highlight this aspect and its implications for feminist philosophy.

Chapter IV analyses three of Lessing's novels, *The Four-Gated City* (1969), *The Memoirs of a Survivor* (1974) and *Briefing for a Descent into Hell* (1971). It also looks at Lessing's experiments with newer narrative forms and the philosophy behind this choice, highlighting her analysis of the world of science and the role of scientific technology in contemporary life. Using science fiction and dystopic modes of storytelling to provide a critique of civilisation, Lessing warns of the potential danger in the complacent acceptance of all scientific intervention as progress. Her narratives show existing modes of perception and value as restrictive and constraining. She is sharply critical of phallocentric and patriarchal perceptions that have been part of the dominant history of Western civilisation for well over 200 years.

Chapter V explores the question of violence. In three of her novels, Lessing raises the issue of recurring violence among humans. This analysis looks closely at the principles of governance and their implications in *The Marriages Between Zones Three, Four and Five* (1980)—the mythic and magical second part of Lessing's Canopus in Argos series. With a changed narrative mode in *The Good Terrorist* (1985)—the second novel under discussion—Lessing offers us an inside view into an ultra-left group in London. In *The Wind Blows Away Our Words* (1987)—the third book under discussion—which is part travelogue and part mythology, Lessing's visit to Afghanistan provides inputs for her examination of the revolution. It indicates that the spectre of violence that emerges in the course of political change is deeply rooted in structured hierarchies of power and control. All three novels can be viewed as test cases through which Lessing highlights the dangers implicit in violent agendas.

Chapter VI looks at the alternatives that Lessing moves towards, anticipating the new theories of the 1980s by speaking of redefining social and ethical constructions.[26] If theories of justice and rights have not contributed to the kind of general happiness and well-being that is enshrined in the constitutions of forward-looking political nations, there is perhaps an urgent need to re-examine why this is so. What precisely has been left out of the picture? Lessing's explorations of the value of care and nurture and her positing of these as providing more holistic alternatives are examined in this chapter. I will discuss two of Lessing's novels here—namely, *The Summer Before the Dark* (1973) and *The Diaries of Jane Somers* (1984). Lessing, in these books, deals with the question of effacing identities and draws attention to ageing as a significant but overlooked aspect of women's experience. She suggests that an understanding of ageing might greatly empower feminism. Providing a detailed reading of these aspects of social existence, she guides her readers to rather new and unusual conjectures.

The explicatory chapters are followed by a conclusion which examines core ideas in Lessing's hitherto undiscussed last novels. These novels voice more emphatically the arguments and perspectives that Lessing has been formulating over the past three decades.

The conclusion traces continuities between *Mara and Dann* (1999) and *The Sweetest Dream* (2001), and the earlier narratives explored by Lessing. Both books subvert older constructions of the domestic sphere and the notions of family life, incessantly examining and unknotting accepted paradigms. Oddly, the timescale highlighted in *The Sweetest Dream* is the period between the 1940s and the 1980s—decades that are historically significant and formative as far as Lessing is concerned. Lessing throws up deeply disturbing questions and anxieties about human life in her treatment of both the household and the public sphere in these novels, unsettling the reader. If the purpose of literature is to enable us to view the world we live in from a different perspective, to push us into asking uncomfortable questions and to redefine our understanding of ourselves and our worlds, Lessing's fiction effectively carries out this function.

Endnotes

1. Sarah Gamble, ed., *The Routledge Companion to Feminism and Postfeminism* (New York and London: Routledge, 2001), vii.
2. Charles Fourier was a nineteenth-century intellectual and political activist who 'imagined a "new woman" who would both transform and be herself

transformed by a society based on association and mutuality', documented in Sheila Rowbotham, *Women in Movement: Feminism and Social Action* (New York and London: Routledge, 1992), 8. Karen Offen opines that the word 'feminist' is erroneously attributed to Fourier and that it was first used by Hubertine Auclerat in 1882, as mentioned in Karen Offen, *European Feminisms, 1700–1950: A Political History* (California: Stanford University Press, 2000), 19. It is possible to look back further into history and trace earlier instances of resistance on the part of women, but for the purposes of this thesis, I will confine myself to a foregrounding of what is politically and historically acknowledged as the beginnings of the modern period.

3. Sheila Rowbotham, *A Century of Women: The History of Women in Britain and the United States* (London and New York: Viking Books, 1997; London and New York: Penguin Books, 1999), 3–5. All further references are from the 1999 edition.
4. See Helen Blackburn, *Women's Suffrage: A Record of the Women's Suffrage Movement in the British Isles, with Biographical Sketches of Miss Becker* (London and Oxford: Williams & Norgate, 1902), 222, for a chart indicating the changes in the activities of women in the years between 1831 and 1901. This was perhaps due to a heightened awareness of the suffrage issue and the coming out of women into public areas for work and their increased mobility as a result of industrial, urban and colonial expansion.
5. Terry Eagleton uses Jürgen Habermas' definition of the intimate sphere—referring to the family and household. He records women's historical exclusion from participation in the public sphere and its culture—social and political functions—as distinctly noticeable in the eighteenth century. This is in spite of the intimate sphere's contribution of impulses and energies to the public sphere in Terry Eagleton, *The Function of Criticism* (London: Verso, 1984), 8–9.
6. Lessing's interviews record her skirmishes with feminism. In one such interview in 1969, Lessing declared, 'I'm impatient with people who emphasize sexual revolution. I say we should all go to bed, shut up about sexual liberation, and go on with the important matters'. Doris Lessing, 'Doris Lessing at Stony Brook,' interview by Jonah Raskin, in *A Small Personal Voice: Essays, Reviews, Interviews*, ed. Paul Schlueter (United States: Alfred A. Knopf, 1974; New York: Vintage Books, 1975), 71. The reference corresponds to the 1975 edition. Again, at the height of the women's movements—when her best-known work, *The Golden Notebook*,

was making waves—Lessing, in her 1971 preface to the novel, was sceptical about the women's movements: 'I don't think that Women's Liberation will change much'. Unwilling to have her book co-opted by the women's liberation movements of the late 1960s and early 1970s, she reiterated that her 'novel was not a trumpet for Women's Liberation'. Doris Lessing, preface to *The Golden Notebook* (New York: Simon & Schuster, 1962; London: Flamingo, 1993), 8. All further references are from the 1993 edition.

7. Hasan Suroor, 'A Feminist Rallies Behind Men,' *The Hindu*, August 16, 2001, 15.
8. See Fiachra Gibbons, 'Lay off men, Lessing tells feminists,' *The Guardian,* August 14, 2001, https://www.theguardian.com/uk/2001/aug/14/edinburghfestival2001.edinburghbookfestival2001.
9. See Jeanette Winterson, 'What planet is Doris on?' *The Guardian,* August 15, 2001, https://www.theguardian.com/books/2001/aug/15/edinburghfestival2001.edinburghfestival.
10. Lessing, *The Golden Notebook*, 8.
11. For a detailed account of the women's rights groups formed in spring 1968 in Hull, and their demands, see Sheila Rowbotham, 'The Beginnings of Women's Liberation in Britain', in *The Body Politic: Writings from the Women's Liberation Movement in Britain, 1969–1972*, ed. Michelene Wandor (London: Stage 1, 1972), 91–102.
12. Stevi Jackson and Sue Scott trace the strongly heterosexual nature of the women's movements in the late 1960s and early 1970s. Political lesbianism made an appearance in Radicalesbians in the US, in 1970, as an escape from and challenge against patriarchal domination as mentioned in Stevi Jackson and Sue Scott, eds., *Feminism and Sexuality: A Reader* (Edinburgh: Edinburgh University Press, 1996), 13–25. Also see the interview where Davis records her total lack of connection with 'what the white women's liberationists were doing'. Angela Y. Davis, 'Complexity, Activism, Optimism: An Interview with Angela Y. Davis,' interview by Kum-Kum Bhavnani, *Feminist Review,* no. 31 (Spring 1989): 69. She draws attention to the absence of Black women in the white women's movements of the 1960s and the completely different orientation of the Black Women's Alliance formed in the late 1970s.
13. Winterson, '*What Planet is Doris on*?'
14. For feminist readings that refuse the essentialist connotations of gender, wherein women are seen as different from men on account of their

biology, see Nancy Chodorow, 'Gender, Relation, and Difference in Psychoanalytic Perspective,' in *Feminist Social Thought: A Reader*, ed. Diana Tietjens Meyers (New York and London: Routledge, 1997), 7–20. See also Joan W. Scott, 'Gender: A Useful Category of Historical Analysis,' *The American Historical Review* 91, no. 5 (December 1986): 1053–1075.

15. Jeannette King makes this point in the preface to her book, Jeannette King, *Doris Lessing* (London and New York: Edward Arnold, 1989), ix, where she locates an incipient feminism in Lessing's fiction. Louise Yelin locates Lessing as a spokesperson for Western, white middle-class women's positions in Lousie Yelin, *From the Margins of Empire: Christina Stead, Doris Lessing, Nadine Gordimer* (Ithaca and London: Cornell University Press, 1998), 55–107.
16. Doris Lessing, 'A Small Personal Voice,' in *Declaration,* ed. Tom Maschler (London: MacGibbon & Kee, 1957), 12–27.
17. Lessing as quoted in Gibbons, 'Lay off men, Lessing tells feminists.'
18. Winterson, 'What planet is Doris on?'
19. The projection of the United States as civilised and representing exalted values of freedom and justice is the running theme of countless speeches by President Bush. There is a recurrent construction of the United States and its allies as part of a civilised world, standing for all manner of good, in the Selected Speeches. See pages 70, 83 and 101 of 'Selected Speeches of President George W. Bush: 2001–2008,' White House Archives, last modified January 19, 2009, https://georgewbush-whitehouse.archives.gov/infocus/bushrecord/documents/Selected_Speeches_George_W_Bush.pdf.
20. For more systematic tabulation of maternity leave and other benefits country-wise, see 'More than 120 Nations Provide Paid Maternity Leave,' ILO Press Release, last modified February 15, 1998, https://www.ilo.org/global/about-the-ilo/newsroom/news/WCMS_008009/lang--en/index.htm. The report points out that despite the gains, the fundamental problem of unequal treatment experienced by all working women in their professional lives remains unresolved. The information provided in the rest of the paragraph is summarised from the same source.
21. Finland granted voting rights to women as early as 1906 and Norway in 1913 while Iceland and Denmark followed suit in 1915. With the exception of Switzerland and Portugal—where women acquired political rights as late as 1971 and 1976 respectively—women in major Western countries acquired political rights between the wars, according to Marriete Sineau,

'Law and Democracy,' in *A History of Women in the West: Toward a Cultural Identity in the Twentieth Century*, ed. Françoise Thébaud, trans. Arthur Goldhammer (1994; Cambridge, Massachusetts and London: Harvard University Press, 1996), 5:500. The reference is from the 1996 edition.

22. Rowbotham, *A Century of Women*, 3.
23. Rowbotham, *A Century of Women*, 3.
24. For an overview on the subject, see Deborah Cameron, ed., *The Feminist Critique of Language: A Reader* (London and New York: Routledge, 1991), 1–31.
25. Eric Hobsbawm, 'The New Woman,' in *The Age of Empire, 1875–1914* (London: Cardinal Books, 1987), 192–242.
26. Nancy Chodorow, *The Reproduction of Mothering: Psychoanalysis and the Sociology of Gender* (Berkeley: University of California Press, 1978) speaks of the relational associations women make as a result of their processes of socialisation. Adding strength to her work is Carol Gilligan's research and documentation of women subjects in Carol Gilligan, *In a Different Voice: Psychological Theory and Women's Development* (Massachusetts and London: Harvard University Press, 1982), that leads her to conclude that women view most given situations very differently from men.

I

Lessing and Feminism

'Women often get dropped from memory, and then history.'[1]

This statement from Lessing's first formal autobiography exemplifies what has been her most singular concern as a writer. Chronicling women's lives, Lessing's work engages with the articulation of women's voices and seeks to retrieve these by bringing them back into focus. She achieves this in her fiction through diverse narrative techniques comprising notebooks, diaries, history, memory, myth, fantasy and memoirs. Lessing's astute grasp of modern politics and social reality is layered and intermeshed with her use of ancient myths and narratives, which can be seen at work in her fiction. Locating her women characters within complex grids and showing them grappling with the dilemmas of race, class, history, sexuality and literary representation, Lessing creates a wide spectrum of female characters in situations ranging from the banal and every day to the mythical and extraterrestrial. Thus, we encounter a continued involvement with the structure of women's lives and experiential reality in her novels. In this chapter, I would like to examine Lessing's work in the broader context of the history of modern feminism in order to make connections between her life and work, draw attention to aspects of the larger historical period she grew up in and show how her oeuvre as a writer maps the developments within feminism in the twentieth century.

My fascination with Lessing's work began as a Third World reader of literature written in English, residing in a postcolonial space. For years I was formed and shaped by the magic of this language and its narratives while I negotiated my daily identity—that of being a female, urban middle-class, upper-caste and independent-from-colonial-rule Indian. Shuttling between my twin identities, one formed by the willing suspension of disbelief between pages of the printed text and the other shaped by my own cultural history, I began to slowly identify points of similarity and difference in the narratives that had so far constructed me. Early enough in my reading, both text and context invariably began to problematise my identity as a female. One was a biological given and another I could feel slowly evolving through the mediations of culture and ritual—that of becoming feminine.

The next step of resisting this newly developing feminine identity and voicing my difference with it was fraught with difficulty. I knew my points of objection, my anger at the inequities and unfair distribution of rights and responsibilities and the need for protest in general. In using the language and literature that I had grown up with to record my protest, I became aware of both slippages and silences.

Intriguingly, the language and literature that had spoken to me so freely in my androgynous identity became constraining when it addressed me in my new identity as a woman. Rejecting confinement within a feminine identity that was becoming prescriptive was my initial response. Moving towards feminism as a starting point from which I could renegotiate and articulate my position became the logical next move. This, however, has been a long and arduous journey and one fraught with many dangers. It was easy enough to identify all that I did not want as part of my personal, professional and intellectual luggage. To speak up clearly for what it was that I wanted and identify it for myself remained an onerous task.

From a personal space, there is an inadvertent slide into questions of history and location. Coming of age in the last quarter of the twentieth century in a modern democratic state, hazily absorbing notions of equality and freedom and women's rights, I also desired to track down the groundswell of my inspiration—seemingly influenced indirectly by the movements for democracy in modern Europe. When I look back at the lives lived by countless women relatives in the generations that preceded mine, I continue to marvel at the power of ideas to circumvent histories and geographies and sow the seeds of change.

This book traces the journey of Western feminism from its Eurocentric origins to the humungous transformative possibilities it has unsheathed in a global context while being absorbed, assimilated and modified by diverse cultures. What have been the significant features of feminism in the modern West? What period in history can one imaginatively push back to, in order to discover this? How did a movement that was originally Eurocentric generate such widespread appeal? These are some of the issues that this preliminary discussion addresses. While it is no longer possible to talk about feminism as a homogeneous movement, one can see a composite development of women's agendas in its exciting propagation and re-propagation in different parts of the world. Widespread dissemination of the political awareness of rights for women has been a major feminist achievement since the time of the suffrage movements at the end of the nineteenth century.

Feminism has shifted the focus of perception by engaging with women's rights and making them the fulcrum from which to re-examine all manner of assumptions. In doing so, feminism has posited a whole new way of looking at the social, political and personal issues that have confronted women. Its significance, not only as a critical literary tool but also as an empowering ideology and philosophy, will be explored through this analysis. This preliminary chapter will provide a working definition of feminism and examine how it has imaginatively reinvented itself in this century.

As a student of literature, some of my most fascinating insights into feminism have been provided by feminist intervention within a coded text. When writers took to writing and wrote in an unrestrained manner, they managed to create a dialogic space in otherwise monolithic structures. Literature enables us to mediate through the hierarchies of experience, albeit in fictional formats. Such intervention on the part of the writer, thus, becomes an act of subversion which provides new perspectives on ordinary and everyday events on offer. This is especially significant given the context of silencing and erasure within which women's lives have usually been lived. In cultural contexts, women's voices can be subsumed, obliterated or simply papered or glossed over. The emergence of a fictional narrative is therefore of great significance in the shaping and articulating of different perspectives or, at best, alterity. This is particularly true of Doris Lessing's fiction, written broadly over seventy years. Acts of prescient subversion punctuate her literary oeuvre, providing critical insights into understanding how feminism is the most significant movement of our times.

Using Lessing's key narratives to highlight the central issues raised by her, I hope to show how her interventions highlight the composite nature of modern feminism.

It would be absurd to suggest that Lessing's narratives address themselves directly to immediate problems in India. However, her birth in the interwar years and her subsequent coming of age in erstwhile Southern Rhodesia, a British colony, establish several correspondences and connections. Again, it is important to remember that colonial laws written in an older England, were the prototype for several laws framed in Independent India. As my examination of her work will show, Lessing's sharply critical enquiry into Western white feminism allows readers to reflect upon and recognise the commonality of shared areas, restrictions and boundaries. Locating herself in opposition to the values of the colonial world in which she grew to adulthood, Lessing continues to move away from its central premises in her early writings—as her first novel demonstrates. Writing as a woman situated within patriarchy, Lessing examines the dilemmas of race, violence, the construction of women's images, oppressive hegemonies and cultural constrictions in a postcolonial world. In her writing, these aspects usually find expression through the perspectives of women. By creating fictional characters to voice these issues, Lessing's fiction becomes an important milestone for modern Western feminist movements in the second half of the twentieth century. Her work—while often being prescient or anticipatory—also provides critical inputs for an understanding of the shifts in Western feminism, sharpening one's perception of critical paradigms within feminist theory and praxis.

Feminism and Eurocentric History

Where exactly does one place the magnifying lens while searching for the roots of the feminist movement in the twentieth century? Does one focus on the suffrage struggles which were a part of the 1890s and continued into the 1900s? Or does one push further to earlier periods in occidental history, locating the women's movements as part of a larger upheaval concerning the rights of specific groups of individuals?

It is pertinent to remind ourselves that although the Industrial Revolution, French Revolution and American War of Independence changed society in Europe and the United States in very tangible ways, paving the way for the larger democratic framework of the twentieth century, they did not create social and political spaces for women inhabitants of the First World. Democratic processes in Europe were also not accompanied by an automatic granting of equal rights to all the citizens of the world. The granting of political rights and their subsequent devolvement remained not merely Eurocentric but also mostly confined to the privileged white male.

This is substantiated not only by accounts of the constricted lives led by women but also by records of the prolonged struggle for political representation by women in Europe and the United States during the nineteenth century. Feminism in Europe and the US began when a large number of protesting women demanded access to social, economic and political spaces. These articulations took considerable time to be incorporated into the fabric of public, legal and cultural life despite the egalitarian revolutions that were the order of the day.

Imaginatively, it is possible to view incipient assertions by women at any point of time in oral and written history. In such accounts, one usually encounters a vibrant tradition of protest by women. As we proceed towards the end of the first quarter of the twenty-first century, hitherto lesser-known narratives documenting the extraordinary and difficult lives led by women continue to surface. However, to record feminism's quantum leap in the second half of the twentieth century, it is useful to look at the ferment around the women's question—especially in England in the nineteenth century. For this reason, most studies on feminism locate the first phase of the feminist movement in the period between 1830 and 1920.[2]

Mary Wollstonecraft's *A Vindication of the Rights of Woman* raised the issue of women's rights as early as 1792. However, it was in the last four decades of the nineteenth century that women's struggles for suffrage were channelised. This struggle was subsequently carried over into the first three decades of the twentieth century before limited franchise for women could become a reality in parts of Europe and North America. Women's agitations over legal and social rights were not only splintered by issues of class and race, but were also invariably subsumed under the onrush of emerging nationalisms on the Continent. Women's participation in public life as a result of the war in the early twentieth century gave them a sense of freedom and financial independence, sowing the seeds of incipient feminism.[3] While the war 'affected the lives of all women' and 'changed the ways in which they carried out their customary tasks', it did little to redefine women's 'overall relationship to the family and the wider society'.[4] Women's movements, at this time, were a long way off from questioning the existing social and cultural structures in which their lives were enmeshed. Such questioning was a much later development in feminist thinking[5] and came from the margins.

It is pertinent to recall at this juncture that feminism began as a protest on the part of both women and men against the subordinate social position that women occupied in industrialised and technologically advanced societies. The attempts to vindicate the rights of woman and citizen were an ongoing process in the home countries during the years of colonial expansion at a time when technologically advanced countries like England, France and Holland furthered their economic interests in the colonies at the expense of the native populations. In hindsight, the ironies of this situation are now only too clear to us. White women, while being disadvantaged in their countries of origin, occupied privileged status in countries where male spouses or kin administered to the affairs of the empire. Thus, women could be second-class citizens in industrial and technological Europe and yet be complicit in the extensive colonisation of vast sections of the world that served as colonies. The articulation of white women's identities, therefore, was complicated by the colonial enterprise.

This created a situation where, ostensibly, a large majority of free men and free women participated in the economic, political and cultural subjugation of men and women who were non-white. Although the category of poor whites in indentured service due to conviction as criminals and white women prostitutes in naval service would not really qualify as part of a privileged group, their existence allows us to see the divisions due to economic and gender differences among the colonisers. This alerts us to the dangers of viewing the colonisers as a single homogeneous group. Nevertheless, the anomalies of fighting for women's rights in one's home country and being part of administrative machinery that suppressed the rights of entire communities based on race on another continent have now become glaringly apparent.

This anomaly went completely undetected for the longest time. It was also compounded by the fact that well into the twentieth century, despite the amelioration of their personal and social positions, women's interests and priorities were still seen as secondary to other national agendas. Women's struggles for political rights were also split by the issues of emerging nationhood in England, France and Germany prior to the First World War. For instance, the agitation by women for political rights in Britain met with incredible resistance from the British government. In 1910, the Liberals in Britain promised home rule to the Irish nationalists if they supported the government in opposing women's suffrage.[6] Women's rights, thus, remained precariously located and could be easily displaced in the wake of issues that were construed as more significant.

Women's entry into the public sphere, their economic ability and their contribution to both imperial and war activity did not ensure them any unique status. Women's issues received lower priority during the world wars, eclipsed as they were by the processes of war-inspired assertions of nationalisms. The shift from an emotive identification with the causes of war to a critique of its policy was also very minimal. As Sheila Rowbotham points out, 'it was militarism rather than anti-militarism, nationalism rather than internationalism which stirred most British women in 1914.'[7]

A vivid sense of women's lives between the wars is created through the details Lessing provides of her mother's life in her autobiographies, anecdotes and other literary genres. Lessing's mother's life is fairly representative of the lives of many British women of her generation and is typical of women whose strength and independence were harnessed by the state during the war. Women in Maud McVeagh's generation were willing to subsume their identities in consolidating the lives of their husbands, having families and, thus, furthering the cause of English nationhood. Maud McVeagh and the fictional May Quest who is modelled on her in *Martha Quest,* one of Lessing's early novels, speak for a generation of visible, independent women who contributed to the growth and consolidation of Britain as a nation and participated in its expansion as an empire with far-flung dominions. Both the real Maud and the fictional May Quest are acutely conscious of being English. They also completely endorse the supremacy of European civilisation.

Maud McVeagh's life typifies that of the educated, white middle-class women of her generation. During the First World War, many women were recruited to the workforce and functioned in important, productive and economic roles. Yet, the limited freedoms of employment and falling in love at the workplace remained constricted by the overarching pressure on women to marry. At the end of the war, Maud McVeagh's decision to marry John Tayler marks the closure of lucrative career options, where she could have risen to the highest position of head nurse in a London hospital. May Quest, her fictional counterpart, fares no better.

Women had limited access to exploring and enjoying their newfound economic identities in the workplace because the state viewed their roles as homemakers and mothers as being of paramount significance. While women received far lower rates of pay in comparison to men and viewed their positions as waged members of a family as a temporary phenomenon, the existence of marriage bars to women's employment imposed its own controls. Work for women who belonged to the middle class or thereabouts 'was not about self-fulfilment and independence',[8] but remained closely enmeshed with older ingrained notions about women's proper sphere—reinforced by policies of the state that sought to curtail the employment of married women. As Pat Thane points out, during 'the inter-war years middle-class women entered the labour market for the years between education and marriage and then overwhelmingly left it permanently'.[9]

European women on the eve of the First World War and between the wars seemed to be caught in a double bind. Their attempts at self-determination were invariably overshadowed by the larger politics of nationhood, and their assertion of their national identities invariably located them within the structure of white hegemonic authority. Thus, despite assertions that Britain's participation in the First World War was 'the beginning of the end of Europe's supremacy, and of the predominance of the white man in the world',[10] notions of Eurocentricity continued to hold sway much longer—both on the Continent and in the colonies, and there have been attempts to consolidate both Eurocentricity and the strength of European nations for decades thereafter. The perpetuation of this ideology continued well beyond the decade of the 1940s, during which decolonisation movements in Asia and Africa gained momentum. Where exactly amongst these new political and international developments does feminism feature? Is it possible to see feminism as bringing something new to this shifting of perspectives?

For our purposes, feminism needs to be viewed as a philosophy that slowly begins to consolidate its position in this period. It would be fruitful to see feminism as etymologically focusing attention on the rights, desires and needs of women that had been subsumed under the rubric of humanism. Feminism could be seen as adding a new dimension to the worldview of humanism. The word humanism has been in use over many centuries as a philosophy pertaining to both men and women, and such usage has been accepted as providing adequate representation for both until recently. Chandra Mohanty defines humanism as 'a Western ideological and political project' and draws our attention to the 'anthropomorphism and ethnocentrism'[11] that has in its wake generated a hegemonic space, with the man and Western versions of history, culture, politics and technology as the clear defining parameters. The identification of feminism and minority discourse as a counter-discourse to humanism has, of course, been the mainstay of much contemporary postmodern philosophy.[12] 'Feminism' then needs to be read as the acting and speaking other of 'humanism' in so far as it orchestrates for itself a whole range of meanings and positions which were not conceivable within humanism but have increasingly been viewed as significant, especially in the here and now of our times.

It is from this perspective that we can understand how Western feminism, at the level of theory and praxis, has played a major role in the percolation of the awareness of women's rights in the cosmopolitan sections of the Third World. Women's agitations for suffrage in the West in the first quarter of the twentieth century bequeathed, quite without knowing it, a valuable legacy to future generations of women the world over. In the new plural spaces created by the achievement of political freedom by erstwhile colonies, the incorporation of political rights for women was made easier—at least on paper. This was possible due to the new legislations enacted during the historic processes of decolonisation in Asia and Africa in the 1940s and 1950s that were modelled on the constitutions of their erstwhile colonial rulers.

Today, with the widespread mobilisation of women's groups at the grassroots level, it is possible to see the distinctly topical and local nature of different movements spearheaded by women's activist groups all over the globe. The feminist movement in this century has made inroads into almost every bastion and questioned and challenged all kinds of assumptions. Unlike other movements, feminism has adopted innumerable forms, imbued and absorbed various discourses and shown itself as capable of speaking in protean ways. Beginning with agitations for political rights, the right to education and the right to paid employment, feminism has moved through formats of liberal feminism, socialist and Marxist feminism and has eventually expanded its boundaries to include the experience of women from different social classes, races and cultures.

Women are now learning to assert their rights in contexts where they are often at a disadvantage. This emphasises the importance of viewing the twentieth century as a kind of churning vat which allowed for the coagulation of women's resistance into a visible and identifiable end product. It would be useful, at this juncture, to look at Lessing's formative years in this period and explore women's articulation of social and sexual identities.

Personal Narratives and Public Histories: From the Centre to the Margins

The story of how Lessing's parents met could easily be seen as the reworking of one of Hemingway's most powerful narratives—*A Farewell to Arms*. John Tayler, Lessing's father, was a soldier wounded in the First World War. He was nursed through the trauma of the war and an amputated leg by Maud McVeagh, Lessing's mother, at the old Royal Free Hospital in London's East End. This wartime interaction between the injured patient and his nurse, over one year, grew into a more serious commitment and subsequently resulted in the nurse marrying the soldier.

Sick of the war, disillusioned by wartime experience, suffering from shell shock and depression and never really recovering from either, John Tayler opted to stay away from England for the rest of his life. Maud McVeagh had already lost her first love, a young doctor, to the war. Her choice of marriage and a family over a career, although in keeping with the decision of many women in her generation, was fraught with difficulty as Lessing tells us in the first volume of her autobiography.

Having chosen marriage, Lessing's mother's acceptance of her new-found identity as John Tayler's wife led her to quit work and follow her husband out of England. It was to Kermanshah in Iran that they first went. John Tayler worked at the Imperial Bank of Persia from 1919 to 1924. The name of the bank itself makes for a most telling account of the politics of Britain at this time. It was in Kermanshah that Maud Tayler had both her babies. Doris Lessing was born in 1919 and Harry followed suit in 1922. Lessing's early infanthood in Iran ended with the Taylers returning to England in 1924, where they spent six months with family in London.[13]

Lessing recounts this period in London from her father's point of view: '[s]ix months of relatives, hell on earth, in snobby, self-important, provincial, parish pump, ignorant, little England.'[14] Cynical about the war, which belied all that he and his generation had fought for, Lessing's father continued to remain extremely critical of England and all things English to the very end. The Taylers' long vacation in London coincided with the British Empire exhibition of 1924. It was a visit to the exhibition that precipitated the family's migration to Southern Rhodesia in the hope of making their fortunes in maize. This decision was to change the nature of Lessing's parents' lives and 'set the course'[15] of her own life and her brother's, as she puts it herself. The Taylers belonged to the generation of white British settlers who were encouraged to participate in the agricultural exploitation of Southern Rhodesia. Lessing's parents settled down at a farm in Umtali (presently Mutare) in Southern Rhodesia in 1924; the year in which the country became a self-governing colony of Britain.

Southern Rhodesia

I would now like to provide a brief capsule on the political history of the region that was once termed Southern Rhodesia and is today known as Zimbabwe. The period that Lessing writes about in her fiction is based broadly in the 1930s and 1940s, well after the British had entrenched themselves as the new power elite in Southern Rhodesia. Lessing's narratives about Africa document the presence of white men and occasionally the Boer and Greek, but predominantly draw attention to the role of the British as the cultural and political elite. This brief outline of the history of Southern Rhodesia seeks to locate the social, cultural and political milieu wherein Lessing grew to maturity.

This history of Southern Rhodesia can be divided into four phases:

(a) The years free from British involvement and control of Southern Africa, pre-1890s.
(b) The period when the British South Africa Company administered over parts of Southern Rhodesia, 1890–1922.
(c) A period of increasing repression of Black people, when white racist politics was at its peak, 1923–1962.
(d) A period that marks the beginnings of active Black subversion of white authority, post-1962.

From the end of the first millennium to the 1830s, an agricultural people called the Mashona settled down south of the Zambezi River and dominated the land in Central Africa. In the 1830s, the Matabele Zulus settled in the south of the area inhabited by the Mashona. Primarily an agricultural and tribal society, the Mashona and the Matabele came in contact with the French Huguenots and the Dutch Boer farmers before Britain eventually established control. Cecil Rhodes—the diamond millionaire from South Africa—and three others, Charles Rudd, Rochfort Maguire and Francis Thompson, negotiated the Rudd concession with Lobengula, the king of the Matabele. The concession, then acquired by the British South Africa Company, facilitated the entry of the British into these areas. Subsequent resistance by both the Mashona and the Matabele was unhesitatingly crushed.[16]

Armed with mineral rights over the territories of Rhodesia and Zambia, Rhodes was granted a royal charter from the British government—paving the way for the British South Africa Company to administer Rhodesia from 1890 to 1923.[17] Rhodes dreamt of repeating the mining success of Witwatersrand but that did not materialise here. The British South Africa Company, which had invested heavily in infrastructures such as roads and railways, decided to open up land for agricultural exploitation to recover its investments. Subsequently, white settlers were encouraged to live in Southern Rhodesia and take up farming as a viable commercial venture. The availability of cheap farming land aided by government subsidies for white settlers was part of the process that eventually led to the extremely unequal distribution of land, contributing to the disruption and eventual destruction of indigenous Black societies.

The best land was distributed among a small number of whites while the dispossessed Blacks were pushed into what came to be called the reserves, which were inferior land areas unfit for cultivation.[18] They were also forced to work as manual labour on white farms or recruited forcibly in the mines. In the year 1922, at the end of a referendum conducted among the white minority, Southern Rhodesia declared itself a self-governing colony of the British Empire. The British government acknowledged Southern Rhodesia as a self-governing colony in 1924.

From 1924 onwards, this white minority community practised a ruthless system of segregation that resulted in the complete domination and suppression of Black people. They were not only done out of their traditional rights to land but were also forced to work for the white minority in a menial capacity. Commercial farming having proved successful, legislation was enacted to appropriate land on a large scale from the indigenous Black people. The returns from agriculture were ploughed into mining and industrial sectors.

Apart from the economic and political deprivation, statutes and regulations were passed to uphold and preserve the racial purity and cultural superiority of the whites. As early as 1903, an ordinance to suppress immorality was passed. As Cyril A. Rogers and C. Frantz point out, '[a] European woman found guilty of illicit intercourse with an African man was liable to two years hard labour, while the African was liable to five years.'[19] In 1916, a further ordinance was passed which made 'acts of indecency between African males and European females an offence'.[20] The sexual taboos and regulations that were put in place by the ruling white elite are important markers of the way in which sexuality was sought to be controlled, policed and placed under the jurisdiction of the state. The bodies of women and those of the colonised became the sites through which the state mediated its authority.

The rigorous policing and control exercised by the white state was so complete that although the Black population outnumbered the white ten times over, they were unable to offer any systematic resistance for a long time. It was in the late 1940s that African political movements began to grow on a mass basis and undertake the kind of propaganda that would seriously influence British opinion and pose a challenge to white settler nationalism.[21] Eventually, the early 1950s saw the beginnings of the resistance movements in Central Africa and Northern and Southern Rhodesia.[22]

The last phase of Southern Rhodesian history deals with the disbanding of subsequent white schemes to hold on to the colony as an outpost of British imperialistic policy. The Central African Federation was created between 1954 and the early 1960s, forming an association between Nyasaland (currently Malawi), Northern Rhodesia (currently Zambia) and Southern Rhodesia (currently Zimbabwe) despite strong opposition from Africans in all these territories. African objections and resentment were ignored both by the white settlers as well as by Great Britain's political parties. The federation was eventually disbanded amidst great violence in 1962, a year that was marked by the banning of the Zimbabwe African People's Union in September and the election of the far right Rhodesian Front to the government in December. The year 1980 saw the birth of modern Zimbabwe as we know it today.

Lessing, despite being the daughter of a white settler, was acutely aware of the exploitative position of authority enjoyed by the white minority in Southern Rhodesia and remained sharply critical of the attitude of the white settler towards the natives. Intensely hostile to the smug and self-righteous perspective of the racist white minority, she was rightly dismissive of 'the soft-mindedness which deplores the colour bar and ideas of white supremacy, hopes they will soften and diminish . . . and yet will not acknowledge the justice of the black nationalism which is its inevitable consequence.'[23]

South Africa and Southern Rhodesia, simmering cauldrons of injustice and atrocity—particularly in the years after the First World War—provided the backdrop against which Lessing grew into a young woman and began to define herself as an adult in her own right. Disagreeing vociferously with her mother's opinion on most things, Lessing found herself at odds with white minority assumptions in Southern Rhodesia. A bid for personal independence made her leave home for a job in the city. Her stay in the city culminated in an early marriage, followed by the pressures of being a young mother with two small children.

The claustrophobia of her marriage to a civil servant and the disintegration of her relationship with her husband, Frank Wisdom, led to their subsequent separation and divorce. By this time Lessing was part of a communist group in South Africa. Lessing's work in the Communist Party of South Africa (CPSA), an identification with the cause of Black people and her subsequent politically expedient marriage to Gottfried Lessing and the birth of her third child did little to dispel her growing conviction about the stifling insularity of colonial life. This eventually proved to be the motivating factor that compelled her to leave for England twenty-four years after her parents moved to Southern Rhodesia.

'I was already formed by the time I arrived in London,'[24] says Doris Lessing. Lessing returned to England in 1949, long after her parents left it, with infant Peter—her son from her second marriage. Armed with her first manuscript, Lessing's literary entry into England heralded newer orientations and fresh contexts. While Lessing's journey to England—where she continued to live until she died in 2013—reversed the journey undertaken by her parents a quarter-century before, her fictional oeuvre continued to absorb and reflect new, robust interests and ideas that were to become the hallmark of her writing.

Lessing's father, who remained traumatised by his war experience, had drifted into ill health. Her mother retained for a while the fond hopes of someday returning to England and sought to preserve as much of English traditions and values as she could and inculcate them in her children. Assimilating vicariously the history of the times her parents lived in, Lessing developed and sharpened her critical understanding of events—mediated on the one hand by her father's anguish and bitterness and on the other by her mother's sense of pride in all things English. Internalising her father's anguish over the war and distancing herself from her mother's implicit belief in the superiority of the white race, Lessing's first-hand witnessing of racism in Southern Rhodesia and the trauma of the Second World War propelled her to be a chronicler and critic of her times, recording, interpreting and making prophecies in her various narratives.

Beginnings: Women's Lives and Representation

What are the significant aspects of Lessing's work as a chronicler of women's lives? Born in October 1919, Lessing grew to adulthood in Southern Rhodesia at a time when political rights framing white women's lives were often simultaneous with similar legislations in Britain. For instance, although full suffrage was granted to all British women under thirty by 1928, only women over the age of thirty had access to the vote in Britain in 1918. Similarly, limited suffrage had been granted to Rhodesian women as early as 1919, 'on the basis of a woman's husband's financial means.'[25] Ground realities in Southern Rhodesia notwithstanding, Lessing's own perceptions were shaped by the impact of the women's movements in Europe and the percolation of their ideas through written materials, pamphlets and books. As has already been pointed out, Lessing was a beneficiary of the achievements of the women's suffrage movements in her formative years. Significantly, these were also the years that saw the beginnings of a redefinition in the perception of women's identities and greater participation of women outside of the home

There was, in particular, a significant shift in the awareness of and responses to matters concerning the female body. The growing demystification of the female body and an understanding of the psyche that based itself less on religious prescriptions and more on the scientific discourses of Havelock Ellis along with the subsequent psychoanalytic interpretations of Freud made a considerable impact.[26]

In her autobiography, Lessing records her eclectic and voracious absorption of ideas originating from books and journals that were regularly ordered from England and delivered to her parental home in Southern Rhodesia. Lessing also recalls her mother's manuals on gynaecology and Marie Stopes' book as important tools of reference. Lessing's easy acceptance of the female body and her effortless recording of its pleasures possibly spring from her early exposure to new ideas that were beginning to gain currency. During this period, birth control measures became accessible to the working classes; Marie Stopes published her book *Married Love* (1918) and opened her first birth control clinic in England in 1921.[27] In the 1920s, new social and sexual spaces suddenly began to be made available for women.

The 1920s also saw an impressive programme of legislation that speedily gave British women many of the rights they were demanding.[28] Despite the granting of suffrage rights to women by 1928 and a marked increase in the number of schools and universities to which women in Britain had access,[29] the perceptions of women's roles and identities remained ambiguous. Sandra Holton has contested the argument put forward by Hobsbawm that 'suffragism' had a middle-class appeal and that it based itself entirely on liberal bourgeois ideology. Holton draws attention to 'a "new feminist" school of suffrage history' that has, in turn, drawn attention to the multidimensional nature of women's participation in order to show how 'the ideology of the suffrage movement was never fixed or monolithic. It was, indeed, often internally contradictory, a contradiction that is intrinsic to the feminist project.'[30]

Despite new research that suggests the involvement of a larger cross section of women who questioned women's economic and cultural confinement, there was little change in the popular perception of women's roles in the interwar years and after. Women had made inroads into the workplace in the absence of men. Yet due to the loss of male lives in the wars, the national anxiety of building families gained greater momentum. This led to an emphasis on the centrality of motherhood and nurture in women's lives. The popular belief articulated in the mid-1940s was that 'in the next thirty years housewives as mothers have vital work to do in ensuring the adequate continuance of the British race and of the British ideal in the world'.[31]

Thus, despite women's continued access to education and employment between the wars, change in perceptions regarding the possibilities of larger social identities for women was minimal. Another significant factor that contributed to the lull in the women's movements was the gradual establishment of a welfare state in Britain by the end of the 1940s. The welfare state began to provide a whole number of services for its citizens, ranging from family allowances, help for children, insurance and health care,[32] many of which had been on the agenda of the women's movements before the world wars.

Lessing's earliest full-length fiction was published in the year 1950. This was almost two decades before the beginnings of the second wave of feminism whose dates can be fixed towards the end of the 1960s to the present.[33] Although women began to be admitted permanently to the police force in 1945 and marriage bars to women's employment as teachers and civil servants were lifted around 1950, women's identities continued to be constructed around their primary familial responsibilities as mothers and caregivers. Protesting against such conventional perception, Lessing's early novels traced the breakdown of marriage in the lives of her protagonists and their escape from the prescriptive confines of domesticity.[34]

A great deal of Lessing's depiction of the oppressive and stifling nature of relationships within the structure of the family also stems from her engagement with communism and left politics as early as 1942. Fifteen years later, acknowledging her inaccurate perception of the development of socialism, she declared herself 'in possession of an optimism about the future' and a recognition that 'we are all of us, directly or indirectly, caught up in a great whirlwind of change.'[35]

Lessing's work in the 1950s seeks to address this 'great whirlwind of change' and traces the limits of liberal feminism, showing how the issue of race complicates its perspective. She highlights the dilemma of the white, middle-class and largely female protagonists of her narratives in the context of colonialism, class and race. Her involvement with the woman question pre-empts and anticipates the revival of the women's movements in the West in the 1960s.

The Grass is Singing, Lessing's first full-length novel, offers a critical commentary on liberal white feminism as a movement largely preoccupied with the problems of white women in the West. *The Grass is Singing* pushes us to re-examine the limited perspective of acquiring rights for white women by drawing attention to the complete absence of rights in the case of Black people. By juxtaposing the issue of women's freedom and rights onto the context of the absence of rights in a colonised continent, Lessing enmeshes the race issue with the question of women's rights. In doing so, she makes us confront the premises of liberal feminism. Showing how feminism merely articulates the desires of a small minority under such circumstances—white women in this case—Lessing's writing highlights the need for feminism to mediate with larger structures of power and control at the level of ideas and praxis. This, Lessing suggests, requires feminism to negotiate with diverse and disparate lives.

The connections that Lessing establishes between race and feminism were made well before Black feminists and women of colour protested their marginalisation in white women's movements.[36] Articulations by Black feminists such as Angela Davis and Amina Mama, in accounts of their lives and formative experiences, reveal their alienation from white women's movements and their affiliation to groups with left-based ideologies due to white feminism's failure to assimilate Black women's perspectives into their agendas.[37] This is the key point of difference that Lessing brings to her writings. Despite engaging largely with the trajectories of white middle-class women, Lessing's fiction highlighted the gaps and caesuras in the white women's movements long before the interventions made by women of colour.

Beginnings: Women and Writing

The novel has been the single most important literary form in the recording of women's experience and also the most accessible, even to the most prosaic of women. It proved itself an invaluable ally for women writers in the nineteenth century. Yet, it was stretched and shaped beyond recognition in the latter part of the twentieth century. The empirical changes and shifts in women's lives as a result of shifts in representation can be easily distinguished when one compares the portrayal of women characters in the nineteenth-century novel with women characters in the twentieth-century novel.

Narratives dealing with women's lives and experiences by Jane Austen, the Brontë sisters and George Eliot form part of the great tradition of the nineteenth-century novel that engaged in the construction of women's identities by looking very closely at certain aspects of women's lives. Austen, Brontë and Eliot engage intently with women's lives within the family or the private realm. This tradition of writing is identified by Nancy Armstrong as that of the domestic novel.[38]

Within the realm of the domestic novel, there was an extensive construction of the inner lives of women as it examined women's psyches and engaged with concerns over their emotions, feelings, moods and affections informed by the overarching penumbra of familial or private space. The novels located within this tradition record the power that the female protagonists exercise over the home and in personal and sexual relationships between men and women. However, the protagonists in such fiction are seldom shown as transcending the domestic realms which they initially set out to define and conquer. The larger world outside—that of political and public space—if it exists at all, does so in the glimpses of men's lives and remains invariably outside women's purview. Thus, Elizabeth Bennet can only share Darcy's estate as his wife in *Pride and Prejudice* while Fanny Price's greatest moment of solace is the possibility of marriage to her clergyman cousin in *Mansfield Park*. Jane Eyre, with an independent fortune, consents to be the eyes of the blind Rochester in the novel bearing her name while Dorothea visualises incredible spiritual and emotional heights through her marriage—first to Casaubon and subsequently to Will Ladislaw—in *Middlemarch*.

It is my submission that this mode of perception which confines women's potential and possibility within the domestic realm is first subjected to analysis and questioning in the popular fiction of the 1890s, which is credited with the creation of the economically independent New Woman. Articulate and highly sexual and espousing free love or adultery in the face of marital breakdown, the New Woman threatened existing domestic structures. Yet, as Gail Cunningham points out, the

New Woman did not last much beyond the Victorian era and much of her energies were absorbed by the suffrage struggle.[39]

Cunningham's reading that the New Woman novels 'broke through the constricting bounds of conventional reticence and helped clear a path for better novelists to tread'[40] is insightful as it suggests future directions made possible by the New Woman novels. The confident articulation of women's issues is subsequently to be found in Virginia Woolf's fiction. Woolf focused on the interiority of women's lives, recording various details and capturing nuances and textures of great complexity. She succeeded in doing away, to some extent, with notions of women's territorial confinement to the domestic realm by introducing her readers to a world that stretched far beyond the domestic sphere viewed by women in earlier narratives.

In *Mrs Dalloway* (1925), Woolf's protagonist Clarissa wanders through sections of London all by herself. Despite her lack of opportunity and limited education, Clarissa Dalloway is a poised and successful hostess. Woolf, while critical of Clarissa Dalloway's immediate social and political world, orchestrates a questioning of marriage as the culmination of female development through several questionable alliances in the novel. *Mrs Dalloway* creatively reinforces Woolf's non-fictional narratives such as *A Room of One's Own* (1929) and *Three Guineas* (1938), where she critiques cultural and societal constrictions imposed on the lives of women and imaginatively traces the history of women's suppression. Woolf's critical and creative inputs into reading women's lives must be seen as the beginning of a larger literary and theoretical tradition within feminism, one that has received much attention—particularly in the second half of the twentieth century.

Woolf's work, both fictional and non-fictional, demands that women should have the right to freedom and equality—which are rights that men have always easily accessed. Highlighting the extended world of London through this experimental novel, Clarissa Dalloway's walk outside her home allows both her and the reader more access to the public world from which they had been shut away for so long. While women's identities come into their own, the novel format itself shifts further from realistic modes of representation to an intense focus on consciousness as a means of organising individuality.[41]

Lessing's novels, I would like to stress, draw sustenance from and then work upon this trajectory.

The differences between Woolf's protagonists and those of Lessing's are the result of the democratic processes of history. The ordinary white woman with a nondescript middle-class background replaces Woolf's upper-class white woman. Unlike Woolf's fictional women with all the infrastructure and cultural cushioning at their disposal, Lessing's heroines have very little in their past that can bolster them. Lessing's protagonists of the 1950s are comparatively poor or come from families subjected to hardship because of war, colonization, and other natural and man-made disasters. The other major dimension, which remains largely unexplored in Woolf's fiction but is central to Lessing's, is the disturbing one of race. Lessing, as subsequent discussions will reveal, locates her characters within domestic and familial situations but uses these situations to raise questions about the larger world connected to the domestic sphere.

Lessing's writing in the post-war period is required to be seen as an important site of critique and subversion. There was a tremendous upsurge in women's creative writing in the period after the wars. Significantly, women's self-expression took emphatic form at a time when occidental national identities had begun to crumble. Can one see this as endowing women's writing with transformative possibilities? Women's narratives at this point seemed to work against the grain of established literary traditions. By writing about their lives, women spoke of their experiences and thereby articulated seldom discussed perspectives. This significant aspect of women's writing provided women with new ways of reading and valuing their experience and also outlined liberating directions. This was furthered by the greater visibility of women. It would be no exaggeration to see women's writing at this stage as a conscious and deliberate questioning and rewriting of their cultural roles and identities.

Feminist Subversions: Lessing's Short Stories

Most of this book will engage with Lessing's full-length novels, doing justice to the literary form in which her output has been prodigious.

It would, however, be remiss to leave out of the discussion some of her short stories—another genre in which Lessing has been prolific. Lessing's short stories form a substantial aspect of her work and have been widely published and disseminated. Lessing's earliest short stories predate the publication of her first novel by almost a decade. Most of her short stories have been anthologised into four volumes: *Collected African Stories Volume One* and *Two* (1973) and *Collected Stories Volume One* and *Two* (1978). Later, collections of stories abound—such as the anthology *London Observed: Stories and Sketches* (1992).[42] Lessing's short stories have also been published prior to these anthologies, either separately or as part of other collections. She has continuously used this pithy genre of the short story with great success.

As a prelude to the discussion of Lessing's novels, I would like to engage with three of her short stories that highlight her acute grasp and understanding of the role and structures of narration for the dissemination of different kinds of ideas. The stories I would like to discuss are 'The Trinket Box' (1964), 'One Off the Short List' (1963) and 'Debbie and Julie' (1989).

Referring to 'The Trinket Box' in 1965, Lessing speaks about two kinds of narrative styles that she distinguishes from one another—terming them *masculine* and *feminine*. Lessing sets up a comparison between an early story called 'The Pig' (1948) and 'The Trinket Box', privileging her narrative style in the former. Terming her style of writing in 'The Trinket Box' as feminine, Lessing declares her intention of eschewing this style for one that is masculine. Further identifying the narrative style of 'The Trinket Box' as 'intense, careful, self-conscious, mannered', Lessing consciously announces her preference for the narrative technique she adopts in 'The Pig' and describes it as 'straight, broad, direct', a 'highway to the kind of writing that has the freedom to develop as it likes.'[43] Lessing's use of the terms feminine and masculine is significant, particularly in the context of sophisticated feminist readings of the politics of writing and the silencing of women's voices.[44] It is also significant that Lessing's dissatisfaction with the narrative experiment in 'The Trinket Box' causes her to validate the writing style that she had initially adopted.

What precisely are the features in 'The Trinket Box' that Lessing identifies as belonging to the feminine style of writing? An elderly aunt, with little means of her own, is taken ill. She has spent most of her years in a life of service and self-effacement amidst her various relatives and has been rather useful to all of them. As she lies dying in hospital, she is solicitously visited by all manner of relatives who had used her services with little compunction and not been particularly sensitive to her dependent position before this. For all of them, she leaves behind gifts in a trinket box which they expect will provide some incontrovertible proof of Aunt Maud's individuality, expressions of her anger, what she thought or felt but could not voice. When she dies, the box reveals nothing at all. There are only neatly labelled trinkets, thoughtfully earmarked for each of them.

Aunt Maud's story is one of self-effacement, both in life and death. The trinket box, tightly closed or subsequently opened, refuses to yield any knowledge of Aunt Maud. It replicates the silence that her life represents in terms of the obliteration of her lived history and memory after her death. Finding this narrative mode self-reflexive, Lessing consciously chooses to write in the masculine tradition, one that is more amenable to all kinds of possibility. The uncomfortable silence around the 'The Trinket Box' is broken sharply by the protagonist of the second short story.

'One Off the Short List' gives a new twist to a story that could have been a stereotypical account of male mastery and control over deviant or errant female behaviour. Graham, a journalist married for twenty years with a history of infidelity, has a personal shortlist of women he finds sexually attractive. He is shown as very fascinated by Barbara Coles and hopes to make a conquest of her. Virtually stalking Barbara, a prominent designer of stage props, Graham begins by inveigling an interview with her. He insists on dropping her home after the dinner and interview and invites himself in for a drink, setting the stage for what could be consensual seduction between two sexually free adults.

The trouble with this whole episode is that Barbara Coles does not want to play the game. Graham's crude refusal to leave without making a conquest despite her unwillingness could have been the high point of tension in the narrative. Instead of a terrified Barbara who could have cried 'rape', we are presented with a pragmatic woman who does not subscribe to any of the cultural codes so blatantly brandished by Graham through his sexist, boorish and arrogant display. Forced into a situation where she must have sex with him irrespective of what she feels, Barbara decides to get it over with. At this crucial juncture, to his horror, Graham finds that he is unable to 'get it up'. This deflation, both literal and metaphorical, is a new moment—one of comic anti-climax that effectively reduces the aspect of penis terror so deeply encoded as cultural fear in every woman's psyche.

Lessing's sense of sheer comedy does not end here. The next morning, Graham—who has stayed on—insists on dropping Barbara to her workplace in order to make a public statement of his conquest. Barbara lets him accompany her and actually draws attention to the fact that Graham is the man she had left the studio with the previous evening. This, however, does not produce the impact that Graham had hoped for. He becomes more and more insignificant and diminished by the end of the story. Lessing's rewriting of the codes of machismo and female acquiescence is a very valuable intervention.

The story not only leads to a diminishing of the aura of male machismo but also shows us what a paltry thing it is after all—built up as it is entirely within the confines of Graham's inflated self-perception. Lessing thus takes the sting out of notions of virile male libido and the consequently vulnerable female and presents a scenario wherein, despite attempts to compromise and humiliate her, the female emerges with her dignity and integrity unscathed. This is not to suggest that the possibility of rape or the danger that sexual assault represents for vulnerable women are issues that can be treated lightly. Especially in the context of vulnerable women whose bodies continue to be defenceless sites for aggression and violence, whether in peacetime or at the time of war, rape is and remains an abhorrent act—one that demands continual policing, intervention and redress. Lessing's story works in a context that is rather distant from these concerns. At a notional level, other things remaining equal, male definitions of sexual interaction with a woman as some kind of conquest are done away with, and instead of the triumphant male, we see one who has been thoroughly deflated.

'Debbie and Julie', one of Lessing's later short stories, speaks of the bonding between two women who meet in the city. Debbie, a prostitute, takes in Julie—a younger girl who is pregnant—and nurtures her. When we meet Julie, Debbie has been away for some time, possibly with a lover who she wistfully hopes will lead her to the paradise of a stable relationship. The event of the birth is at hand and Julie tries to minimally organise a place where she will have her baby.

The echoes between this twentieth-century birth and that of older mythological births are too obvious to be missed. Alone, with no place to go to and suffering the pressures of having no money, Julie decides to have her baby in a derelict shed where she is kept company by a visiting stray dog. The birth over, she cuts the umbilical cord, wraps the baby in swaddling clothes and leaves it—not in a basket of rushes but in a telephone box. Hoping that the baby will be rescued and looked after, Julie makes the long journey back to her maternal home. Her parents, who are unaware of the infant she has left behind or the past they have not been privy to, welcome her. The parents are grateful to have their daughter back home, apparently unharmed, especially when they were expecting the worst.

The biblical parallels and parodies notwithstanding, this story is not merely a graphic account of the processes of childbirth and the physical and emotional state of a woman at such a juncture. It speaks of yet another 'immaculate conception' where Julie's pregnancy is seen as an accident during a chance sexual encounter, part of teenage experimentation. Aware of the pressures in her provincial surroundings, Julie fled to the anonymity of the town—away from the presence of censorious and moralistic eyes. Here she gives birth to her child, watches it being taken to safety and then returns to her original moorings.

Julie's story is reminiscent of the narratives of several unfortunate women; including her father's sister. It highlights the fact that the onus of responsibility continues to rest with the woman. Julie remains vulnerable despite the possibilities of anonymity in modern life, as does her friend Debbie who fervently seeks a full-time relationship with one man. While 'One Off the Short List' punctured an inflated male ego mercilessly, 'Debbie and Julie' is a poignant indicator of women's anguish in the face of constraining societal prescriptions and expectations.

Conclusive Beginnings

Lessing's short stories, which I have discussed here, draw attention to the myths and stereotypes structuring female identity. They pay great attention to patterns of monitoring that modulate the behaviour of women irrespective of their diverse cultural environments. In the specific context of the stories, all the three women are from white middle-class backgrounds. However, by disrupting conventional narrative expectations and following them up with unexpected endings, Lessing's short stories signal the processes of rewriting. The reader achieves new insights. The fresh perspectives succeed in directing the thinking process away from earlier, well-worn narrative conclusions which have structured meaning and boundaries in women's lives. This analysis is only a point of entry which highlights Lessing's quiet and relentless chipping away at obsolete and hidebound structures and ideologies that have sought to either stereotype women or modulate their behaviour along well-marked grooves. Lessing's subversive feminist position is often indicated through such narratives.

Lessing's examination of the limits of white middle-class feminism is ahead of its time. It anticipates developments in the future where white feminism will be attacked for its solipsistic tendencies. Projecting itself initially as a monolithic structure, white middle-class feminism's recognition of the exclusion of other feminisms of colour and class was a gradual but extremely significant process. One of the important interventions that provided for a paradigmatic shift in feminist theory, as I have previously mentioned, occurred in the 1970s. This was an attack directed at the women's movement, accusing it of being centred on white women. This accusation was followed up with protests that were launched by women of colour. Subsequently, it was no longer possible to posit a universal or essentialist reading of *woman* as an *a priori* category.

This has definitively made possible the recognition of the diversity and plurality of women's experience and the multiplicity of sites wherein women's identities are constructed. It has simultaneously allowed for a more critical analysis of the overarching role played by political and cultural ideologies, enabling feminist theory to critically examine the factors that made such constructions possible in the first place. This new perspective is possibly the first step towards the emergence of non-Western, non-white feminism. Suddenly, the emphasis has shifted to evaluating experience through an understanding of the registers that inscribe women's experience, instead of through patriarchal perspectives.

Seismic points in history have contributed towards the evolving of such perspective and critique, and these remain significant for feminists who seek to locate the new ground covered by feminism in the last few decades of the twentieth century. I would like to draw attention to the fact that the limitations of white middle-class feminism were spelt out at a point when Eurocentric perceptions were being theoretically contested as well.[45] Alongside the contestation of Eurocentricity, feminism also came in for reassessment. This will be examined at length in the succeeding chapters.

Endnotes

1. Doris Lessing, *Under My Skin: Volume One of My Autobiography, to 1949* (New York: HarperCollins, 1994), 12.
2. Sandra Kemp and Judith Squires, eds., *Feminisms* (Oxford and New York: Oxford University Press, 1997), 7.
3. Françoise Thébaud, 'The Great War and the Triumph of Sexual Division,' in *A History of Women in the West: Toward a Cultural Identity in the Twentieth Century*, ed. Françoise Thébaud, trans. Arthur Goldhammer (1994; Cambridge, Massachusetts and London: Harvard University Press, 1996), 5: 21–75. The reference is from the 1996 edition.
4. Barbara Caine, 'Feminism and the Woman Citizen in the Interwar Years,' in *English Feminism, 1780–1980* (Oxford: Oxford University Press, 1997), 179.
5. Françoise Thébaud, 'Explorations of Gender,' in *A History of Women in the West: Toward a Cultural Identity in the Twentieth Century*, ed. Françoise Thébaud, trans. Arthur Goldhammer (1994; Cambridge, Massachusetts and London: Harvard University Press, 1996), 5: 9. The reference is from the 1996 edition.
6. Sheila Rowbotham, *A Century of Women: The History of Women in Britain and the United States* (London and New York: Viking Books, 1997; London and New York: Penguin Books, 1999), 14. All further references are from the 1999 edition.

7. Rowbotham, *A Century of Women,* 71.
8. Rowbotham, *A Century of Women,* 22.
9. Pat Thane, 'Women since 1945,' in *20th Century Britain: Economic, Social and Cultural Change*, ed. Paul Johnson (Harlow: Longman, 1994), 395.
10. Harold Macmillan reproduced in Peter King, *Twentieth-Century British History Made Simple* (London: W.H. Allen, 1980), 1.
11. Chandra Talpade Mohanty, 'Under Western Eyes: Feminist Scholarship and Colonial Discourses,' in *Third World Women and the Politics of Feminism,* eds. Chandra Talpade Mohanty, Ann Russo and Lourdes Torres (Bloomington and Indianapolis: Indiana University Press, 1991), 73.
12. For a specific critique of humanism, see Ania Loomba, *Colonialism/ Postcolonialism* (New York: Routledge, 1998).
13. These details of Lessing's life are to be found in most introductions to her life and work. For the most recent and authoritative version, see Lessing, *Under My Skin,* 37.
14. Lessing, *Under My Skin,* 37.
15. Lessing, *Under My Skin,* 46.
16. Henry O. Thompson, Jan Knappert, and Helen Bell Feddema, eds., *Africa: Land and People* (Delhi: ISPCK, 1995), 66.
17. Leonard T. Kapungu, *Rhodesia: The Struggle for Freedom* (Maryknoll, New York: Orbis Books, 1974), 6–24.
18. This information on South Rhodesian history is a paraphrasing of Larry W. Bowman, *Politics in Rhodesia: White Power in an African State* (Cambridge, Massachusetts: Harvard University Press, 1973), 1–8. Under the Land Apportionment Act of 1930, 46% of Southern Rhodesia's total land area was designated as African reserve land. Ninety-five per cent of the entire Black population was to be accommodated there. The whites constituted 4% of the total population and occupied over 37% of the land area of Southern Rhodesia. This was the first of a series of acts that formed the basis of much of the political unrest leading to armed struggle against white minority rule. Subsequent acts like the Maize Control Act of 1934, Native Land Husbandry Act of 1951 and the Land Tenure Act of 1969 contributed their share to the enhancement of European agriculture.
19. Cyril A. Rogers and C. Frantz, *Racial Themes in Southern Rhodesia: The Attitudes and Behaviour of the White Population* (New Haven and London: Yale University Press, 1962), 137.
20. Rogers and Frantz, *Racial Themes,* 137–138.

21. John Darwin, *Britain and Decolonisation: The Retreat from Empire in the Post-War World* (London: Macmillan, 1988), 195–199.
22. Doris Lessing, *African Laughter: Four Visits to Zimbabwe* (New York: HarperCollins, 1992), 6.
23. Doris Lessing, *Going Home* (Great Britain: Michael Joseph 1957; London: Panther Books 1968; repr., London: Grafton Books, 1989), 225. References are from the 1989 edition.
24. Doris Lessing, 'The Progressive Interview,' interview by Jonah Raskin, *The Progressive*, June, 1999, https://progressive.org/dispatches/doris-lessing-progressive-interview/.
25. See Caroline Daley and Melanie Nolan, eds., *Suffrage and Beyond: International Feminist Perspectives* (Auckland: Auckland University Press, 1994), 350.
26. Stevi Jackson and Sue Scott, eds., *Feminism and Sexuality: A Reader* (Edinburgh: Edinburgh University Press, 1996), 13.
27. Rowbotham, A *Century of Women,* 140.
28. Olive Banks, *Faces of Feminism: A Study of Feminism as a Social Movement* (New York: St. Martin's Press, 1981), 164.
29. For a detailed study on this, see Helen Blackburn, *Women's Suffrage: A Record of the Women's Suffrage Movement in the British Isles, With Biographical Sketches of Miss Becker* (London and Oxford: Williams & Norgate, 1902), 223 onwards.
30. See Eric Hobsbawm, *The Age of Empire, 1875–1914* (London: Cardinal Books, 1987), 201. The expression, 'new feminist' is used in Sandra Holton, 'The making of suffrage history,' in *Votes for Women,* eds. June Purvis and Sandra Stanley Holton (London and New York: Routledge, 2000), 26. The quotation is from the chapter called 'Introduction: The campaigns for votes for women' in the same book.
31. Rowbotham records popular belief in the mid-1940s about motherhood being the crucial work that housewives were required to undertake for the next thirty years, thereby ensuring the continuance of both British ideals and subjects throughout the world. This is a paraphrasing of William Beveridge's viewpoint as reproduced in Rowbotham, *A Century of Women*, 247. Beveridge was one of the liberal reformers and proponents of the welfare plan. For a detailed mapping of the prevalent belief that the family provided the key to a better society in this period, see 242–248.
32. The welfare state was established in Britain around 1950. The Family Allowances Act (1945), The Children Act (1948), Industrial Injuries Act (1946), National Insurance (1946) and National Health Act (1948) were

some of the salient features of the benefits provided by the welfare state as stated in King, *Twentieth-Century British History*, 267–270.

33. Kemp and Squires, introduction to *Feminisms*, 7.
34. The search for spaces outside of marriage and reproduction by Anna and Molly of *The Golden Notebook* is seen as a reaction to the post-war family policy by Louise Yelin, *From the Margins Of Empire: Christina Stead, Doris Lessing, Nadine Gordimer* (Ithaca and London: Cornell University Press, 1998), 184.
35. Doris Lessing, 'The Small Personal Voice,' in *A Small Personal Voice: Essays, Reviews and Interviews*, ed. Paul Schlueter (United States: Alfred A. Knopf, 1974; New York: Vintage Books, 1975), 20. The reference corresponds to the 1975 edition.
36. Deborah King, 'Multiple Jeopardy, Multiple Consciousness: The Context of a Black Feminist Ideology,' in *Feminist Theory in Practice and Process*, eds. Michelene R. Malson, Jean F. O'Barr, Sarah Westphal-Wihl and Mary Wyer (Chicago and London: University of Chicago Press, 1989), 75–106.
37. See Angela Y. Davis, *Women, Race & Class* (New York: Random House, 1981) where she speaks of the occluding of the experiences of Black women and the operative role of both racism and sexism in this context. Racist practice which implicitly takes the white perspective as universal is termed as 'white solipsism' by Adrienne Rich, 'Disloyal to Civilization: Feminism, Racism, Gynephobia' in *On Lies, Secrets and Silence: Selected Prose, 1966–1978* (New York: W.W. Norton Company, 1979), 299. Amina Mama, recollecting her experience as a part of the civil rights movements organised by the Black community in the United States, speaks of the impossibility of a Black woman ever being part of the white-dominated women's movements in the late 1960s in Amina Mama, *Beyond the Masks: Race, Gender and Subjectivity* (London: Routledge, 1995).
38. Nancy Armstrong, *Desire and Domestic Fiction: A Political History of the Novel* (New York: Oxford University Press, 1987).
39. Gail Cunningham, *The New Woman and the Victorian Novel* (London and Basingstoke: Macmillan, 1978), 152–156.
40. Cunningham, *The New Woman*, 79.
41. Sydney Janet Kaplan, introduction to *Feminine Consciousness in the Modern British Novel* (Urbana: University of Illinois Press, 1975), 1–7.
42. The publication details of these volumes of short stories are as follows: *This Was the Old Chief's Country*, vol. 1, *Collected African Stories* (Great Britain: Michael Joseph, 1973; London: Triad/Granada, 1979); *The Sun*

Between Their Feet, vol. 2, *Collected African Stories* (Great Britain: Michael Joseph, 1973; London: Triad/Granada, 1979); *To Room Nineteen*, vol. 1, *Collected Stories* (Great Britain: Jonathan Cape, 1978; London: Triad/Panther Books, 1979); *The Temptation of Jack Orkney*, vol. 2, *Collected Stories* (Great Britain: Jonathan Cape, 1978; London: Triad/Panther Books, 1979); *London Observed: Stories and Sketches* (Great Britain: HarperCollins, 1992; London: Flamingo, 1993).

43. Doris Lessing cited in Margaret K. Butcher, '"Two Forks of a Road": Divergence and Convergence in the Short Stories of Doris Lessing,' *Modern Fiction Studies* 26, no. 1 (Spring 1980): 56.
44. Josephine Donovan, 'The Silence is Broken,' in *The Feminist Critique of Language: A Reader*, ed. Deborah Cameron (London and New York: Routledge, 1990), 42.
45. I am thinking in particular of Edward Said, *Orientalism* (London: Routledge & Kegan Paul, 1978). This path-breaking work highlighted the construction of the non-Western as the other as part of a deliberate and long-drawn-out discourse and strategy.

II

The Interrogation of Liberal White Feminism: Race and Colonialism in *The Grass is Singing*

'The master's tools will never dismantle the master's house.'[1]

This observation by Audre Lorde is central to the issue of redefining value from the perspective of women in this discussion. Despite comprising a sizeable percentage in all communities, women have invariably had little say in important policy decisions and have more often than not gone along with decisions they had very little to do with in the first place. Women's acceptance of the *status quo* very often sprung from either an internalisation of the rules in place or from intense social pressure. For any change to happen or for new construction, there is an urgent requirement for new implements and in the context of the literary text, new perspectives.

In *The Grass is Singing* (1950),[2] Lessing addresses Mary Turner's attempts at self-transformation and shows how her failure stems from having deeply internalised the ideologies of colonial and racial superiority. Lessing draws attention to the need for dismantling extant hierarchies and belief systems in her documentation of Mary's life. Women as subalterns need new tools and mechanisms that will enable them to dismantle old structures and build new ones.

Written at a time of decolonisation struggles in Asia and Africa and published in 1950, *The Grass is Singing* created a literary sensation in the United States and England and definitively launched Lessing's writing career. The narrative was located in South Africa—unfamiliar territory for most readers in England—and was about the personal relationship between a white woman and her Black servant. This was an explosive subject since it dealt with the forbidden and relatively less discussed issue of race and gender in a colonial context.

Lessing's book was by no means the first to deal with these issues. Earlier novels such as E.M. Forster's *A Passage to India* (1924) and Alan Paton's *Cry, the Beloved Country* (1948) also dealt with the colonial encounter. By contrasting *The Grass is Singing* with these earlier novels and V.S. Naipaul's *Guerrillas* (1975), a novel written much later, it becomes possible to see the new aspects that *The Grass is Singing* draws attention to while engaging with the questions of race and gender.

Written at the end of Forster's experiences in India, *A Passage to India* is an exploration of the lives of the British in an India they had colonised and their interaction with the subject race of Indians. Published at a time when India was in the thick of nationalist agitations and protests against colonial rule that turned bloody, such as the Jallianwala Bagh massacre of 1919, *A Passage to India* introduces us to a white woman who is visiting India for the first time. Positioning a sensitive and vulnerable Adela Quested against the dominant ideology of colonial arrogance, Forster examines entrenched notions of racial superiority and white insecurity when faced with the possibility of miscegenation.

Adela comes to India to marry her chosen Englishman, Ronnie Heaslop. Striking an acquaintance with an Indian Muslim doctor called Aziz, she goes off on an expedition to the Marabar Caves—a nearby tourist attraction—along with some of her own compatriots. This episode, central to the novel, has Adela accusing Aziz of attempting to assault her. When Aziz faces formal charges of assault, colonial constructions of the native as a potential sexually aggressive male immediately come into play. The white community rallies around Adela and other vulnerable women, ready to protect and defend racial purity. When Adela inexplicably withdraws her accusation, the court acquits Aziz. Eventually, nothing really emerges to ratify white preconceptions about the native male, in the instance of this novel.

Now, Adela ceases to be of further narrative interest. The plot never highlights the nature of the violence she faced nor does it offer any concrete reasons for her withdrawal of charges. In the third section, the narrative unfolds at a new location, at a later period in time. It speculates on the possibility of friendship between English and Indian men on terms of equality—presumably in free India, non-existent at this point. Adela is briefly mentioned when Aziz wonders mistakenly if Fielding is now married to her. It transpires that Fielding has not married Adela at all. Both Fielding and Aziz communicate a sense of relief, as for both of them as also for Forster, Adela has now become a source of embarrassment and awkwardness.

In this novel, Forster does not look at the question of heterosexual intimacy between persons belonging to different racial groups. Adela's interest in Aziz, which could have been a narrative possibility, is never developed. How do we view Adela's inexplicable withdrawal of charges and Aziz's subsequent acquittal? While Forster may have quelled new constructions of the bestial Indian native, he does not engage or elaborate on the gendered race issue. Instead of enlarging on this theme, Forster drops the subject altogether.

Meanwhile, Fielding and Mrs Moore, two white figures, are shifted centre stage to endorse Forster's liberal philosophy of reaching out emotionally and intellectually across the racial divide, rather than in the flesh. Mrs Moore leaves for England and dies at sea around the time that Aziz faces trial. However, the goodwill represented by Mrs Moore makes jubilant Indians evoke her name as a positive incantation. In this episode, is Forster conferring a quasi-mystical identity upon Mrs Moore? Hard-pressed for any other evidence, one can only conjecture that Mrs Moore's advanced age renders her sexless and, consequently, her attempts to bridge the interracial divide do not pose a threat. Eventually, it is the perspective of empathy that emerges as a solution to the colonial dilemma. Through such a conclusion in *A Passage to India*, Forster also skirts around the issue of women's implication in the colonial enterprise and evades the vexed question of sexuality in the colonial context.

Alan Paton's well-known novel *Cry, the Beloved Country* also addresses racial tension in South Africa. Paton does not really engage with the question of gender or the marginalisation of women; instead, he focuses on the colonial, religious and racial divide. The central narrative is about a Black man's search for his son in the big city of Johannesburg. It highlights the slow but steady erosion of the Black way of life and the exploitative and dehumanising face of white imperialism, also recording the beginnings of Black dissent in the face of poor wages and a steady decimation of tradition. In *Cry, the Beloved Country*, Paton invests hope in the relationship of mutual succour established between Stephen Kumalo, a Zulu priest, and James Jarvis, a white landowner, after Kumalo Junior kills Jarvis Junior. James Jarvis turns benevolent messiah for the Zulu community at Ndotsheni after his son's death and the Black community responds to his overtures under the guidance of Stephen Kumalo, their parish priest. Subsequently, all manner of good things come their way. Suddenly, provision is made for the material and financial comfort of the Black community. Protests and agitations about delayed white paternalism are only distant rumblings, barely heard in the last chapter. In *Cry, the Beloved Country*, Paton's reading of racial tension and the possibility of resolving it at the level of interpersonal bonhomie without political alternatives has much in common with Forster's resolution of race relations in *A Passage to India*.

The treatment of women characters and the roles allotted to them in Paton's novel highlights women's secondary status. While there is no suggestion of any kind of frisson between men and women from opposite sides of the racial divide, the novel gives us many vignettes of Black women who lead subjugated and exploited lives within their communities—in both rural and urban areas. A raging Stephen, in a moment of gratuitous cruelty, can ask the young girl upon whom his son has fathered a child whether she would be willing to accept him, Stephen, sexually if he desired her. Although her scared and startled acceptance highlights the vulnerability of her position, it also spells out the fact that there are very limited possibilities for women in such a situation. Within the world of the novel, women can either be victims of male indifference and callousness or subsist under the benevolent patriarchal gaze. In Paton's narrative, women are of interest as long as they are affiliated to or associated with men. They are expected to fulfil the secondary roles of providing nurture, care and service to the dominant males in their lives as wife, mistress, whore, destitute, deserted woman, and so on. This holds even for the minor white woman characters we come across. The novel remains centred around the destinies of male characters, regardless of race.

A Passage to India and *Cry, the Beloved Country* heralded new directions for fiction in their exploration of colonial and racial tensions. Yet, neither Forster nor Paton engages with women's lives, either within the novel or within the colonial context itself. Their novels work within stereotypical narrative constructs structured around male destinies and echo earlier narrative trajectories in which the delineation of the male characters remains paramount. Centring their narratives on male protagonists and male experience, both narratives sideline the issue of women's enmeshment in the colonial context.

It is true that Forster touches upon the issue of sexual assault. Rape, both real and symbolic, is often a marker of the inherent violence in the colonial encounter. However, in keeping with his liberal political position, Forster makes little attempt to sustain this line of thinking. Instead, he makes the account fuzzy, allows Adela to retract her position and reduces her to an ineffectual figure. When Adela loses the sympathy of the supportive whites and is also dismissed derisively by the natives, Forster ships her back to England. It is almost as if Adela's quest is over and therefore relegated to the past—a fact reiterated perhaps by her surname, Quested. The question of interracial mingling, miscegenation and the threat to racial purity, a central preoccupation in the colonial context, remains unanswered.[3] Adela's retraction also makes it possible for Forster to veer away from the complex issues of interracial heterosexual intimacy.

An important departure from *A Passage to India* and *Cry, the Beloved Country* is V.S. Naipaul's *Guerrillas* which shares more common ground with *The Grass is Singing*. In this novel located in the Caribbean, Naipaul analyses more explicitly the issues of race and sexuality within the structures of neocolonialism. Naipaul's critique of colonialism, like Lessing's in *The Grass is Singing*, is direct and hard-hitting. Both Lessing and Naipaul share the chilling intuition that political resolutions in the colonial context are likely to be bloody and brutal, and this is emphasised very categorically in their novels.

Lessing and Naipaul mediate their presentation of the colonial encounter by building narrative action around the experiences of white women. In the novels under discussion, there is a focus on the forbidden intimacy between white women and native men. Both

Lessing and Naipaul portray privileged white women who make overtures to a native male. Coincidentally, Mary is the name of the central protagonist in both novels. An African native, Moses, murders Lessing's protagonist, a South African white woman. The white woman in Naipaul's narrative has a sexual liaison with a Caribbean native who murders her on the eve of her departure from the island. In *The Grass is Singing* and in *Guerrillas*, although the white women are brutally murdered, the idea of rape is not used to suggest the violence inherent in the colonial encounter. Instead, these two novels about the colonial situation focus on the murder of a white woman by a non-white native. Lessing and Naipaul suggest the possibility of physical liaisons and unsentimentally examine the reasons for violence in the context of interracial heterosexual contact.

The central plot of the two novels is both compelling and intriguing. Why is it that Lessing and Naipaul choose to portray a relationship between a white woman and a Black man? Within the interstices of racial interaction, such activity is not only culturally taboo but also punishable as a crime. Historical and material evidence throws light on the fact that initial interaction between members of different racial groups was far from hostile. Eventually, policing and monitoring of racial identity gradually replaced early interracial mingling. This was a part of the colonial project. However, despite all manner of laws and restrictions forbidding interracial sexual encounters, the sexual exploitation of the native women by the white coloniser was prevalent.[4]

I would argue that Lessing and Naipaul's analysis of the politics of colonialism and racial conquest in the realm of fiction draws our attention to the layering of the hierarchies of power and control. In other words, we have the old patriarchal structures at work where men are invariably in control, economically and socially, while women are confined to subordinate positions. This hegemonic structure of relationships also replicates itself in the relationship between the white community and the colonised people. Thus, the cultural structuring of relationships between women and men within a bourgeois hierarchy of class and gender is further complicated by the question of race relations and interracial relationships.

Lessing's novel adds further complexity by its detailing of the white woman's life, an aspect that Naipaul's *Guerrillas* does not address. Is it possible to stipulate that Lessing is a woman writer and, therefore, she operates from a different trajectory? Could one suggest that Lessing's positionality in the history of her times as a white woman allows her to read the questions of race and gender differently?

This could be resolved by looking at *The Grass is Singing* alongside two very popular and significant novels written by two white women whose work preceded Lessing's and encapsulated their experiences of Africa. These are Olive Schreiner's *The Story of an African Farm* (1883) and Karen Blixen's *Out of Africa* (1937). Schreiner and Blixen published their novels under the male pseudonyms of Ralph Iron and Isak Dinesen respectively. Their intention of deflecting attention from their identity as women novelists could be seen as an indicator of the continuing unease felt by women writers while negotiating the realms of public discourse such as the writing of novels. In portraying their women protagonists in new geographical locales, both Schreiner and Blixen—possibly nervous about their radical intention—chose the safety of male pseudonyms. Olive Schreiner (1855–1920)[5] was perhaps the earliest white woman to write about Africa. Schreiner's novel and Karen Blixen's[6] book, written at the high point of British and European colonial history, make for compelling reading.

Born in the second half of the nineteenth century, Olive Schreiner saw the subsuming of women's political rights under the more urgent rubric of the First World War. She lived through years of colonial conquest in South Africa, protesting against the exploitation of the natives. She participated enthusiastically in what were the beginnings of the Afrikaner women's movements, joining their protests and speaking at the Women's Enfranchisement League as its Vice President.[7] Schreiner's novel belongs to the period of the women's suffrage movements, while Blixen wrote *Out of Africa* in the 1930s when women were in the process of arriving at full suffrage. The central protagonist in both *The Story of an African Farm* and *Out of Africa* is a white woman. Since Schreiner and Blixen's writing comes out of a period of colonial imperialism, their novels show how patriarchal societies structure women's identities. Schreiner and Blixen exhibit tremendous personal grit and courage in their personal lives. However, their delineation of the white female protagonist in the two novels under discussion completely overlooks the fact that white women's histories formed part of a larger context of racial exploitation.

In *The Story of an African Farm* (1883), Schreiner's primary concern is about her female protagonist, the beautiful and rebellious white girl Lyndall. The narrative records Lyndall's passionate and intense life, starting with her childhood as an orphan, her education and subsequent rebellion and her eventual death after the birth of an illegitimate child. Schreiner's politicisation made her acutely aware of the cultural pressure to conform to prescribed roles that women faced in her time and her protagonist Lyndall is, therefore, equipped with a thirst for knowledge, travel and adventure and the desire to lead a less conventional life. The novel provides an emotive delineation of the restrictions inhibiting a woman's life and the trials and tribulations of intelligent and sensitive women thereof. *The Story of an African Farm* and *Women and Labour* (1911), Schreiner's influential tract, had a tremendous impact upon subsequent generations of women. Lessing read *The Story of an African Farm* intently when she was in her teens and speaks of the indelible impression the book left upon her: '[h]ere was the substance of truth, and not from England or Russia or France or America, necessitating all kinds of mental translations, switches, correspondences, but reflecting what I knew and could see.'[8] Lessing speaks of the extraordinary influence of Schreiner's *Women and Labour* in the 'Afterword' she wrote for *The Story of an African Farm*, corroborating that it 'became a kind of bible for the feminists.'[9]

The important thing to note about Schreiner's narrative is that although the Boer and the native African feature in her novel, their roles remain minimal. They function as shadowy figures on the periphery of the narrative. Despite her radical political position and her deep sympathy for the exploited African in real life, Schreiner's novel does not engage sufficiently with the African dilemma. In the final analysis, *The Story of an African Farm* is not a novel about race relations.[10] Schreiner's moving narrative and powerful protagonists notwithstanding, her focus is solely on the white woman's predicament.

Karen Blixen writes passionately about women's need for equality in her *Letters from Africa, 1914–1931.* Her letters also look closely at the white woman's rights and expectations within the institution of marriage.[11] When she speaks of native men and women in her letters, however, Blixen's interest in them parallels the sentiment she displays for her numerous pet animals. In Blixen's novel, the white woman character retains a larger than life representation with her individual story subsuming everything else. Lessing's review of Karen Blixen's *Out of Africa* takes exception to Blixen's narrative and describes it as 'a tale much concentrated, like a myth'.[12] Here too, the white woman's personal and financial preoccupations take on a disproportionate significance. By comparison, there is an exotic and diminutive presentation of the histories of the people of Central Africa. It is almost as if in Blixen's narrative, the hegemonic feudal class shifts from Europe and is reinstated in Africa. Lower down the feudal social order, the ordinary white person is replaced by exotic Black characters in an African milieu.

In her fiction and non-fiction writing, Blixen is critical of the oppressive racial and imperialistic policies that formed part of her life as a white woman in Africa. Despite dealing with race relations in her novel, Blixen's approach to Black people remains reductive. She views them as a subspecies, deeming their lives as significant only to the extent that she takes notice of them and incorporates them in her entourage. This is probably because Blixen has an inflated notion of her mission as cultural ambassadress to Africa. Her letters communicate the significance of the role of the white in bringing civilisation and empowerment to the natives. Her attitude towards the Black people she encounters, as well as those she fictionalises, is extremely paternalistic. Her treatment of Black males, in particular, deserves mention. Blixen deals with them indulgently and displays an amused tolerance of the kind extended to children.

Both Schreiner's and Blixen's engagement with the political debates on white middle-class women's rights allows them to adjudicate sensitively on behalf of white women in different ways. Yet, in their treatment of women's lives and destinies, they confine their protagonists' areas of authority within domestic and emotive boundaries. Both Schreiner and Blixen in the delineation of their female protagonists seem to echo the trajectory of the domestic novel. The actions of their central characters are circumscribed by the fact that they are women. In *The Story of an African Farm,* Lyndall dies after childbirth while her self-effacing cousin experiences repeated disappointments in her expectations of a happy domestic conjugality.

In *Out of Africa*, the Baroness who chooses to stay on and run a coffee estate draws strength from the loyalty and service of the Black men living on it. The high points of the narrative always remain her interaction with white friends. In the film based on the book, much is made of her friendship with the romantic white man who dies tragically in an air crash. The baroness' relationship with this man holds great promise and she is plunged into a void at his unexpected death. The personal and the sexual in both novels compellingly remain the centre of focus; these are the defining and circumscribing dilemmas of women's lives. This perception is reinforced by the film *Out of Africa*. In Schreiner's and Blixen's narratives, women's lives continue to be structured by the older boundaries of private space which the nineteenth-century novel had explored at length as women's domain. In both novels, the larger questions of race and colonialism and white women's complicity remain unexamined.

In its privileging of female experience, *The Grass is Singing* shares similarities with Schreiner's and Blixen's work. Yet, Lessing's novel also marks a clear shift from their work. By embroiling her female protagonist into the dilemmas of race and presenting the reader with a rather unsympathetic portrayal of her female protagonist, Lessing deliberately shifts the focus elsewhere. As readers, the author does not invite us to identify emotionally with the central character. While Lessing recognises the pressures at work upon middle-class women within white society and shows how these operate upon her central character, she creates a sense of distance by starting the narration towards the end of the story rather than at its commencement. Using the technique of analysis after the event to scrutinise the malaise of colonialism and racial exploitation, Lessing, through this narrative methodology, questions the premises of the cultural codes under operation in racial South Africa. To examine these aspects, it would be useful to look at the publication history of *The Grass is Singing*.

The Grass is Singing

Lessing drew upon her own experiences as part of the settler community in Southern Rhodesia and South Africa in her fictional writing. She resigned from a job at a law firm in Salisbury to write this first novel. A publisher in Johannesburg accepted the manuscript, took a large percentage of possible proceeds for himself and then delayed publication, attributing it to the subversive nature of the book. Lessing eventually left for England along with her copy of the unpublished manuscript in 1949.

In England, Lessing's manuscript generated a lot of interest and Knopf eventually indicated acceptance. Lessing recounts how they suggested that she rewrite the novel to present an explicit rape scene since this was very much 'in accordance with the mores of that country'.[13] Although she refused to alter her narrative, her publishers got round this by producing an edition with an outrageous cover of a 'blonde cowering terrified while a big buck nigger . . . stood over her, threatening her with a panga'; Lessing's protests that she had not intended the Black man to be 'a great, stupid, murderous thug' were ignored.[14]

The book had a wonderful reception, winning accolades on both sides of the continent, and it was 'reprinted seven times in five months'.[15] Largely because of her successful book, Lessing became a visible public figure and managed to attract the ire and indignation of white authorities in Southern Rhodesia and other parts of Africa. By 1956, Lessing was a Prohibited Immigrant and could not enter most parts of Africa due to her indictment of white attitudes in South Africa in her novel. To keep her out of Africa seemed to be the best way of dealing with her and of ensuring that she did not make any further trouble.

This brief publishing history and the political fallout thereof draws attention to the attempts to silence Lessing on part of the publisher she had approached in Johannesburg and the white political regime. It is easy to understand why *The Grass is Singing* set up certain kinds of expectations and elicited a particular kind of response. The usual way of reading any narrative dealing with race and gender is deeply conditioned such that to say 'race' is to mean a 'Black man' and to say 'gender' is to mean a 'white woman'. The dynamics of this interface tend to be those of power and sexuality. Either the Black man is seen as a threat to the white woman—in which case we deal with the issue of sexuality. If it is a question of power, then we are looking at the logistics of control exercised by a white woman over a Black man. Lessing's publishers played up the first stereotype by using a jacket illustration showing a Black man in an aggressive and threatening posture behind a cowering blonde. The political authorities responded to the second stereotype by declaring the country out of bounds for Lessing.

Lessing's narrative does lend itself to the possibility of such an interpretation at one level. This is perhaps due to the portrayal of the Black man in the novel. As readers, we are not part of the interiority of the Black man's experience. From the perspective of the white community which views him within the narrative, his presence tends to perpetuate imperialistic myths of Black savageness and sexual aggression. Alongside, there also exists the element of intimacy with a white woman. On the face of it, therefore, we have within the novel all the conventional ingredients for a racy narrative. Lessing herself points out that the element of explicit rape would have 'been a novelty'.[16] Such a reading would then have reiterated ill-founded but deep-rooted stereotypes about the lustful Black man and the vulnerable white woman in a colonial encounter.[17]

My reading of this novel sees it as the earliest indicator of Lessing's feminist interventions. Lessing's focus on a white woman's story within a colonial framework is a questioning of the premises of white middle-class feminism much ahead of its time. I would argue that in this first novel, Lessing records her discomfort with the limitations of a perspective that engages solely with the interiority of white middle-class women. A brief outline of the plot of *The Grass is Singing* and a quick review of earlier criticism on this novel will help to illustrate the point.

The Grass is Singing: Plotting Mary's Story

This is the story of a white woman called Mary Turner and her transition from a life on the fringes of poverty to one with employment—providing her with minimal economic security. Mary's story, however, emerges from within the complex and complicating hierarchies of class, race and gender. Mary's personal success does not make for any site of feminist resistance. Lessing shows Mary as deeply grounded in the prejudices and biases of her class and race.

Single, employed and unattached, Mary's perception of herself undergoes a major alteration when she overhears unpleasant opinions voiced about her. Women she has thought of as friends discuss her nature, clothes and lifestyle threadbare, even hinting at her possible abnormality. First, Mary goes into deep shock; next, she accepts a proposal of marriage that comes her way from Dick Turner. Both of them barely know each other at the time of marriage. They live hard lives on a farm and the attendant poverty and extreme heat do not improve things. The marriage slides from bad to worse. Dick falls ill and events on the farm drive Mary into the hopelessness of despair.

On the farm, Mary interacts daily with Black people whose existence had never impinged on her consciousness earlier. Mary eventually slides into an uneasy intimacy with Moses, her houseboy, after displaying initial racial hatred. The local doctor recommends a holiday away from the farm for both the Turners. Marston, the fresh-from-England overseer hired to take charge of the farm during Dick Turner's absence, observes Mary's relationship with her houseboy. Marston's stumbling upon the intimacy between Mary and her houseboy makes her dismiss Moses. Angered by Mary's slighting of him, Moses hides and hovers around the farm and eventually murders her. Having done so, he waits near the dead body until the police come and then surrenders.

Earlier Criticism on the Novel

The Grass is Singing lent itself very early to a film production that provided insights into the race question.[18] Early criticism of the novel tends to view it in the light of its observations on the race issue.[19] Seen as drawing heavily from a tradition of realism,[20] the novel firmly places Lessing as the literary successor of Olive Schreiner and D.H. Lawrence.[21] Early criticism also tends to mine the novel for its critique of colonialism and for prophesying the doom of empire in the tradition of Forster.[22] Recent criticism has offered psychoanalytic readings of its central character[23] and analysed the narrative as indicative of Lessing's deep-seated 'matrophobia'.[24] Eve Bertelsen sees the novel's conclusion leading to 'a mystical and deterministic resignation in the face of the forces of savage nature'[25] while Shadia Fahim's Sufi reading deems Mary's tragedy as emanating from the 'negative result' of never undertaking the 'arduous journey' of the inner realm.[26]

Curiously, while the novel invariably finds mention in most accounts dealing with the question of race or colonialism, *The Grass is Singing* is seldom included in discussions that see Lessing's early work as feminist. It is Lessing's treatment of the 'generational conflict' in the Children of Violence series and her experiments with form and narration in *The Golden Notebook* that are usually identified as her primary feminist expositions.[27]

My point of departure from earlier criticism on *The Grass is Singing* is in reading gender and race together and studying the implications thereof. I intend to show how Lessing works her way through the accretions of the past to draw attention to the traditions she consciously sidesteps or reformulates in the portrayal of woman characters in her novels. An understanding of Lessing's novel also involves a reading back into her own lived experience. I contend that in *The Grass is Singing,* Lessing's juxtaposing of the issues of feminism alongside those of race is a very significant intervention. In doing so, Lessing's first novel signals the limitations of white feminism whenever it encounters the question of race.

Lessing wrote her novel in the late 1940s in South Africa. This was a time when race was not a significant issue, as she points out herself.[28] By this time, women had won the right to vote. They had more equality based on laws and enjoyed greater economic freedom bolstered further by the welfare state's incorporation of most of the demands made by women's groups. The women's movements were also yet to regroup around newer agendas.

While some issues pertaining to women seemed to be on the back burner, what remained an ongoing process was the participation of women in the promulgation and continuation of colonial empires. On the Continent, women came out of domestic spaces not only to support the war but also to contribute variously to the imperial effort. A large number of women moved to the colonies as wives, teachers, employees and homemakers. They did so as privileged Europeans belonging to a culture supposedly far superior to the Black culture they would be presiding over. Their geographical relocation did not necessarily entail a dislocation of their belief in a feminism that focused primarily on the rights of white women. It is this belief that both Schreiner and Blixen endorse in their narratives. A major feature in the grouping and regrouping of women's interests at this point is that in mainstream white culture, women had been battling with class and gender and agitating over more equitable distribution of the resources, benefits and laws in their societies for a very long time. Yet, the moment it became a question of national and cultural identity, women tacitly reaffirmed their support to familiar and hallowed patriarchal pursuits. Thus, women were invariably co-opted into the larger agendas of colonial expansion that were the driving impetus of their society. Most women implicated themselves as collaborators in the colonial enterprise.

Small groups of pacifists and anti-abolitionists existed and they resisted both war and racial inequity. However, it took much longer to articulate a questioning of the structure and policies of the colonial state and its dispensations. In fact, an examination of the rigorous cultural policy implemented by the colonial state was yet to take place. While struggling to achieve equal status within their own cultural community, white women tended to overlook the inequities that they sanctioned and supported when dealing with people of colour.

The processes of decolonisation in the 1940s probably played a significant role in highlighting this issue. The ferment of Third World nationalisms introduced an element of cultural relativity into otherwise impermeable occidental perspectives. The colonies increasingly became important sites where this issue was to surface repeatedly after the Second World War. Emergent nationalisms in Asia and Africa began to question the arrogation of racial and cultural privilege that had allowed the whites to construct and maintain an unequal system. Ann Stoler documents how notions of monolithic white imperial authority were also under strain in this period. A large number of poor whites and women within the white community increasingly undercut predominant white notions of cultural superiority and authority.

Due to the economic impoverishment and deviation from the norm, this group of poor whites and women was socially and economically at par with the native.[29]

The citation at the beginning of *The Grass is Singing* takes note of these schisms within white culture and mocks the assumptions of Western civilisation by declaring that it is the trajectory of 'the failures and misfits'[30] produced by a civilisation that enables us to understand it. With this headnote, Lessing alerts the reader to her critical location vis-à-vis Eurocentric cultural ideology.

In raising the question of the rights of a white woman in a racial society, Lessing relocates older debates about women's roles and identities in a very new political context. *The Grass is Singing* takes issue with the limited Eurocentric notions of women's quest for equality that existed well into the 1950s and draws attention to the singularly occidental and largely middle-class nature of the struggle for women's rights to franchise. She also highlights how processes of identity formation prevail insidiously for both men and women and remain significant cultural determinants.

The Grass is Singing: Historical and Political Contexts

The geographical boundaries of Lessing's early novels are located within South Africa. This continent, in her novels, also operates as a new fictive site that raises fresh queries about race and gender. Knowledge about the political and historical past of South Africa becomes indispensable to an understanding of the conflict between the Black man and the white man as well as the differences within the settler class, which Lessing's novel addresses.

Lessing observes that 'Southern Rhodesia is self-consciously British' and 'came into existence as a British colony, opposed to the Boer-dominated Union of South Africa . . . she has taken her political structure from the Union'.[31] This is pertinent to our understanding of the similar nature of the racial conflagration, both in Southern Rhodesia and South Africa.

European intervention in South Africa started at the beginning of the nineteenth century, much earlier than it did in Southern Rhodesia.

The Dutch Boers, the French Huguenots and the British were visible in Cape Town in the latter part of the eighteenth century. Britain took over the administration of Cape Colony in 1795. The Dutch took back the colony in 1803; the British recaptured it in 1806 and subsequently administered it in various ways.

There was also a far greater investment of white capital in South Africa. The discovery of diamonds in Kimberley in 1867 and gold-bearing reefs in Witwatersrand in 1886 provided great returns to infrastructural investment. The predominantly agricultural land was, as a matter of policy, earmarked for commercial exploitation. Production of crops for export played a major role in transforming the character of a backward, rural society. With the advent of domestic manufacturing and modern agriculture, there was also the displacement of the Blacks from their lands and their earlier way of life. Mining towns sprang up and reserves housed the Black population far away from their traditional living spaces. Dislocated from familiar landscapes and living patterns and forced into cheap unskilled labour, the natives were subjected to ruthless exploitation.

The Union of South Africa, dominated by the Boers and the British—all male—formed in 1910 made the region into a self-governing British dominion. Parliament was limited to the whites. The success and control achieved by the white minority was termed 'a marriage of maize and gold'.[32] *The Grass is Singing* also draws attention to this in the reference to Charlie Slatter as one of the 'enriched . . . farmers because of the sharp rise in the price of maize' around the First World War.[33]

The Native Land Act, limiting the purchase of land by Africans, was in place by 1913. Around 70% of the Black population was pushed to live in the reserves that comprised around 7% of the total land. The Act made it illegal for Africans to purchase or lease land anywhere except within the designated reserves. Politically, socially, culturally and economically, Black people were alienated from their land and their way of life in a systematic manner. By 1914, the whites owned 90% of the land. Unable to live on their lands and sustain themselves, the majority of Black men worked either on white men's farms, in the towns or in the mines and were subject to compound and migrant labour laws. Whites owned, financed and provided technical skills and retained the well-paid, skilled jobs for themselves.

Although Black South African organised resistance to white rule and the South African Native National Congress (SANNC)—later renamed to African National Congress (ANC)—came into being in 1912, white settlers continued to carry out economic, social, political and racial rampage with great aplomb and authority. This reached new heights with the election victory of the right-wing Afrikaner Party in 1948 and its introduction of 'apartheid'. Translating roughly as 'separateness' in English, this term encompasses the complete and systematic exclusion of Black people from access to any kind of social, political and economic participation alongside the whites. Apartheid ushered in more than four decades of institutionalised racial discrimination.

Acts and statutes such as the Prohibition of Mixed Marriages Act (1949), Immorality Act (1950), Population Registration Act (1950), Group Areas Act (1950), Bantu Authorities Act (1951) and Reservation of Separate Amenities Act (1953) enabled the government to implement a physical separation between the races. While these acts and statutes further consolidated white hegemony, they dealt a death blow to the Black community. Black women and children were the worst hit, being the most vulnerable group under this new dispensation. Organised resistance by Black men was crushed effectively in the initial years after Union.

The greater part of the twentieth century elapsed before democratic processes held sway in South Africa because the strategies and policies governing the colonial state rationalised this commercial and cultural exploitation. It was as late as 1994 that South Africa achieved democratic changes. This saw the end of apartheid and the beginnings of universal enfranchisement, national elections, as well as constitutional reform.

It is perhaps feasible to look at the entire colonial venture as a masculine operation—beginning with the conquest of a land and its people, followed by the subsequent exploitation of its land for agricultural export to the mother country and the mining of its mineral resources. Arguably, such activities are part of a patriarchal, male trajectory of praxis that incorporates women into it. Colonialism, in its administrative and political control over the colonies, replicates the patriarchal control within bourgeois society. As Ann Stoler points out, 'distinctions of color joined with those of religion and culture to distinguish the ruler from the ruled.'[34] Women's roles within the colonial enterprise need examination, keeping this framework in mind.

Women and the Colonial Situation

The larger question one must address has to do with the roles played by women on either side of the colour bar in the history of colonisation. My argument draws both from Ann Stoler's analysis of the schisms within the colonial enterprise—from the days of the Imperial British East Africa Company (IBEAC) as a trading company to the time that it began to effectively monitor the exploitative structures of colonial rule—and from Anne McClintock's reading of the colonial woman. Speaking of the role of white women within the colonial state, Anne McClintock states that white women 'barred from the corridors of formal power . . . experienced the privileges and contradictions of imperialism very differently from colonial men.'[35] White women, while negotiating their own spaces in a male-dominated society, were not often aware of or sensitive to the whole question of what colonial exploitation actually entailed.

McClintock's observation regarding the ambiguity of the positioning of white women within the processes of imperialism is a moot point. They did not directly deal with the economic or military decisions of the empire and seldom reaped its direct profits. However, white women were complicit in what can be termed as dual roles. They enjoyed positions of power vis-à-vis the colonised. Within their own racial group, they occupied very limited and circumscribed roles. It is possible to see this as a crucial period wherein women began to tentatively realise that their agendas did not necessarily need to imitate male trajectories of experience and understanding. The theoretical formulation of such ideas is a much later event and it took place only around the feminist movements of the 1970s.

The colonial encounter, then, operates as a cathartic geographical space. It is responsible for bringing new life and perspective to the rendering of women's experience by expressing women's unease or discomfort in the double bind of colonial patriarchy while articulating that women's experience cannot be isolated or viewed in seclusion from everything else that is going on in the world any longer. At such a juncture, the possibilities for feminism become enormous. It is this new envisioning that Lessing hints at in *The Grass is Singing*.

In *The Grass is Singing,* Lessing shows how women's lives and identities can no longer be confined to the private realm of domestic experiences but must be analysed alongside the discourses of race. By foregrounding race and gender, Lessing unfixes the notion of colonialism as part of the large, historical public domain where questions of race can be minimally located, if at all. I contend that she affects a clear rupture of the segregated public and private realms where the constitution of male and female subjectivities took place, thereby extending the ambit of the fictional representation of women.

Mary Turner's story is about a female protagonist who is part of a narrative that focuses directly upon the issue of race. Lessing posits that questions about women's subjectivity can no longer be raised without taking into account the other divides of race and class. This insistence on the constitutive connections between race and gender along with that of gender and sexuality frees female subjectivity from the constricting spaces of the private and personal realms. This not only metaphorically expands the range of women's participation and responsibility but also exposes the relative positioning of white middle-class feminism. Thus, Lessing's novel calls into question entrenched notions of Eurocentric women's movements as a unified monolithic entity.

Lessing's narrative explores the links between culturally sanctioned hierarchical roles for men and women and their replication within racial structures. This allows for a rereading of colonialism and enables us to re-examine the cultural construction of male and female identities. I would now like to draw attention to the formal narrative structure of *The Grass is Singing* in order to discuss Lessing's negative portrayal of Mary Turner.

Forms, Narratives and Oppressions

The thematic content itself is inadequate to an understanding of the novel. Its formal aspects are also crucial to the development of the narrative. Given the context of tropical Africa and a landscape of extreme heat and dust, the novel invites comparison with an older tradition of realistic and naturalistic writing. Depicting the failures of individuals in a closed society and the inability of its central characters to do very much with their lives, the deterministic nature of their existence and its conclusion can easily be located within the naturalist tradition. Yet, in terms of the conclusions that the narrative directs us towards, there is a criticism of certain kinds of life and certain kinds of choices imposed by a particular sociopolitical ethos.

Despite showing us Mary's struggle out of poverty, Lessing is critical of Mary and draws our attention to Mary's short-sightedness and insularity in most situations. Lessing's treatment of Mary's sexuality is also rather different from the treatment meted out to the woman figure, say, in a novel such as *Madame Bovary* (1856). Unlike Emma Bovary—the female protagonist of Flaubert's novel—who is passionate, amoral and sexually promiscuous, in keeping with the tradition of the naturalistic novel, Mary Turner in *The Grass is Singing* displays repugnance for any kind of sexual overtures. It is rather late in her life that Mary wakes up to the fact of the compulsory heterosexuality internalised by men and women in her culture. In recording Mary's aversion to heterosexual encounters and drawing our attention to the fact that heterosexuality is a compulsive marker of adult behaviour, Lessing's narrative seems to echo Foucault's viewpoint on state-monitored sexual mores.[36]

Her discussion of Mary Turner's life does not endorse the conventional male point of view. Emma Bovary, in *Madame Bovary*, drifts into amorous relationships in search of true love, propelled apparently by the boredom of provincial life—thereby neglecting a devoted but ordinary husband. The reasons offered up by Flaubert for Emma's transformation strain credibility, given women's agency in those times. Arguably, Emma's portrait resembles the idle wealthy young men of her times more than it reflects the life of dependent young women. Lessing's protagonist Mary is preoccupied with a different angst, that of fitting in and receiving the approval of her community.

Lessing's location of her text in South Africa—or as she put it, 'anywhere south of the Zambezi'[37]—is part of her decision to chart newer and less familiar territory. Outside of Europe and England, the home to progressive democratic movements, *The Grass is Singing* highlights the precarious location of both reason and equality when measured alongside imperial and racial stratagems. The novel, I would argue, shows that Mary Turner's bid for equality and personal freedom remains extremely limited, given the new complexities thrown up by the dimensions of race and colonialism. Lessing's Mary Turner is not pushed into grandiose, delusionary acts of self-aggrandisement of the kind that Emma Bovary is made to undertake by Flaubert.

The Limits of Liberal White Feminism

In *The Grass is Singing,* Lessing makes us look anew at the political and cultural connotations of the word 'woman'. She shows us the larger ideology that nurtures the achievements of individual women and subsequently feeds into the construction of the categories of race and colonialism. Mary Turner, the central protagonist, does not begin as the prototype of a subjugated or oppressed woman. Nevertheless, her personal, social and economic gains involve the taking on of an identity sanctioned to her by the structures of civilised white society. As a free white woman, Mary works and socialises within her class and race. Yet, her own group does not allow her to retain this identity. Conventionally, women must settle down, marry and then raise a family. By accepting such precepts and internalising them, Mary shows how the cultural codes scripted by her specific white society act upon her. These codes that come into operation for white women in their private lives subsequently form and shape male and female conduct at the social and political level. It becomes incumbent upon Mary to lead a heterosexual life and quit her job upon marrying to follow her husband to his home. Outside of this personal structure, Mary's interaction with Black people is in keeping with the dictates of colonial ideology. Her actions and decisions echo the ideology of the ruling whites.

Drawing attention to the colonial politics of South Africa, Lessing relocates the female subject in the narrative to a space fraught with much more than domestic or economic frisson. Mary's personal drama is deeply enmeshed within the larger structures of race and colonialism. Mary Turner's trajectory of personal gains and achievements is in the context of Africa and therefore very different from earlier stories of personable young women who draw up new trajectories for themselves in familiar, recognisable England. Lessing's first novel does not engage merely with the construction of Mary's social self. Instead, it shows how the compelling ideology of imperialism pushes Mary towards a particular identity formation. In *The Grass is Singing*, Lessing interrogates the notions of freedom and equality as they are available to Mary and looks beyond her immediate story, drawing attention to the larger ideologies within which notions of liberal feminism are enshrined.

Mary Turner is economically independent. She has worked her way up from being the poor daughter of a petty railway official. Instead of a celebratory tone, the authorial voice focuses on her limited exposure and insularity. Mary inherits 'an arid feminism'[38] from her mother and does not possess any kind of sensitivity to her father's suffering. 'About what?' She retorts. 'He's a man, isn't he? He can do as he likes.'[39] The authorial voice also comments on Mary's lack of awareness of her good fortune as a single woman in South Africa and her ignorance of conditions in other countries. At this stage in the narrative, Mary leads a privileged life that is confined to the city limits of the white population. Mary plays sports and socialises at the sports club. She resides at a hostel for working women when she is employed as a secretary in an office.

In her portrayal of her female protagonist, Lessing's intention is not to show her as representative of the 'New Woman'. Mary's is an ironic portrayal, one that shows up the limitations of white middle-class feminism. Mary, despite being free and economically independent, is still very deeply rooted in her community's ideologies. Having internalised the common assumptions of her community, she continues to postpone acting upon them for the greater part of her privileged and singular adult life. Lessing's focus on this problem indicates that older patterns of thought and narratives, where women's identities remained part of a constricting private world, are no longer adequate for an understanding of how newer women's identities can be arrived at. With new geographical boundaries and newer political roles, women's lives and histories take on a new perspective and involve a search for newer orientations.

Mary's achievements themselves are not so minimal if one were to read against the grain of the narrative voice. Even though she was a white woman, she was part of the poor white community. She survived against great odds. Her younger siblings had succumbed to dysentery. A shortage of money and domestic friction between her parents was the past from which she escaped to economic independence as an adult. However, Mary's individual achievement when viewed beside a larger colonial history merits only a diminutive status. For this reason, Lessing does not intend us to see in her story the possibility of individual growth and success. In *The Grass is Singing*, Mary's story is a case study and a critique of the notion of feminism as operational at the level of limited individual success. Through Mary's story, Lessing suggests a drastic re-examination of this notion.

The Grass is Singing is a prototypical study of how social codes and prescriptions distort and thwart possibility. By critically examining the structures through which the self is constructed, Lessing shows such constructions to be based on several extraneous considerations. The sympathy that the reader might feel for Mary due to the uncharitable treatment meted out to her by her peer group alternates with the hostility evoked by Mary's attitude to Black people. Mary is no lover of Black people, nor does her discomfort within her social group spring from deep-seated anti-racism. The narrative voice does not allow us to forget that Mary completely subscribes to the stereotype of the oppressive white in a colonial situation. Mary's initial response to the Black people she encounters echoes and mirrors the white community's attitude towards the Black population. This is a hostile colonial society, insular and hemmed in by its parochial norms, prejudices and brutal assumptions. When compared to the white community in *The Grass is Singing*, the community of whites portrayed in *A Passage to India* come across as far more sociable, capable of amicable interaction and therefore more receptive to forging interracial connections.

Within the white community to which she belongs, Mary is subject to unpleasant and unflattering scrutiny. By the end of the novel it is made amply clear that she is disliked and disapproved of by the entire white community whether it is her social circle of male and female friends, her husband Dick, their neighbours, the local police officer or, for that matter, the author herself.

Within the boundaries of this white racial group, Mary's life and the event of her death remain an aberration. For the whites, Mary is not an acceptable representative at all. Mary's difference lies in her being single and female and not aspiring to a happy marriage like women in her social group. It also lies in her uneasiness with heterosexuality. Her immediate social circle views her repugnance to conventional heterosexuality as an illustration of her abnormality. The fact that she leads her own life with a measure of independence is clearly not enough in a compulsively heterosexual society where 'all women become conscious, sooner or later, of that impalpable but steel-strong pressure to get married'.[40] Deeply affected by the criticism levelled at her, Mary's 'idea of herself was destroyed and she was not fitted to recreate herself.'[41]

Her bewildered haste to win social acceptance pushes her into a marriage with Dick Turner and further impoverishes her financially. In the close-ups of Dick and Mary's marriage, Lessing divests this socially sanctioned heterosexual relationship of all traces of romance. We take a hard look at the power structures that operate within any conventional marriage in most cultures. Dick makes little money from the farm and invests in too many impractical schemes; yet, he continues to make all the major financial decisions. Mary, despite her shrewdness, does not offer advice since she 'needed to think of Dick, the man to whom she was irrevocably married, as a person on his own account, a success from his own efforts. . . . She needed a man stronger than herself'.[42] Madame Bovary, we need to recall, is made to embark upon sexual dalliances and expenditure and has little qualms about using her husband's money, hoodwinking him or neglecting her child.

While such cultural pressures dictate Mary's actions, they also guide and shape Dick Turner's worldview. For instance, Dick's notion of women is very conventional and stereotypical. His interest in Mary develops because a trick of light makes him fall in love with Mary's profile while watching a film in a cinema hall. He also proposes to her largely because of his loneliness. Bracing himself to be the provider of the family, Dick—prior to his marriage—draws strength from two pictures on his bedroom wall: 'one was of a chocolate-box lady with a rose in her hand; and the other was of a child of about six'.[43] He tears down these pictures upon Mary's arrival but is unable to put up anything new in their place. While he welcomes Mary's participation, he is not keen on management that will reduce his authority.

One of the most telling episodes in the novel is when Mary asks if they might have a child. Dick, who has always wanted children, is pleased but when he sees that Mary 'was desiring a child for her own sake, and that he still meant nothing to her, not in any real way', he obdurately refuses.[44] Both Mary and Dick are constrained by the cultural codes and assumptions that they must follow. Lessing explores a similar theme in Martha's marriage to Douglas Knowell in *Martha Quest*. In both these novels, Lessing traces the hierarchical structures that are set in place within a marriage and shows how these continue to be shaped and sanctioned by cultural expectations.

While the exterior narrative charts the failure of the Turners and shows up their abysmal record as colonising subjects, there is an interior narrative of Mary's inner life which examines Mary's transformation from a passive colonial subject into someone who is at odds with the system itself. From an initial repugnance of heterosexuality and contempt towards Black people, Mary moves into a relationship of dependence with Moses. She eventually offers her relationship with Moses as proof of her sexual normalcy—she 'was not like that'[45] after all. Does a Black man enable Mary's discovery of her sexuality? The answer to this rests in speculation or in the shadowy realms of Mary's mind. What the text records more forcefully is Marston's shock that 'one of the guarded, a white woman',[46] had so easily evaded the barriers to cross-racial intercourse set up through stringent statutes and policing.

This is precisely why the news of Mary's death evokes complete silence from both her neighbour Slatter as well as the police officials. A 'vicious grimace'[47] contorts the faces of these men as they view her dead body. They show very little sympathy for Mary as, from their point of view, she has let the white 'side down'.[48] Mary's not conforming to the 'esprit de corps'[49] of white Africa evokes 'instinctive horror and fear'.[50] It puts great pressure on the Slatters and Marston who have to work hard at 'preserving appearances'.[51] A Black man kills Mary, presumably in search of valuables. This is the officially circulated account of Mary's murder. The particulars of Mary's case—that this was not a random killing by a passing stranger, that the Black man was a known employee, that she herself was sexually deviant and that she had gone 'native', wearing material and jewellery usually sold to native women at the stores—were suppressed, so that they never formed part of any official report.

The narrative voice explains why Mary's murder was hushed up. The anxiety and insecurity of the white elite was the cause. Even the very suspicion that other interpretations existed would push the beleaguered white civilisation into further consternation. It could never admit to the possibility of human intimacy existing between a white woman and a Black man. This would lead to the crashing down of its elaborately constructed and administered racial ideology. Mary's very existence becomes an aberration when viewed through the eyes of the white rulers. Mary is thus doubly silenced. First, by the fact of her physical death and later by the deliberate quashing of the actual details around her death.

Within the structure of white colonial patriarchy, women have very limited roles to play. They contribute to the efficient building of the empire with their domestic support. This quality is shared by Mrs Slatter and her wide circle of acquaintances, with the exception of Mary. Mary's inability to play this role makes her presence irrelevant.

We observe Mary's loss of identity and moorings. Having given up her job in the city to marry Dick, Mary is now completely at sea. 'She felt, rather, as if she had been lifted from the part fitted to her, in a play she understood, and made suddenly to act one unfamiliar to her'.[52] At this point in Mary's life, her expectations no longer correspond to the codes and rules she has so far followed. An aborted attempt to find a job, yet another to wield the *sjambok* and capitalise on her white authority, the continual economic disasters that Dick's schemes end up in, the irregular farm labour and her inability to get on with her Black servants—these are played out in a continuous cycle. Mary's last-ditch attempt to escape from the farm falls through when Dick follows her to town after she flees and entreats her to return.

The narrative voice records the change that she undergoes on the last day of her life. Mary moves from the blankness and despair that has characterised her years on the farm. A mist seems to have cleared and she seems to emerge from the stupor brought on by her loneliness and isolation. 'Today she was vastly peaceful and rested. Her mind was clear, and her body comfortable'.[53] While wandering about the farm, she suddenly stumbles upon the hiding Moses. Aware that Moses will exact his revenge, she wonders if she should appeal to Marston for help. At this point, the repetitive nature of her experience strikes her. Recollecting that her earlier attempt to save herself and function according to prescribed codes had brought her to the unending years on the farm, she resolves that '[s]he would walk out her road alone. . . . That was the lesson she had to learn.'[54] This decision marks the beginnings of Mary's self-understanding.

As she says later to Marston who is unable to comprehend her, 'I have been ill for years. . . . Inside, somewhere. Inside. Not *ill*, you understand. Everything wrong, somewhere'.[55] This is an important moment of knowledge for Mary. It is a moment of understanding and acceptance of her guilt and complicity. She can no longer go back or ask for help. The novel now hurtles towards its conclusion which is pessimistic and grim. Mary is brutally murdered and Dick becomes insane. Why is it that of all the white characters in the narrative, only these two suffer? Dick's empathy for the land he cultivates is not seen in the other successful farmers who make profits from their holdings. Why are the other whites let off scot-free? These questions plague the reader. One way of getting round this is to see Moses' revenge, Mary's death at his hands and the lack of reverence for agricultural land itself as a prophecy of the state of things to come. This bleak and violent conclusion is Lessing's prediction of what colonialism and racism in South Africa will lead to eventually. The novel, like the world it recreates, no longer lends itself to an equitable dispensation of rewards and punishments.

Conclusions, Insertions and Openings

If we were to read the novel's conclusion as a 'resignation in the face of the forces of savage nature,'[56] it would mean overlooking the irony that Lessing brings to bear upon the narrative. Such a reading views Lessing's novel as complicit in the production of knowledge whereby the Occident views, interprets or analyses the non-Occident. The construction of the myth of the noble savage, one must remember, originated when differences in technological development exacerbated the differences in community and colour. Colonialism at its most rudimentary meant the control and domination of human and economic resources for the benefit of the coloniser. The coloniser's superiority was projected by creating a hierarchy within the differences pertaining to culture and race. Simultaneously, mechanical advances, success in sea travel, ability to transport material and people and access to powerful and more advanced weapons endorsed and strengthened this primary domination. The emphasis on the cultural superiority of the coloniser enabled the perpetuation of the belief that the native was backward and inferior. This discourse of colonialism reinforced ideas of the superiority of the white civilisation over that of its colonies. To perpetuate the sense of superiority, there were constant checks on interracial encounters.

The Grass is Singing's engagement with the inner life of its white protagonist and its portrayal of the colonised subject poses a challenge to imperial and colonial ideology to 'sustain the identity of the ideological or discursive image it has created of the colonized and of the depreciated image the colonized have of themselves'.[57] How does the novel do this? By drawing attention to the schisms and hierarchies among the colonials themselves, providing a record of Turner's financial failure and the references to 'the growing army of poor whites'.[58]

An entire spectrum separates Dick from Slatter, who is quintessentially the successful white settler who has managed to exploit the land for agricultural and mineral returns. Slatter is at the opposite end from Dick Turner who, despite his real love for the land and resistance to the idea of farming as an aggressive commercial venture, is shown as unable to survive. Dick's economic failure, physical ill health and breakdown point to the inexorable machinery that is in place to deal ruthlessly with people who do not fall in line. Slatter is a harsh, insensitive man; cruel to both the country and the people he exerts supremacy over. His material success outweighs the finer sensibilities of Dick Turner. Slatter's success embodies the machismo of settler colonialism. Dick is simply not masculine enough.

This brings us to question of the cracks and fissures in the citadel of white racial superiority in the novel. The white settler community is extremely unsympathetic to the presence of poor whites since this undermines their wonted superiority vis-à-vis the Blacks. What the novel also draws attention to is that despite harsh and inequitable legislation designed to crush and subjugate Black people, poor whites still existed and were on the rise within the settler community. Poor whites evoked great hostility and contempt since they were always seen as letting the white side down. Their presence upset projections by the whites concerning their cultural and racial superiority over the natives. This is true of the general response the Turners evoked amongst the farming community during the period of their stay. Mary and Dick's continued struggle and failure added more reasons for despising them, while increasing the hope of buying Turner out cheaply. To add to this, Mary is seen as aloof and arrogant and seems rather odd in the way she dresses and keeps house. Her choice of a Black male servant as a constant companion is seen as abnormal. This makes her poor material for a possible icon of white cultural identity.

The novel records the systematic exploitation of Black people, their displacement from their homelands and confinement into dwindling reserves.[59] It makes mention of the ruthless press gangs that kidnapped Black men and sold them to white men on annual contracts for five pounds a head, forcing them to work for a pittance.[60] It draws attention to their cramped and unsanitary living conditions in ugly compounds on farms belonging to white settlers. The novel thus enables us to see how the colonial system oppressively disempowers the poor white male, the oddball white woman and Black persons.

Lessing highlights the subject position of both men and women whose identities evolve within the structures of imperialism. Seen in this light, Moses and the other Black men in the narrative represent not so much noble savages but men who have been dislocated from their traditional mores and customs and have been dehumanised to further the commercial and imperial ambitions of the settlers. The Black men in the narrative, then, are not some exotic species discovered by the white race but a people reduced to an abject state by repressive political, economic, social and cultural control on the part of the whites.

Moses' violence at the end of the narrative lends itself to meaningful interpretation in the light of Frantz Fanon's analysis of the Black man's anger. Lessing's novel's publication in England is followed closely by Fanon's book *Black Skin, White Masks* (1952). Lessing's formative years in Southern Rhodesia as a displaced white woman allow her to capture the dilemma of the doubly dispossessed Black man effectively. Her portrayal of Moses' dilemma and the violent act of killing that he performs echoes Fanon's viewpoint presciently.

Although Fanon's work draws upon the experience of being Black in Martinique and France, it provides valuable insights into readings of colonial interaction. Fanon's book discounts the possibility of a normal relationship existing between a Black man and a white woman, given the dynamics of their acculturation. Fanon's conclusion that the problem is not so much with individuals as with the system itself plays out in the relationship between a Black man and a white woman poisoned by the system in *The Grass is Singing*.

Fanon's articulation of the interiority of the Black man who wishes to be white enables us to read Moses' predicament. Educated at a mission with limited access to the white man's world, uprooted from his own traditions and full of half-formed anxieties, Moses has often been debased and insulted. He establishes a rapport with Mary, makes her tea and sees that she eats her meals, tends to her sick husband and brings her offerings of eggs and flowers. These propitiatory gestures by Moses uncannily parallel the following lines from Fanon's book:

> I wish to be acknowledged not as black but as white. . . .[W]ho but a white woman can do this for me? By loving me she proves that I am worthy of white love. . . . I marry white culture, white beauty, white whiteness. When my restless hands caress those white breasts, they grasp white civilization and dignity and make them mine.[61]

Marston's intervention makes Moses react to what he sees as Mary's rejection of him and her plan of leaving the farm, snaps the precarious control Moses has maintained all through the narrative. Could we interpret his killing of Mary as a reclaiming of his own identity? As he leaves the compound, Moses ignores a sleeping Dick 'since he had been defeated long ago' and is contemptuously dismissive of Marston, the enemy, 'whom he had outwitted'.[62] Albeit brutal, Moses' act of self-assertion prophecies the future course of violent action that the Black population would be forced to follow—both in Southern Rhodesia and in South Africa. Psychologically, it also works as a form of ideological revenge through which the Black man seeks to assert himself. This countering of the white man's violence with the Black man's reprisal, we must note, also leads to the silencing of the white woman, who is half reluctant and half complicit in the enterprise of empire.

In *Black Skin, White Masks,* Fanon does not address the interiority of women's experience, white or Black, or even seek to place it within a historical context. Lessing's narratives, all of which engage with the interiority of women's lives, fill this lacuna. Yet, she allows Mary to be murdered by Moses. Neither Moses nor Mary has much agency in the social and political context of the novel. Mary's brutal death remains disturbing and, arguably, Lessing chooses to offer Mary up as an iconic sacrifice. Mary wanted to have a child and Dick did not want to include a child in their economic struggles. Drawing attention to the bleak, postlapsarian world that the Turners inhabit, Lessing excludes the regenerative possibilities of birth and sets up a blood sacrifice involving the spilling of Mary's blood. This is a grim conclusion but in the world of the novel, Mary's story becomes a cautionary tale in the context of colonial control. While Dick and Moses are left behind to suffer, Mary is swiftly rescued by death.

Lessing addresses the absence of choice in Mary's life and her inability to find a suitable role through the character of Martha in *Martha Quest* (1952). Young, white, adolescent and on the threshold of experience, Martha journeys confidently towards economic independence, friendships and marriage. Unlike Mary, Lessing provides her with more space and more sympathy as she travels across two continents over several decades in search of similar answers. It is possible to see Martha's journey as a continuing quest for meaning and connections. It is not a coincidence that Lessing's Martha Quest begins her journey in Africa around the time that Forster's Adela Quested, in *A Passage to India*, comes to the end of her travels; she 'quested no more' and stayed put in England.

Mary's death concludes Lessing's critique of individual white middle-class feminism, both literally and metaphorically. At this point, it would be pertinent to examine how the novel deals with the subject position of the Black female. In the course of Mary's life, the Black woman remains unspeaking. We view the doubly silenced Black woman twice in the novel through Mary's eyes. On the first occasion, when Mary goes into the compound to find the men, the narrative voice briefly encapsulates conditions of extreme poverty and squalor. The second time is when they come with their babies clinging to their bodies to the store to buy beads and baubles. The authorial voice records Mary's disgust at these women: 'they were alien and primitive creatures with ugly desires she could not bear to think about.'[63] The Black women function merely as sexual female bodies with frightening procreative and maternal energies. This construction of Black women in the colonial tradition changes very little when it comes to the implementation of policy outside of the colonies. Black feminists have documented how Black women have been treated unfairly by the 'state which is not only patriarchal, but also imperialist and racist'.[64]

While the novel does not deal with the interiority of the Black man's experience, the Black woman's life is one that remains doubly distanced. Probably, Black women were of even less relevance in a white settler culture that depended on Black male labour for agricultural and mining activities.

A Proper Marriage (1954) records racist white sentiment directed at Black women and shows their inadequate access to gynaecological services. In the short novelette *Hunger*, Lessing looks at the paucity of options available to Black women as the result of colonial practice. Women in the rural sector cope with the break-up of the family with little money available to feed mouths. In the city, one Black woman makes money by running a *shebeen*. Another young Black woman is plunged into a life of petty crime and prostitution. The story also records a Black movement with both men and women working towards Black nationalism. In her novels, Lessing shows how the process of colonialism—based as it is on racial differences—turns Black women into the alien and the 'other,' hardening and strengthening racial divides. While the short novelette focuses a little more on Black women's lives, Lessing's novels themselves do not engage with the interiority of their lives.

Lessing's work in the 1950s is significant as she juxtaposes the dilemma of white middle-class feminism with questions about the larger rights of 'other women' who are not white or middle class and are therefore rendered insignificant. Her fiction warns of the dangers of universalising fictional contexts. One runs the risk of subsuming significant topical references through such means of falsification, thereby leading to the total erasure of ground realities.

A case in point is Adrienne Rich's poem 'The Diamond Cutters' (1955), where Africa is invoked as a metaphor for the mining of untold riches: 'And know that Africa / Will yield you more to do'.[65] The mineable diamonds are seen as 'expensive fires / Fit to enamor Shebas'.[66] Within the poem, Rich equates the complex process of poetry making to the act of polishing the diamond. The metaphorical depths of the self, plumbed in the course of poetic self-expression, become comparable to the factual depths from which mining processes operate. Rich's use of this metaphor signals her ignorance of the exploitative contexts of diamond mining and the heavy price paid by generations of Africans as a result of the discovery of mineral wealth in Africa. Rich's reference to adorned and powerful Black women, mythologised 'Shebas', continues to juxtapose women with precious ornaments. Rich's perspective recalls earlier associations that portrayed imperialism as a project accumulating untold wealth on behalf of desiring women subjects, resulting in the obscene collection of riches on Belinda's dressing table dating as far back as Pope's *Rape of the Lock*.

Investing the Black woman in 'The Diamond Cutters' with mythical and historical power renders her actual alienation and acute poverty invisible. More revealing than the poem is the later commentary that a politically correct Rich offers in 1984:

> I was drawing, quite ignorantly on the long tradition of domination, according to which the precious resource is yielded up into the hands of the dominator as if by a natural event. The enforced and exploited labour of actual Africans in actual diamond mines was invisible

> to me and, therefore, invisible in the poem, which does not take responsibility for its own metaphor. . . . [T]his kind of metaphor is still widely accepted, and I still have to struggle against it in my work.[67]

Adrienne Rich's acknowledgement of this error in literary representation is now grist in the mill of Black feminist theorists. Rich's earlier 'ignorance' was symptomatic of the blinkered perception of white middle-class feminist agendas well into the 1970s. It also recalls feminist theorising within the white male dominated realms of class and gender and the silence around the issues of Black women. Feminists of colour brought this conspicuous absence of Black women's experiences and lives to the notice of white feminists in 1978.[68] Subsequently, Hazel Carby's interrogation of white feminists in 1981 proved to be an important intervention that transformed feminist theory in the early 1980s.[69] Speaking of how they have been silenced in colonial and white women's narratives and theory, Black feminists then began the slow process of recovering and tracing their 'herstories'.

Endnotes

1. Audre Lorde cited in Nada Elia, 'Violent Women: Surging into Forbidden Quarters,' in *Fanon: A Critical Reader*, eds. Lewis R Gordon, T. Denean Sharpley-Whiting and Renée T. White (Oxford and Cambridge, Massachusetts: Blackwell Publishers, 1996), 163.
2. Doris Lessing, *The Grass is Singing* (Great Britain: Michael Joseph, 1950; London: Grafton Books, 1980; repr., Paladin/Grafton Books, 1989). All references to the novel are from the 1989 edition. In this chapter, my discussion of *The Grass is Singing* will be informed with references to other related texts, both fiction and non-fiction, written by Lessing in the 1950s. Other Lessing texts dealing with Africa that were published in the 1950s include the first three volumes of The Children of Violence series—namely, *Martha Quest* (1952), *A Proper Marriage* (1954) and *A Ripple from the Storm* (1958)—and the two volumes of the *Collected African Stories*. These collected stories, written much earlier, appeared in their current format only in 1973. Her non-fiction writing dealing with this period of her life includes *Going Home* (1957) *African Laughter: Four Visits to Zimbabwe* (1992) and *Under My Skin* (1994). It is at this juncture of the decentring of nationalisms and the rising crescendo of women's

articulations that I would locate the significance of Lessing's narratives. In this chapter, I would like to explore the decade of the 1950s by analysing *The Grass is Singing.*

3. For a reading of how colonial authorities 'conjured up the supposed moral bankruptcy of culturally dissonant populations, distinguishing them from the interests of those that ruled', saw them as posing sexual and racial affronts to European identity and how they sought to impose control over this by monitoring adult bodies on the lines of bourgeois heterosexual relationships already in practice, see Ann Laura Stoler, *Race and the Education of Desire: Foucault's History of Sexuality and the Colonial Order of Things* (Durham and London: Duke University Press, 1995), 10. See also Cyril A. Rogers and C. Frantz, *Racial Themes in Southern Rhodesia: The Attitudes and Behaviour of the White Population* (New Haven and London: Yale University Press, 1962).
4. In the documentation of colonial histories, we see a shift from the intermixing of different races to a rigid policy of monitoring the sexuality of people in the Victorian period. What were once amicable racial interpolations, became matters of rigid colonial policy in the context of a Eurocentric perspective. On the one hand, we have the emphasis on racial purity while on the other hand, despite the existence of laws and prohibitions, we have instances of colonised women being subjected to sexual attention by the coloniser. For a detailed documentation of the implementation of laws to preserve racial purity, see Rogers and Frantz, *Racial Themes in Southern Rhodesia,* 137. See also Stoler, *Race and the Education of Desire*, 26–28.
5. Schreiner grew up on several mission stations in South Africa. She left for England in 1881 with *The Story of an African Farm,* her first novel, whose publication in 1883 established her as a literary figure both in England and in the United States. Schreiner stayed in England for about eight years before returning to South Africa, where she married a farmer–politician. Her subsequent trip to England was in 1913. She left for Cape Town in 1920 and died shortly thereafter.
6. Karen Blixen was married in 1914 to one Baron Blixen and moved to British East Africa subsequently, successfully running a coffee plantation till 1931 when financial losses made her sell the estate and return to Denmark. She wrote *Out of Africa,* published in Denmark and England in 1937, a few years after she left Kenya to resume life on the Continent. A valuable source for the material that went into the writing of her novel is her *Letters from Africa, 1914–1931* (1981).

7. In 1899, Schreiner delivered speeches as part of women's protest movements in the Cape, participated in the women's congress and was hailed by the Women's Enfranchisement League as a motivating and inspiring figure in the suffrage movement of South Africa. However, she withdrew her support when franchise rights were not extended to women of other races. For a passionate and vivid account of Schreiner's life and politics see Anne McClintock in *Imperial Leather: Race, Gender and Sexuality in the Colonial Contest* (New York and London: Routledge 1995), 258–295.
8. Doris Lessing, 'Afterword to *The Story of an African Farm* by Olive Schreiner,' in *The Doris Lessing Reader* (Great Britain: Jonathan Cape, 1989; London and Toronto: Paladin/Grafton Books, 1991), 494. All references are from the 1991 edition.
9. Lessing, 'Afterword,' 509.
10. Dan Jacobson, introduction to *The Story of an African Farm,* by Olive Schreiner (Great Britain: Chapman & Hall, 1883; London: Penguin Books, 1939; repr., London, New York and Australia: Penguin Classics, 1986), 21. The reference is from the 1986 edition. See also Anne McClintock for her brilliant analyses of all of Schreiner's writing in this light in McClintock, *Imperial Leather,* 267–288.
11. Isak Dinesen, *Letters from Africa, 1914–1931*, trans. Anne Born, ed. Frans Lasson (London: Weidenfeld & Nicolson, 1978).
12. See Doris Lessing, 'A Deep Darkness: A Review of *Out of Africa* by Karen Blixen,' in *A Small Personal Voice: Essays, Reviews, Interviews,* ed. Paul Schlueter (United States: Alfred A. Knopf, 1974; New York: Vintage Books, 1975), 147–150. The reference corresponds to the 1975 edition. Here she sums up the novel as reflecting Blixen's identification with 'nobility, noble behaviour' and 'feudal' airs. Calling her 'an enemy of the commonplace', Lessing draws attention to the Baroness' 'view of people as items in a high drama' she participated in and that 'while the idea that a man has rights was not one she could hold, she could not stand that he should be hurt or insulted.'
13. See Doris Lessing, *Walking in the Shade: Volume Two of My Autobiography, 1949–1962* (New York: HarperCollins, 1997), 8.
14. Lessing, *Walking in the Shade,* 8–9.
15. Martin Green, *The English Novel in the Twentieth Century: The Doom of Empire* (London: Routledge & Kegan Paul, 1984), 175.
16. Lessing, *Walking in the Shade,* 9.

17. The classic stereotypes of the sexually potent native male and his savage sexuality are part of the structures of colonial codification. For an extended history of this discourse which saw 'the colonized native American, African and Asian as eroticised savage or barbarian', see Stoler, *Race and the Education of Desire,* 124.
18. *The Grass is Singing* was made into a film called *Killing Heat.* For reviews and further information, see https://www.imdb.com/title/tt0084033/externalreviews?ref_=tt_ov_rt.
19. See Michael Thorpe, *Doris Lessing's Africa,* Modern African Writers (London: Evan Brothers, 1978).
20. Jeannette King makes this observation in her discussion of the novel in Jeannette King, *Doris Lessing* (London and New York: Edward Arnold, 1989), 1–7.
21. See Charles Sarvan and Liebetraut Sarvan, 'D.H. Lawrence and Doris Lessing's *The Grass is Singing,*' *Modern Fiction Studies* 24, no. 4 (Winter 1978–1979): 533–537.
22. See Green, *The Doom of Empire,* 168.
23. See King, *Doris Lessing,* 7–13.
24. Gayle Greene, *Doris Lessing: The Poetics of Change* (Ann Arbor: University of Michigan Press, 1994) 25.
25. Eve Bertelsen, 'Veldtanschauung: Doris Lessing's Savage Africa,' *Modern Fiction Studies* 37, no. 4 (Winter 1991): 647–658.
26. See Shadia Fahim, *Doris Lessing and Sufi Equilibrium: The Evolving Form of the Novel* (New York: St. Martin's Press, 1994), 50.
27. *The Grass is Singing* is usually seen as belonging to Lessing's African period while her subsequent novels written in the 1950s—from *Martha Quest* and *A Proper Marriage* up to *The Golden Notebook*—are seen as addressing the question of women's self-assertion and liberation.
28. In *Going Home,* Lessing's critical insight into the plight of Black people in Africa punctuates accounts of her actual visit to parts of Africa. In an afterword titled 'Eleven Years Later', added on in 1968, Lessing records the apathy to the African crisis in the House of Commons and observes that it 'was not until the 'fifties that any section of British opinion took an interest in Rhodesia, let alone any action.' Doris Lessing, *Going Home* (Great Britain: Michael Joseph 1957; London: Panther Books 1968; repr., London: Grafton Books, 1989). All references to the book are from the 1989 edition.
29. Stoler, *Race and the Education of Desire,* 26–32.

30. Citation by an unknown author in Lessing, *The Grass is Singing*, 7.
31. Lessing, *Going Home*, 64.
32. Alex Callinicos, *Southern Africa: After Zimbabwe* (London: Pluto Press, 1981), 74. My account of South African history draws from this work as well as from Howard Brotz, *The Politics of South Africa: Democracy and Racial Diversity* (London: Oxford University Press, 1977) and Heather Deegan, *South Africa Reborn: Building a New Democracy* (London: UCL Press, 1999).
33. Lessing, *The Grass is Singing*, 170.
34. Stoler, *Race and the Education of Desire*, 27.
35. McClintock, *Imperial Leather*, 6.
36. For this reading, I am indebted to Ann Stoler's extensive analysis of Foucault, in Stoler, *Race and the Education of Desire*, 10–15, where she discusses Foucault readings of sexuality as providing a formative system of control and policing.
37. Said by Doris Lessing in an interview. 'Interview with Doris Lessing by Roy Newquist,' in *A Small Personal Voice: Essays, Reviews, Interviews*, ed. Paul Schlueter (United States: Alfred A. Knopf, 1974; New York: Vintage Books, 1975), 46. The reference corresponds to the 1975 edition.
38. Lessing, *The Grass is Singing*, 35.
39. Lessing, *The Grass is Singing*, 35.
40. Lessing, *The Grass is Singing*, 40.
41. Lessing, *The Grass is Singing*, 43.
42. Lessing, *The Grass is Singing*, 127.
43. Lessing, *The Grass is Singing*, 53.
44. Lessing, *The Grass is Singing*, 135.
45. Lessing, *The Grass is Singing*, 186.
46. Lessing, *The Grass is Singing*, 186.
47. Lessing, *The Grass is Singing*, 21.
48. Lessing, *The Grass is Singing*, 25.
49. Lessing, *The Grass is Singing*, 11.
50. Lessing, *The Grass is Singing*, 20.
51. Lessing, *The Grass is Singing*, 25.
52. Lessing, *The Grass is Singing*, 97.
53. Lessing, *The Grass is Singing*, 190.
54. Lessing, *The Grass is Singing*, 200.
55. Lessing, *The Grass is Singing*, 201.
56. Bertelsen, 'Veldtanschauung,' 648.

57. See David Theo Goldberg, 'In/visibility and Super/vision: Fanon on Race, Veils, and Discourses of Resistance,' in *Fanon: A Critical Reader,* eds. Lewis R. Gordon, T. Denean Sharpley-Whiting and Renée T. White (Oxford and Cambridge, Massachusetts: Blackwell Publishers, 1996), 179–200.
58. Lessing, *The Grass is Singing,* 181.
59. Lessing, *The Grass is Singing,* 181.
60. Lessing, *The Grass is Singing,* 114.
61. Frantz Fanon, *Black Skin, White Masks,* trans. Charles Lam Markmann (New York: Grove Press, 1967), 63.
62. Lessing, *The Grass is Singing,* 206.
63. Lessing, *The Grass is Singing,* 95.
64. See Amina Mama, 'Violence against Black Women: Gender, Race and State Responses,' *Feminist Review,* no. 32 (Summer 1989): 35.
65. Adrienne Rich, 'The Diamond Cutters,' in *Collected Early Poems, 1950–1970* (London and New York: W.W. Norton & Company, 1993), 132.
66. Rich, *Collected Early Poems,* 131.
67. Rich, notes to *Collected Early Poems,* 423.
68. Pratibha Parmar and Kumkum Bhavnani wrote a tentative article for discussion on 'Racism and the Women's Movement' for a workshop on Women Against Racism and Fascism at the 1978 Socialist-Feminist conference, expressing their anguish over the failure of the British women's movements to take up the issue of racism that impacted all Black women. Declaring that such an attitude ensured 'that the Women's Liberation movement as a whole is irrelevant to the needs and demands of most black women', they stressed differences by concluding that it 'is clear that we are not "all sisters together".' See Pratibha Parmar, 'Other Kinds of Dreams,' *Feminist Review*, no. 31 (Spring 1989): 56.
69. Carby, amongst others, initiated the theoretical development of a Black critique of white feminist theory in her hard-hitting essay. Hazel V. Carby, 'White Woman Listen! Black Feminism and the Boundaries of Sisterhood,' reproduced in *Black British Cultural Studies: A Reader,* ed. Houston A. Baker, Jr, Manthia Diawara and Ruth H. Lindeborg (Chicago and London: University of Chicago Press, 1996), 61–86.

III

Tracing Older Histories: Marking Continuities in *The Golden Notebook*

Lessing's first novel *The Grass is Singing* drew attention to the silences outside of the boundaries that white liberal feminism demarcated. Lessing's novels of the 1950s—namely, the Children of Violence series, continue to touch upon the issue of race. However, there is a shift in focus and we are now introduced to Martha Quest, an engaging young woman who comes of age amidst the complexities of war, racism and colonial struggle in Southern Rhodesia. Martha, unlike Mary, is a favoured protagonist and appeals far more to Lessing and her readers. Through stories woven around Martha, Lessing deals with an enormous cultural matrix that highlights women's lives in all five books in the series. The worlds of *Martha Quest* and *A Proper Marriage*, the first and second books of the series, involve an articulate and restless heroine who plunges into the complexities of modern living. In its inception, the *Martha Quest* series can be seen as a forerunner of *The Golden Notebook*—Lessing's *magnum opus*—where modern lives are situated and read primarily through women characters. By increasing the number of women characters in *The Golden Notebook,* Lessing simultaneously records the plurality of women's existence and allows us to make imaginative leaps into women's historical and literary pasts.

The Golden Notebook[1] (1962) is the most popular and well-known of Lessing's novels. Discussing women's lives and framing them within a new narrative technique,[2] *The Golden Notebook*'s form and content draw attention to the subjectivities and experiential realities of women. Dealing unabashedly with women's private, personal, sexual and psychic experiences, the contents of *The Golden Notebook* expose us as readers to new dimensions of women's lives in a modern world. This chapter will look at Lessing's focus on women in her fifth full-length novel, published long before the feminist movements of the late 1960s.

The novel, at its time of publication, was prophetic in its visualisation of women's lives in the decades to come. It may be recalled that *The Golden Notebook* evoked tremendous interest among large numbers of women readers. Carey Kaplan and Ellen Cronan Rose, women who came of age in the 1960s and the 1970s, spoke of how this novel changed their perceptions of themselves, declaring that Lessing was a 'writer who, it seemed, knew us better than we knew ourselves.'[3] Readers responded emotionally to the book as it addressed 'many female emotions of aggression, hostility, resentment'.[4] Its focus on women's lives was seen as empowering and it has been co-opted as playing a formative role in modern feminism.[5] The book eventually achieved cult status and is now regarded by feminists as being a forerunner of the women's movements of the 1960s.[6]

While acknowledging its frank explorations of female sexuality and its significance in an era that heralded 'sexual liberation', this initial reading of the novel cannot be the basis of one's appropriation of it as a feminist text decades after its entrance into the literary scene. The prophetic insights offered by the novel at the time of its publication are no longer new or extraordinary in the year 2020, given the fact that fifty-eight years have elapsed. How then does one revisit this book from our current location?

The Golden Notebook is of relevance today if we read it as a primary text for second-wave feminism—first, by placing it in its historical context of the 1960s and second, by examining it in the light of Lessing's claim for it being 'a novel of ideas'.[7] My reading of the novel seeks to place it both as an extraordinary new arrival heralding second-wave feminism, as well as a novel whose central ideas and images grapple with concepts—such as individual freedom—that were articulated at the beginning of modern democratic movements in Europe at the end of the eighteenth century and the impact of these movements and ideas on the lives of women. By referring to this history of ideas, *The Golden Notebook* consciously draws our attention to an older tradition and history of women's lives and experiences, inaugurating an era of women's liberation and tracing connections with the past. While on the face of it *The Golden Notebook* can be seen as futuristic, my reading of the novel also seeks to highlight its evocation of a forgotten and overlooked past in which women played a central role. The novel's content and structure allow us to imaginatively recall an older period, replete with instances of women's communities.

The novel links contemporary women's lives and experiences and suggests associations with earlier history. Lessing's conscious use of structure enables us to see the connections between modern women and women from the past. *The Golden Notebook* records women's participation in the social life and political struggle of the twentieth century and imaginatively harks back to the time of the French Revolution. This evocation of a forgotten past provides for a retracing of historical and literary continuities which spill over into the present. Women's histories form part of the dense interweaving of the novel and these are retrieved and presented centre stage with an altogether new focus and energy.

The Golden Notebook shares familiar ground with other seminal texts that sought to examine closely women's roles and identities in Western societies. The impact created by its detailed examination of women's lives within the matrix of patriarchal structures has much in common with earlier writings such as Mary Wollstonecraft's essay 'A Vindication of the Rights of Woman' (1792), Virginia Woolf's *A Room of One's Own* (1929) and Simone de Beauvoir's *The Second Sex* (1952). While these aforementioned feminist tracts are in the form of pamphlets, essays and non-fictional prose, *The Golden Notebook*—introduced by a longish preface—is primarily a work of fiction. Lessing's novel extends the arguments raised by seminal non-fictional tracts into fiction. Her emphatic assertion is that it has much in common with these older traditions of writing and interrogation. Lessing's preface maps out the role she envisaged for her novel and the perspective she had written it from. The generic form of the novel, the use of polemic through the techniques of fiction and the imaginative rendering of experience into fiction allows Lessing to espouse various arguments on behalf of women and provide endless play with possibilities. In the case of *The Golden Notebook,* Lessing deliberately sets up connections between free women in the second half of the twentieth century to interrogate older traditions of writing. I will begin by prising out the older historical and literary connections that this novel is enmeshed in and subsequently place it in the historical and literary context of the 1950s and 1960s.

Women's Lives and Notebooks: Lesser-known Patriarchal and Literary Traditions

Lessing's retrieval of women in *The Golden Notebook* allows a close look at roles that devolve on women in modern life, as well as those which have been recorded within literary traditions. Her women characters address this older history along with the demands of their complex present. When Anna declares in the Blue Notebook that she is 'living the kind of life women never lived before',[8] Mother Sugar's rebuke is a sharp rejoinder:

> In what way are you different? Are you saying there haven't been artist-women before? There haven't been women who were independent? There haven't been women who insisted on sexual freedom! I tell you, there are a great line of women stretching out behind you into the past, and you have to seek them out and find them in yourself and be conscious of them.[9]

This exchange provides a crucial marker in reaching an understanding of the novel's structure.

One of the significant features of *The Golden Notebook* is that it makes women's presence visible despite the overriding pressure exerted by all kinds of political, cultural and patriarchal ideologies—ones that have greatly contributed towards the creation of reductive identities of women. The private sphere remains the culturally demarcated realm for women despite the continuing entry of women into the public world. This cultural demarcation exercise a powerful hold over the average imagination, despite women's participation in and for the war effort, their slow but eventual winning of suffrage rights and their active participation in the paid labour market. Within narrative strategies, the stories of individual women's personal growth and development are invariably lost; individual case studies get subsumed in the larger cultural processes that shape women's lives. As feminist readers, we repeatedly encounter the presence of strong powerful women who dot narratives and histories and are subsequently obliterated from memory and narrative. How does one check the sedimentation of women in history? One possible way of retrieving women's history would be to look at groups instead of individual women. *The Golden Notebook* does this through a location of women's experiences as stories of multiple women living and interacting in an androcentric world instead of as one isolated story under close scrutiny. In doing so, the novel dredges up women's lives buried within history.

Louise Yelin draws attention to 'the radically divergent place of men and women' in *The Golden Notebook,* where men are identified with 'national or transcultural political cultures' while women 'are situated in a chronotype—a narrative articulation of time and space—defined by gender.'[10] However, she does not view the 'chronotype' provided by the novel as offering any readings outside of contemporaneous English politics. I would argue that the impetus of this novel can be located within a much larger framework, not merely in the here and now of British politics in the 1950s and early 1960s.[11] The novel harks back to a much older tradition—one that Mother Sugar refers to as 'a great line of women stretching out . . . into the past.' This, I would like to reiterate, is the central idea behind the structure of *The Golden Notebook.*

Lessing discusses her technique of incorporating the four Notebooks in the preface to *The Golden Notebook,* allowing us to consider that her use of the 'Notebooks' as a new structural innovation was quite possibly impelled by her going back to the origins of the modern period in European history. Lessing's incorporation of this historical moment into a new literary tradition provides impetus to her narrative. Engaging with the disappearance of women from the annals of history, *The Golden Notebook* seeks to redress this by rewriting women's lives in contemporary times. The nomenclature—Notebooks—recalls the role they played in an important historical event.

Lessing states succinctly that one of her aims in *The Golden Notebook* was to record women's experiences based on the premise that the '*filter which is a woman's way of looking at life has the same validity as the filter which is a man's way*'[12] [emphasis added]. Lessing brings into central focus *narratives, events, histories and stories from a woman's point of view.* Women are central to this novel that records the lives of obscure women.

Her aspiration to write a novel that would express the 'ideological feel of our mid-century' is also pertinent. *The Golden Notebook*, Lessing goes on to add, was intended as 'a novel of ideas' 'more in the European tradition . . . of the novel'.[13] It would be fruitful to follow up Lessing's references to the 'European tradition' and 'novel of ideas' in connection with this book. Lessing's preface locates the novel in an older history and imaginatively evokes 'the various chapters of socialism' within which 'the great debates of our time have gone on.'[14] Lessing's adjustment of the 'filter' through which a woman views life, in *The Golden Notebook*, enables us to recall women as acting, thinking, speaking and writing agents part of a much older and lesser-known history.

The Golden Notebook and the French Revolution

While recreating and refashioning Western women's collective and collaborative efforts in the twentieth century in *The Golden Notebook*, Lessing also places the novel against a backdrop of a history of ideas that dates back to the French Revolution. In her preface, Lessing refers to four major revolutions: the English, French, Marxist and Russian Revolutions. She pertinently identifies all four as important formative influences in the shaping of European society. A significant feature of all these movements has been the impetus towards larger human freedoms envisaged by each one of them. Another common factor linking them is that despite the larger movements toward democracy promised by each of these revolutions in the modern historical period, women and their histories remained submerged within these revolutions. Women's lives and issues have always been relegated to minimum levels of discussion despite their active participation and involvement.[15]

By juxtaposing the narratives of the Notebooks within the interstices of a compact novel, Lessing draws our attention to the similarities between notebooks in a tradition of writing and record-keeping and women's work in a patriarchal world. Women's work and the work done by notebooks are part of an invisible life that the everyday male world and the format of the book tend to overlook. Readings of the novel repeatedly draw attention to the Notebooks that look back into different pasts—emotional, political and literary.[16]

The Notebooks by themselves record a very private and very different kind of experience. They are often used to jot down things, to voice personal comprehension for one's own clarification. A notebook is also a way in which one can informally engage with any given text and interpret its experience or truth for oneself or even extend the scope of the argument. Lessing makes effective use of this to demonstrate the differences in the two sections of her narrative. The use of a dual scheme of narration disrupts and shifts our focus repeatedly from the events in the 'conventional novel'. The Notebooks—despite their demarcated space—constantly intrude into the conventional novel, providing for a nuanced reading experience. The Notebooks challenge the assumptions of compact narrative repeatedly by their presence. While this can be seen as spelling out 'the false dichotomy between outer and inner action',[17] it enables us to see how language is used in the Notebooks by Lessing 'to ground her work in solidly established social and psychological reality'.[18]

Interspersed within the main narrative, Lessing's Notebooks replicate women's lived histories. Lacking authority and subservient to the main novel, the Notebooks—pretty much like women in history—remain confined to the realm of unofficial discourse. Yet the notebooks present the chaos and the contradictions, documenting all manner of dissent and difference that the finished narrative of the novel can never allow. Lessing records the dichotomy between the novel in its finished form available as *Free Women* and the unfinished chaotic narrative that comprises the Notebooks. The novel becomes a fascinating coding of what is located within the realm of finished, organised text and what remains outside of it. The spillover recorded by notebooks is usually edited out of the realm of what is officially termed literature. Any complete book, once it is processed and produced for the market, seldom adds on the loose pages from notebooks. Or as Anna puts it, '[l]iterature is analysis after the event.'[19] To legitimise the formal structure of the novel, notebook jottings are often invariably sidelined.

The marginalisation and silencing of notebooks within systems of writing and production echo the treatment meted out to women within history. Within structures of signification set up by language, the reality documented by notebooks in the realms of mainstream publication undergoes an erasure that mimics women's experience. This analogy between women's lives and notebooks reverberates not only within fiction but also through history. The Notebooks themselves can be traced back to the French Revolution, the same political and historic juncture that Lessing indicates as one of the important events against whose backdrop *The Golden Notebook* must be read.

The French Revolution is the forerunner of modern political movements insofar as it provides a record of the participation of women from different social classes, as well as their subsequent erasure when rules and charters were framed around the issues that had led to the protests in the first place. While this has set the pattern for subsequent political revolutions, the events leading up to the French Revolution provide a fascinating interstice wherein women's protest and articulation has been recorded.

It is a well-documented fact that on the eve of the revolution in 1789, Louis the XVI summoned the Estates-General to reactivate systems of administrative and political control that had been in disuse since the year 1614. Within an ostensibly formal structure of governance, he sanctioned the writing of *cahiers de doléances*. This informal system of addressing one's grievances directly to the monarch, without any intermediaries, was an unusual occurrence—an event without precedence. Women wrote out their grievances in *cahiers,* the French equivalent for the English term notebooks. These *cahiers* or notebooks were unofficial and addressed to the King or the Estates-General, largely petitioning for aid. Women writing these letters were mostly middle class, and they demanded legal equality, equal education and reform of marriage laws.[20] This departure from the traditional scenario was an 'unprecedented radicalizing experience' and along with the use of the *cahiers* 'suggest a never realized potential for women to have been included in the "official" political process.[21]

Like the *cahiers*, which provided a space for unofficial political discourse, Lessing's notebooks are made to operate as unofficial versions of the novel. They also speak of whatever cannot be voiced in the official version of the linear novel. *The Golden Notebook*'s narrative structure reverses the hierarchy, and the *cahiers* that registered the undercurrents of women's grievances well over 200 years ago are presented centre stage as Notebooks, lending primacy to experiences that form an integral part of women's lives.

The association between the *cahiers* and the Notebooks thus imaginatively evokes an older, forgotten history of women's solidarity and reminds us of its subsequent erasure. It was in the years of the French Revolution that women from the salon, the middle class and the working class participated in the popular movements, agitations, marches and protests. Women's participation at this time cut across class boundaries.[22]

The Golden Notebook fruitfully forges an imaginative link between the earlier histories of women and the present. Women's earlier history, despite being recorded, did not receive adequate succour but remained buried in notebooks or *cahiers*. In contemporary times, in *The Golden Notebook*, it is primarily the Notebooks that draw attention to women's stories. What the *cahiers* could not do for women in the 1790s, *The Golden Notebook* tries to do imaginatively almost 200 years later—by allowing the Notebooks to stand along with the conventional novel in decoding women's experience.

This time, unlike the historical *cahiers, The Golden Notebook* as a literary work creates a space wherein women's plural and multiple voices can be heard. The different Notebooks with the further fictionalised personas of Anna and Molly, that also occasionally transmute into Ella and Julia, contribute to a sense of rich interpenetration. The continuum of narratives that Lessing presents in *The Golden Notebook* is evocative of the large numbers of women whose visibility during the French Revolution can perhaps be seen as one of the earliest statements of women's solidarity in the modern period.

In *The Golden Notebook,* Anna's experience in Africa and newspaper reports from all over the world punctuate our reading experience and highlight the novel's new geopolitical moorings. For every story in the *Free Women* sections, we have four more variations offered by the Notebooks along with a host of characters. The distinctions between the narrative strategies of fiction in the *Free Women* sections and the further fictionalised accounts in the various Notebooks—ostensibly written by Anna—often tend to blur, creating a 'non-chronological matrix' wherein scenes and characters are juxtaposed freely.[23] The experiences of Anna and Molly are echoed or contrasted with their fictional counterparts in the other Notebooks. We deal with an enormous expanse of history through a wealth and welter of characters. It is almost as if characters that dot the peripheries of the usual narrative—that deals with one or more central characters—had unexpectedly decided to occupy centre stage and deflect all the attention to themselves.

Suddenly, in *The Golden Notebook*, the margins have shifted to the centre. Our interest in the main narrative is constantly punctuated by the stories of the Notebooks that either add to the complexity of the experience or deviate from the main narrative altogether. This gains particular significance when the novel is viewed in the historical and literary context of the 1960s.

The Golden Notebook and Women's Writing in the 1960s

Lessing wrote the preface to *The Golden Notebook* in 1971, almost a decade after the novel's publication, at the height of the second wave of the women's movements in the West. While unequivocally championing women's liberation—'I support it, of course, because women are second-class citizens, as they are saying energetically and competently in many countries'[24]—Lessing also articulated her unwillingness to have *The Golden Notebook* interpreted as 'a trumpet for Women's Liberation'.[25] This was particularly intriguing, given the fact that the 1960s ushered in a marked shift in personal, economic and sexual freedom for women in the early years of the decade.

For perhaps the first time in history, technological breakthroughs had contributed to the enabling of women to gain control over their bodies. Freeing women from the threat of pregnancy and the fears of unwanted conception, the advent of the pill made safe and discreet contraception available—thereby laying the material basis for women's sexual equality with men, against a backdrop of centuries of sexual double standards.[26]

Around the 1960s, the participation of women in the workplace was much greater. The 1960s was a period when prosperous, educated, middle-class women were ideologically motivated to move out of the confines of domesticity into the paid labour market. Women's desire to find themselves outside of their homes sprang from the discovery of their potential for economic independence. Bolstered by their newly found sexual freedom, they strove for greater personal freedom and autonomy in place of an undifferentiated earlier existence in the roles of wives and domestic appendages. Hobsbawm points out that it was only when 'middle-class feminism, or the movement of educated or intellectual women, broadened out into a sort of generic sense that the time for women's liberation or women's self-assertion had come'.[27] This change in women's perception of themselves raised urgent questions and contributed to a dramatic transformation of the conventions of social and personal behaviour that led to the transformation of the 1960s.

Lessing's insistence in her 1971 preface that this heady space was not the site of her narrative projection needs to be understood in the context of what she defines as 'Women's Liberation'. When Lessing made this statement, the women's liberation movements in England, Europe and America staged visibly articulate protests. Coalescing objectives garnered from several meetings of women's rights groups from 1968 onwards, four essential prerequisites were put forward by the women's liberation groups. These were 'equal pay', 'equal education and opportunity', '24-hour nurseries' and 'free contraception and abortion on demand.'[28] According to Lessing, *The Golden Notebook* cannot be read as simply endorsing the requirements identified by the women's liberation movements that were rapidly gaining momentum and establishing a wider base. The journey that Lessing charts through her narrative is far more ambitious. While *The Golden Notebook* does raise issues of female sexuality and economic independence, its ambit goes well beyond the scope outlined by the women's liberation movements.

To spell out more distinctly the shift in focus in Lessing's novel, it would be useful to look at other fiction dealing with women's self-assertion written around the same time. The 1960s saw the appearance of a spate of novels written by women writers such as Margaret Drabble (1939–), Sylvia Plath (1932–1963) and Penelope Mortimer (1918–1999), to name a few. Dealing with socio-psychic change, these novelists focused on middle-class women characters that negotiated their new-found female sexuality and suffered anguish over means of attaining economic independence.

Given such a context, it is unsurprising that *The Golden Notebook*'s unconventional representation of women allowed it to be read as a pioneering novel that dealt with the intricate details of women's lives. Preceding the work of a new crop of women writers who wrote and published in the 1960s, *The Golden Notebook* has been firmly embedded in the cultural and social matrix of the period. A recent survey by Sheila Rowbotham reiterates that *The Golden Notebook* not only represents the decade of the 1960s but also epitomises 'Doris Lessing's lusts'.[29] This observation draws attention to Lessing's explorations of female sexuality in the novel and moors it in the ambience of the 'swinging sixties'. Rowbotham's summing up of Lessing's novels with this expression is yet another indicator that draws attention to Lessing's female protagonists' strident articulations about their bodies and their sexuality.

Lessing's central characters Anna and Molly enjoy sexual freedom as a matter of course in the *Free Women* sections. The fictional and fictionalised experiences recorded in the various notebooks also demonstrate Anna and Molly's lack of inhibition in exploring their sexuality. Anna's sexual relationships with Steven, Willi, Michael, Paul, Nelson and Saul, frank and detailed accounts of her response to sexual intercourse, menstruation, debates on the vaginal orgasm and so on form part of the content of the various Notebooks. These aspects of Anna's life are shown as being central to her material existence in London as the author of a bestselling novel and a single parent raising her daughter. Molly, Anna's closest female friend, sublets her flat to Anna in the early years of their friendship. She works as an actress and is also a single parent. Living in a London flat, their economic independence and comparable sexual freedom is in keeping with the changes that begin to characterise personal relations in the late 1960s. Lessing's book is a futuristic portrayal of women's lives that goes on to become a reality only in the decade of the 1970s.

This, however, is not the only interpretation that *The Golden Notebook* lends itself to. It is markedly different from contemporary novels on women that superficially resemble it. For example, Sylvia Plath's *The Bell Jar* (1963) and Margaret Drabble's *The Millstone* (1965) also look closely at the issues of female sexuality and economic independence. I will take them up for discussion here to show both the commonality and differences in interests that Plath and Drabble share with Lessing on the question of women's lives and women's writing.

Plath sees *The Bell-Jar* 'as an autobiographical apprentice work . . . to free [her]self from the past'.[30] Her novel traces the breakdown of Esther Greenwood, a promising undergraduate at an American college. Esther's critical inner life reveals to us the discrepancies between her aspirations and the actual external events that surround her life. Her days spent as a clothes horse in New York and her crush on Buddy—which develops into an unsatisfactory relationship—are determining experiences, hinging around important decisions of vocation and marriage. Both are shown up as false and oppressive. Esther is appalled at the paucity of outlets available to her: 'I began to think maybe it was true that when you were married and had children it was like being brainwashed, and afterward you went about numb as a slave in some private totalitarian state.'[31]

The bell jar within which Esther sees herself enclosed becomes a powerful metaphor for the invisible but suffocating spaces in which women are confined. Juxtaposed against women's vulnerability is the power and control that characterises men's lives. Unable to reconcile to this, Esther attempts to kill herself; she is rescued and subjected to prolonged psychiatric treatment. Long after her breakdown and after her so-called recovery, Esther remains astute in her analysis of the precarious nature of the freedom achieved by women.

See, for instance, Esther's attempts at circumventing the biological trap by getting herself a 'fitting': 'I climbed up on the examination table, thinking," I am climbing to freedom, freedom from fear, freedom from marrying the wrong person. . . . I was my own woman.'[32] Yet her subsequent haemorrhaging after her first sexual encounter and her friend Joan's suicide shortly after seeing Esther's condition reveal that sexual freedom has its underlying emotional costs. At the end of the narrative, leaving the asylum to resume her life armed with far more questions about her female identity than when she had started, Esther observes: 'The eyes and the faces all turned themselves toward me, and guiding myself by them, as by a magical thread, I stepped into the room.'[33] The novel's conclusion captures Esther's continuing surveillance and monitoring very effectively.

The Millstone[34] explores similar issues of female sexuality, sexual freedom and economic independence. Rosamund, whose life is 'marked by a strange mixture of confidence and cowardice',[35] conceives at the end of a chance encounter with George. She goes ahead with her pregnancy, leaving the biological father in ignorance about the baby whom she names Octavia Hill—associating the name with one of the 'heroines of feminism and socialism'.[36] Rosamund brings up her daughter as a single parent, finishes her research, publishes her novel and lands a job. All this is admirably fine-tuned, and Rosamund's sense of well-being and achievement is brought out by her confident assertion at the end of the novel when another chance meeting with George makes her invite him over to see her daughter. Deciding against letting him know of his paternity, she measures herself against George and concludes, 'I neither envied nor pitied his indifference, for he was myself, the self that but for accident, but for fate, but for chance, but for womanhood, I would still have been.'[37] The resolutions provided in Drabble's novel provide a sense of liberating direction. While Esther's experience charts a shift from buoyant self-confidence to an awareness of vulnerability, Rosemary's trajectory moves in the opposite direction—towards an assertion of her new-found freedom as a woman.

The protagonists of all three novels, Esther, Rosemary and Anna, share a love for language and literature and are aware of its formative role in shaping their experience. Esther's writing skills have great potential; they win her the literary patronage of an older woman writer and catapult her to the upper echelons of New York. Rosamund's writing enables her to pay for herself, initially through research grants—later gaining more permanent employment, based on her publication of a book. This concern with the material basis of women's existence is reflected in *The Golden Notebook* as well, wherein Anna Wulf—the author of a successful novel—continues to struggle with writer's block.

All three novels highlight the fact that the act of writing is inherently political. Writing, at the most elementary level, provides possibilities for material sustenance. More significantly, it enables the protagonists to sublimate and articulate their psychic selves. The self-reflexive nature of writing, its relationship with the characters and the novels' referential link to their authors thereby become important markers in the history of middle-class women's struggle for self-determination in the 1960s.

Lessing's, Plath's and Drabble's novels also draw from the authors' lives and are, to some extent, a reworking of their lived experiences. It is relevant to note here that the intervention of women's writing in the 1960s thus marks the possibility of shifting the boundaries between fiction, prescription and politics. The writing of oneself into fiction becomes a political act of constructing women's lives and voices. By focusing on women's interiority, the writing interrogates existing cultural boundaries and restructures them in the realm of fiction. In doing so, women's writing often hints at transformative possibilities and a definitive shift in perception.

Let us now look at the differences that mark off Lessing's novel from the ones written by Plath and Drabble. All three novels use fiction as a space for exploring possibilities. The autobiographical connections between each novel and its author can be easily established. Yet, the narratives written by Plath and Drabble move towards tendentious endings. Plath's novel provides an extreme viewpoint by staging Esther's suicide. In highlighting Rosamund's successful evolution as an unwed single parent, Drabble pushes for an apposite perspective. Lessing's *Golden Notebook* does not push towards any such clear-cut conclusions. It remains more ambivalent about judging success or failure. Plath and Drabble create the individualistic and singular female protagonist in their novels, thereby allowing for a more explicit feminist agenda.

Paradoxically, *The Golden Notebook* seems far less representative of conventional tradition in its creation of two women characters as alter egos, its juxtaposition of innumerable characters throughout the Notebooks, its further attempts at fictionalising the central characters—Ella and Julia of the Yellow Notebook who are fictionalised versions of Anna and Molly—its focus on the subjectivity of memory, its insistence on the 'thinning of language against the density of experience'[38] and its bewildering array of data and narratives, when examined alongside the journeys charted out for women in the fiction of Plath and Drabble. Its departure from the newly devolving tradition that we have seen in the novels by Plath and Drabble under discussion also has to do with the fact that Lessing had, by this time, finished with the writing of novels that shared the perspectives of *The Bell Jar* and *The Millstone.*

Martha's Quest and Other Journeys Preceding *The Golden Notebook*

The construction of personal experience into fiction is an aspect that can be traced back to Lessing's earlier novels. In a series that she began in the early 1950s entitled The Children of Violence, a similar enmeshing of lived experience and fictionality can be observed. Lessing's earlier narratives, preceding *The Golden Notebook,* are centred around a single female protagonist and these earlier novels share much in common with *The Bell Jar* and *The Millstone.*

Lessing began work on *The Golden Notebook* in the late 1950s. By the time she began this novel, she had already concluded work on three of her five-part Children of Violence series. *The Golden Notebook* is preceded by three of the novels from this series, namely *Martha Quest*[39] (1952), *A Proper Marriage*[40] (1954) and *A Ripple from the Storm* (1958).[41] Written as straightforward, linear and realist narratives, these three novels deal with the coming of age of their central protagonist—Martha Quest.

In *Martha Quest* and *A Proper Marriage,* Lessing engages with an exploration of women's roles and identities. Located in South Africa instead of England, these two novels trace the development of a young, white girl through a stormy and turbulent adolescence. Martha is an attractive role model in 'quest' mode. Personable, delighting in her female body and uninhibited about her sexuality, Martha's response to her body's desires is delightful and new. There is a lot of material in these texts that is fundamentally experiential. Lessing's delineation of Martha's buoyant celebration of her sexuality, her self-absorption in her youthful form or her increasing absorption with the baby growing in her womb is new subject material for the novel. Martha's trajectory, which explores the minutiae of what it means to be a woman, is a very valuable record presented for public consumption. Aspects of women's bodies and lives were seldom engaged with, in such detail, or deemed fit for literary or fictional discussion.[42]

Martha Quest is a tracing and a placing of Lessing's literary roots. It also charts out a new journey, one where the old myths of personal and cultural roles played by women are re-examined. Martha's personal life, the choices she has to make, the directions she needs to take and the honest and detailed observation of this adolescent girl as she grows into adulthood is a very new exploration of a woman's personal and private life. Lessing traces the development of a young girl through her adolescence—the discovery of her sexuality; the pressures of being young, dependent and woman; the pleasures of the female body and the constrictions created by marriage and childcare.

In marked contrast to the nineteenth-century literary tradition where women's lives culminated in marriages—consider Austen, Brontë and Eliot—Lessing discards the notion of marriage as providing a fulfilling point of closure early on, in the second novel of the Children of Violence series. Self-conscious about her inherited literary tradition, Lessing's fiction constantly attempts to reframe boundaries.

Lessing's depiction of Martha's pleasure in her sexuality, child-rearing and domesticity and her full and richly sensuous life as a woman has evoked inevitable comparisons with Lawrence.[43] Lessing, however, shows that this aspect of Martha's life—despite its *jouissance*—confines and restricts female identity within prescriptive roles in the domestic sphere.

Freeing herself from parental authority as an economically independent young adult, Martha subsequently walks out of the culturally prescribed confines of marriage and motherhood. Martha's bid for individuality and freedom is enacted against the backdrop of a larger world at war. She exchanges her restricted identity within the domestic sphere for a more tenuous identity in the larger public world of which she is a citizen.

In many ways, Martha's story echoes that of Lessing's. Lessing dropped out of formal schooling and found herself a job in the city, away from the protected and solitary life on the farm in Banket. Marrying early like Martha, Lessing also opted out of marriage to join the CPSA—leaving behind two small children. *Martha Quest* and *A Proper Marriage* provide a valuable entry into Lessing's exploration of the female psyche and provide an important sociological record of what it meant to be a young, white woman in South Africa in the late 1940s. Lessing points out that in writing these novels she was taking 'the story out of the personal into the general' and that her interest 'in the series was a historical one.'[44]

Martha's story, like that of other young, white women at this point in history, reflects the tensions that surface in the rewriting of new roles for middle-class white women. Both novels provide significant fictional evidence of shifting identities and interest in middle-class white women's lives. This was made possible by the changes in women's lives after the First World War. Greater access to education, greater opportunities for employment, economic independence and symbolic political power achieved through the winning of suffrage rights contributed in no small measure.

By reworking her personal narrative into a historical epoch, Lessing makes available a body of literature that records the shifting and expanding boundaries between domestic and public spheres, with women reclaiming the latter. By showing that marriage and domestic life are no longer the only markers of female identity, both *Martha Quest* and *A Proper Marriage* highlight the unfixing of traditional identities and territories. Demonstrating that the boundaries of the domestic sphere can no longer contain the female protagonist, both novels remain open-ended despite dealing with different phases of Martha's life. Also, they resonate with issues raised by women's fiction and anticipate the demands of the women's movement of the late 1960s.

In the construction of a female subject who breaks the silence to tell her tale, Martha's narrative journey in the first two books of the

Children of Violence series shares common ground with Plath's and Drabble's protagonists, Esther and Rosamund. Their individual experiences can be seen as having contributed to the consciousness-raising and identity formation processes that were central to the women's movements in the 1960s.

Women's movements, women's novels and an increase in economic and sexual freedom were an intrinsic part of the 1960s. *Martha Quest* and *A Proper Marriage*—Lessing's novels that precede *The Golden Notebook*—engage with the question of women's rights and identities. The reason why Lessing addressed these issues a decade ahead of her contemporaries has much to do with her positionality as a writer. Being a new entrant to England in the 1950s, Lessing's interest in women's lives and writing was shaped by influences outside of the then prevailing literary establishment in England.

The literary scenario in England in the late 1950s was yet to take stock of the shift in England's political climate. While England's international role as an imperial power had diminished, it had also firmly established itself as a welfare state. Lessing's immediate contemporaries who comprised the generation of the 'Angry Young Men'—Kingsley Amis, John Wain, John Braine, William Cooper and Alan Sillitoe to name a few—were drawn to the economic and social reshuffling on the domestic scene. They took potshots at the establishment but their work confined itself largely to political and social criticism at home, focusing their disgust and anger at the establishment and institutionalised bureaucracy in England.[45]

The orbits of their narratives revolved largely around British life and its nuances. It is only reasonable to surmise that as they did not straddle two continents and two different worlds as Lessing did, their work provided little or no new impetus to the novel tradition. Unlike her peers and contemporaries writing in English, Lessing's novels in this period are not England-centred. Her first-hand experience of life in an African colony allowed her to grasp far more firmly the fact of Britain's diminishing control as a colonial world power. As a writer with an anti-colonial slant, Lessing's narrative canvas in the 1950s was far wider than many of her contemporaries. Her novels are not only deeply critical of the cultural complacence of English civilisation[46] but also provide an effective counterpoint by chronicling women's lives very closely. Most of the male novelists referred to previously do not engage with the woman question as a central feature of their narratives in the way that Lessing does.

Lessing's focus on women brings new inputs to the tradition of novel writing in English in the 1950s. Her female protagonists, however, do not base themselves entirely on the assumptions of self-assertion and self-construction that seem to be the central thrust of a great deal of women's writing in the 1960s. Having spent her formative years in white Southern Rhodesia, Lessing's internalising and understanding of women's experience springs from a different epicentre. Thus, in *Martha Quest,* Lessing's protagonist Martha defines herself against her social and cultural space:

> And from these books Martha had gained a clear picture of herself, from the outside. She was adolescent, and therefore bound to be unhappy; British, and therefore uneasy and defensive; in the fourth decade of the twentieth century, and therefore inescapably beset with problems of race and class; female, and obliged to repudiate the shackled women of the past. She was tormented with guilt and responsibility and self-consciousness; and she did not regret the torment.[47]

In this self-conscious analysis, Martha is shown as being formed both by her reading and by her immediate historicity. Martha's awareness of herself as a white middle-class woman is punctuated by her knowledge of a world intersected by race and class.

Martha Quest and *A Proper Marriage* are *bildungsromans* or novels of education, centred on a female whose subject formation takes place in the interstices of class, race and history. It is from this space of the relative position of Martha's self-knowledge that Lessing allows Martha's story to be inscribed. Martha's narrative is punctuated with the presence of other subjects such as the Black woman, the Black male and the Jew, offering glimpses of their interiority. Lessing's location of shifting points of view through her creation of multiple characters even in the single female-subject narrative anticipates the plurality of perspectives that *The Golden Notebook* leads up to.

Older Echoes: Woolf and Lessing

Despite Lessing's status as a new entrant to the English literary world in the 1950s, her familiarity with and exposure to fiction written in English enabled her to assimilate earlier traditions of portraying women and move further in her representations of female experience. The literary echoes in her work demonstrate the self-conscious and self-reflexive nature of her enterprise. Women portrayed in *The Golden Notebook* highlight the difficulties of female self-representation, given the backdrop of cultural and historical stereotypes. Lessing's women characters raise questions of women's representation. How have women been presented in fiction? How are women viewed culturally? How do such portrayals frame women's identities? These issues, which preoccupied feminist theory in the 1970s, have been an ongoing part of Lessing's creative endeavour and she has drawn from extant traditions of representation and writing.

Out of her largely eclectic reading, undoubtedly Virginia Woolf's work has had the most significant impact on Lessing's fiction when it comes to the portrayal of women. *Martha Quest, A Proper Marriage* and *The Golden Notebook* provide crucial links that establish Lessing's indebtedness to Woolf. In her autobiography, speaking of the new writers who formed part of her staple reading in the late 1930s, Lessing refers to the impact Woolf's work had on her. 'Virginia Woolf had joined Olive Schreiner. I felt I had two elder sisters. . . . If the people I was surrounded by did not understand me, then Virginia and Olive would.[48] Woolf's influence on Lessing's work in the 1950s can be traced through a series of monologues that Martha is made to voice.

In *Martha Quest,* Martha is made to record her dissatisfaction with the fictional representation of women that she has so far encountered. She finds no role models for herself in the text she reads, nor does she discover any promising direction. Lessing writes, '[h]er mind turned towards the heroines she had been offered, and discarded them. There seemed to be a gap between herself and the past, and so her thoughts swam in a mazed and unfed way through her mind'.[49]

An older Martha confronts a similar dilemma in *A Proper Marriage*. Lessing adopts the authorial voice as she peers over Martha's shoulder interpreting her anxieties for us:

> Martha turned from the novelists and tale tellers . . . with the half-formulated thought that the novelists had not caught up with life; for there was no doubt that the sort of things she or Stella or Alice talked about found no reflection in literature—or rather, it was the attitudes of mind they took for granted that did not appear there, from which she deduced that women in literature were still what men, or the men-women wished they were.[50]

Martha's observation that women were presented in a particular manner in literature and that neither men nor 'men-women' writers succeeded in addressing real women in her generation is significant in its echoing of Woolf's anxieties. Through Martha's reiteration, Lessing draws our attention to the limited roles and expectations that dogged the portrayal of women characters in fiction.

One does not have a reference list of the books that Martha read that left her feeling so dissatisfied, as far as female portrayal was concerned. Yet in the 1940s, the years in which Martha is growing into a young adult, there is no dearth of strong and independent women—even within the narratives of *The Children of Violence* series. Surrounded by older and younger women who lead difficult lives and make important decisions, what Martha is naturally puzzled by is the absence of such women in the fiction she reads. Fact and fiction confront each other as Martha juxtaposes the history of her lived experience with that of her reading experience:

> Is it really conceivable that we should have turned into something quite different in the space of about fifty years? Or do you suppose they didn't tell the truth, the novelists? . . . Because either that's the truth or there is a completely new kind of woman in the world, and surely that isn't possible . . .?[51]

Through Martha's soliloquy, Lessing draws the reader's attention to the inadequacy of women's representation in fiction. Fiction apparently has not been telling the whole truth.

Martha's queries are not addressed merely to the alert feminist reader. Through Martha, Lessing is responding to an earlier dialogue set up by Virginia Woolf, who also strove to authenticate women's experience in her fiction. In 1931, Woolf visualised the woman novelist in the powerful image of a fisherwoman who must fish into the depths 'of the world that lies submerged in our unconscious being' with the aid of the hook of her imagination. Narrating an imaginary conversation between the woman novelist's reason and her imagination, Woolf articulates the dilemmas that she probably faced in her own delineation of women characters. In this passage, reason tells the imagination:

> Calm yourself. . . . In fifty years I shall be able to use all this very queer knowledge that you are ready to bring me. But not now. . . . I cannot make use of what you tell me—about women's bodies for instance—their passions—and so on, because the conventions are still very strong.[52]

Woolf and Lessing write themselves into fiction through their strong and unconventional women characters. Between Woolf's London of the 1930s and Lessing's London of the 1950s we can record substantial shifts in the lives of the women. Clarissa Dalloway voices the limitations of being female, her lack of access to education, her anxiety over a life where she achieves little beyond marriage, motherhood and being a good hostess and her inability to participate in the ferment and change in the political and public world except at second hand.[53]

Woolf wrote her most consummate fiction in-between the world wars though she did not live to see the end of the Second World War, whose conclusion played a significant role in shaping women's lives and destinies. Twenty-odd years elapse between Woolf's prophecy and the commencement of Lessing's writing career in the 1950s wherein she speaks freely of women's bodies and their passions. Lessing is able to achieve this not only because the conventions have changed and she is living in a new historical era but also because she brings new inputs to the novel being written in the 1950s in England, as discussed earlier. In fact, barely nine years separate Woolf's suicide in 1941 from Lessing's arrival in London in 1949. These details highlight the continuity of tradition and the new space that both writers negotiate in their writing, as they highlight the codes that confine women.

Lessing's protagonist Martha is freer than most of Woolf's protagonists. A white-colonial from South Africa, Martha has access to education and far greater personal and social mobility. As a young woman, she can choose a career for herself and no longer has to obliquely deal with issues pertaining to her sexuality. Yet even at this later point, Martha's break with the prescriptive codes that structure female identity comes at considerable personal cost and trauma. Despite the passing of decades, despite the introduction of more equitable legislation, Martha's straddling of both public and private spheres is neither easy nor effortless—even within the realms of fiction.

Lessing's writing from the 1950s, I would argue, is a conscious taking on of Woolf's literary mantle. It is also very much a part of the continued tradition of intellectual succession recommended by T.S. Eliot in 'Tradition and the Individual Talent'.[54] The exception, in this case, is that here it is a tradition of women writers which is being uncovered. As Roberta Rubenstein points out, '[b]y absorbing Woolf into her own work. . . . Lessing is confirming to some extent Woolf's belief that "we think back through our mothers if we are women".'[55]

The central women characters in *The Golden Notebook* are not merely free women celebrating their economic and sexual freedom in the late 1950s. Lessing's women characters deliberately recall earlier fictional figures and writers. Lessing intends us to quickly identify their antecedents in earlier literature. For instance, it is possible to read the two main female characters in the novel, Anna Wulf and Molly Jacobs, as literary reincarnations from the life and work of Virginia Woolf and James Joyce, respectively. Anna and Molly in their London flat enact Woolf's recommendation that women should have their own income as well as *A Room of One's Own*. The names of Lessing's protagonists, Anna Wulf and Molly, are evocative and reminiscent of an earlier literary tradition. Jocelyn Harris' observation that the name Anna Wulf works effectively by fusing a character and an author from an earlier literary tradition to form a combination of two names is valuable. It evokes an immediate association with strident author Virginia

Woolf and Anna Karenina, Tolstoy's fictional creation 'dependent on relationships and love'.[56]

In *The Golden Notebook*, Virginia Woolf is reincarnated as Anna Wulf. Anna in her Woolf identity is a high-strung and intense writer, subject to breakdowns, whose emotional and intellectual life is presented to us through the form of both notebooks and novel. Consumed by an incredible emotional need for her various lovers and highly dependent on them, Anna evokes her namesake Anna Karenina—Tolstoy's representation of a woman who allowed passion to pursue her to death. Anna Karenina opts out of a conventional marriage, elopes with another man and has a child born out of wedlock. Later, she feels guilty and rejected by her lover and whips up a rage that pushes her to take her own life rather violently. Lessing questions the experience that has so far been culturally allocated to women and has also been enshrined in fiction. Surely a woman can be in love and stay alive, even if love fails her? Tolstoy's Anna Karenina is thus replaced by Anna Wulf, into whose portrayal Lessing also weaves in associations of a writer of fiction whose identity is suggested through echoes of the famous surname—Woolf. Anna is vulnerable in love and contemplates ending her life but does not follow her instinct. This amalgamation of both fictional character and literary ancestor evoked by a protagonist of *The Golden Notebook* marks Lessing's attempts to forge a new dynamic—with both narrative and characters.

A similar case could be argued for Molly Jacobs who could easily be a take-off on Molly Bloom in James Joyce's *Ulysses*. Richard, Molly Jacob's ex-husband, has a second wife who is called Marion—Molly Bloom's given name in *Ulysses*. Molly Jacobs, unlike her literary namesake, is not consumed by guilt, has a grown-up son and is free from a marriage that could have become oppressive or deadening had she chosen to stay on in it. Molly's parents are described as having glittered 'in the intellectual and bohemian circles that had spun around the great central lights of Huxley, Lawrence, Joyce, etc.'[57] The cultural history of Lessing's protagonists evokes the continuities between the immediate present that they occupy and the literary past that travels alongside them.

Molly and Anna are portrayed as being physically very different from one another. Molly is 'a tallish woman, and big-boned, but she appear[s] slight, and even boyish' while Anna is 'small, thin, dark, brittle, with large black always-on-guard eyes, and a fluffy haircut.'[58] Yet the narrative tells us they are often mistaken for each other. This happens perhaps because both Anna and Molly share similar values. In making them operate interchangeably in terms of how people see them, Lessing does away with the conventional framing and fixing of identities through which women characters are usually represented in fiction.

Framing Friendships: Women's Communities Then and Now

The themes of romance, marriage or vocation are not the primary features of *The Golden Notebook*. Instead, we are invited to look at women's lives in London in the late 1950s. Anna and Molly represent different facets of women's experience and they also function outside of any prescriptive categories. They have in common their immersion in experience and their non-judgemental attitude towards situations. Molly and Anna's lives are multiplied and refracted through their representation, both factual and fictional, in the four notebooks.

Other than placing these women in a male world, Lessing also makes their bonding with one another a significant feature of the narrative. The interiority of Anna and Molly's experience is the inside story of *The Golden Notebook*. This story is narrated from the perspective of how women see themselves in a predominantly male world. Despite their differences and tensions, Lessing shows their relationship as one of care and nurture and mutual support. *The Golden Notebook* is perhaps one of the earliest novels that explores female friendship in such detail. It shows that heterosexual women can have intense female friendships and do not need to be pitted against each other, as authors have been wont to do in an earlier narrative tradition, irrespective of whether they were friends or sisters. For instance, consider Fanny Price and Mary Crawford, or Fanny and her cousins in *Mansfield Park* or Becky and Amelia in *Vanity Fair*.

Lessing's portrayal of the intense friendship and camaraderie of Anna and Molly is the first building block that she puts in towards constructing communities of women in *The Golden Notebook*. When a fictionalised Ella leaves Julia's flat to move into her own, she records feeling like a 'daughter leaving a mother'.[59] Ella believes that their separation is similar to 'the break-up of a marriage'.[60] The only similar supportive example that one can think of is that of the two sisters in Christina Rossetti's poem 'The Goblin Market'. However, it must be remembered that the two sisters achieve tremendous solidarity and strength in the poem only by shutting out the public world and creating a world of domesticity, away from the site of activity—the market place. Also, no men are glimpsed in the rustic domestic space occupied by the two sisters.

Female bonding, the finer details of women's responsibilities and what they do each day are chronicled and 'herstories' become the point of focus in *The Golden Notebook*. Women's lives, punctuated by a criss-cross of interpersonal relationships, are documented at length—how they bring up their children, cook for their lovers and offer support systems for each other from babysitting to socialising, providing mental and emotional support and discussing personal and political issues.

Lessing focuses on women's roles of nurture and secondary support instead of tremendous corporate building or other traditional male activities. She reveals that roles of nurture, despite being pivotal to the future of the world, are not perceived to be of great significance. Female bonding becomes a central and important relationship—one that is supportive of women, especially in the absence of other support systems. This is true not only for Anna and Molly but also for Marion, Sarah and the other fictionalised women in the notebooks—Julia, Ella and Muriel—whose years of childcare and nurture are rendered invisible and inconsequential in mainstream history texts and literary narratives.

Lessing's text not only indicts such practice but also creates a literary precedent. We are made to look closely at the effort that goes into the bringing up of children and the unaccounted woman-hours invested in it. So far, in mainstream narratives, the actual spaces where women's work is carried out have remained largely unseen and irrelevant.

In *The Golden Notebook,* Lessing makes such space and such work the centre of her narrative focus. She also documents how society allows men access to a variety of activities—ranging from the personal to the professional—with an ease which is not granted to women.

The Golden Notebook also charts the story of men. Richard, Molly's ex-husband, spends considerable time outside of his work in a string of affairs and romantic entanglements. Clearly distinguishing between the cultural roles allotted for men and women, when Richard's second wife, Marion, takes to drinking on account of his infidelity, Richard views his actions in all of this as being of little consequence. Marion's drinking becomes a source of anxiety to Richard only when it interferes with the children's nurture. Richard sees little need to be accountable to Marion or to consider her emotional needs. Yet, when Marion finds herself a lover, Richard possessively persuades her to break off her affair. He feels no qualms in pursuing younger women or in declaring himself sexually unexcited by Marion, to whom he has been married for over fifteen years. Again, the onus of bringing up Tommy badly, as far as Richard is concerned, rests primarily with his first wife Molly.

Richard's double standards also hold for Michael. In her relationship with Michael, it is Anna who worries about positioning her sexual and adult life in a manner that will not disturb her daughter's everyday routine. Michael, Anna's lover, turns up at Anna's flat at his convenience. Michael's wife takes care of their children and the housekeeping back in his home, making dalliance with Anna easy and possible for him. As Anna observes in The Blue Notebook, 'he will spend his day, served by secretaries, nurses, women in all kinds of capacities, who will take this weight off him.'[61] Both his wife and his mistress have little to do with any of his decisions, personal or professional. Lessing shows how childcare in the context of a marriage gone awry rests primarily with the mother, irrespective of whether she is living with her husband or not.

Lessing highlights the urgent need to look closely at cultural codes. *The Golden Notebook* is peopled with articulate and intelligent women skilled enough to provide themselves with a room of their own if needed. What is perhaps of significance is that the tremendous support and bonding that these women provide for each other frees them from the guilt faced by their literary predecessors. It is for this reason that neither Anna nor Molly, though under intense pressure, end up destroying themselves. Lessing is able to factor in more options for them. They possess reserves of energy and unencumbered thought that allow them to break free of older stereotypic roles and believe in nebulous possibilities, even in the face of stiff opposition. Thus, they rally around Marion, who moves in with Tommy after the break-up of her marriage. Molly and Anna also accept new relationships despite having come to grief in older ones and are reconciled to the inevitability of change.

Negotiating Freud and Marx

It is not merely the relational domestic lives of middle-class white women that *The Golden Notebook* documents. It marks a major shift in narrative intention by juxtaposing snippets of information relating to events taking place all over the world alongside the life of its protagonists, particularly through the four Notebooks. What are we to make of Anna's experiences in Africa? Of Molly's experiences as an actress; fictional accounts of Anna and Molly's lives; their involvement with communism; the angst of women from the working class; Black men and women and their lives; violence and war in different parts of Europe, Asia and America—all of which the novel documents? Discussing this aspect, Claire Sprague observes that Lessing has 'developed a unique multi-personal mode'.[62]

Lessing uses this mode to engage with two influential ideologies—namely, psychoanalysis and Marxism; these have dominated Western thought from the end of the last century. It is not merely Saul Green who recognises that 'he never had a thought, or an emotion, that didn't instantly fall into pigeon-holes, one marked "Marx" and one marked "Freud".'[63] The authorial intention is aimed at directing the reader into a space 'not willed . . . by Grandfathers Marx and Freud.'[64] Lessing, in this novel, recognises the very powerful impact that Marxism and Freudianism have exercised on the minds and psyches of Europe.

Lessing highlights the fact that Marx and Freud have shaped the political and intellectual fabric of the West and framed the outer boundaries within which thought processes have been structured. Marxism and Freudianism, then, are seen as extremely pivotal ideologies around which political and psychological understanding has evolved since the end of the nineteenth century. Political movements based on socialist belief pervaded large parts of the world in the twentieth century and seem to provide hope even in the twenty-first century. Socialism also added to the tumult in the 1950s, the years that the novel documents. Freud's focus on sexuality and his readings of women's psyche was also the subject of widespread debate and discussion. While Marxist theories structured the contours of the larger political world, those of psychosexual behaviour were modulated by Freudianism.

The significance of these two figures from the nineteenth century and their continuing relevance to feminist ideology and fiction needs to be noted here. Feminist theory draws upon Lacan's analysis that women are culturally and socially at a disadvantage. Reinterpreting Freud's essentialist readings of women's self-construction, feminists show how women's sense of inferiority stems not from penis envy but from their understanding that the phallus is the dominant signifier in a patriarchal culture.[65] *The Golden Notebook* also follows this trajectory.

The fictionalised account of Ella in the Yellow Notebook parodies conventional stereotypes associated with female sexual behaviour. Ella's identity, formed by being in love and having it reciprocated, is a stereotypic rendering of how women are viewed within phallocentric traditions. Showing how assumptions about female sexuality remain extremely phallocentric within structured readings of Marxism and Freudianism, *The Golden Notebook* remains dismissive of such readings. The novel is critical of male anger and frustration when faced with emotionally and economically independent women.

Richard's resentment of Molly's unconventional lifestyle and her having 'a whale of a good time junketting all over Europe',[66] despite leaving her nineteen-year-old son at home in England for a year, is shown as petty and unjustified. In conventional life, such options did not exist for women. An episode in the Notebooks reiterates the absurdity of Richard's accusations. There, Julia's independence immediately becomes a malefic power that can turn men impotent—she is accused by a visiting male acquaintance of being 'a castrating woman'.[67]

Again, during his extramarital relationship with Anna, Michael's commendation of Anna's cool and composed pragmatism is shown to be incredibly insensitive. Michael's observations, we are made to realise, are not true of Anna's actual condition but a callous generalisation that allows him to feel little qualms about exploiting a woman he has no intentions of marrying. Anna feels extremely vulnerable in this relationship that has been steadfastly monogamous from her side. Unwarranted generalisations about women based on their unconventional sexual behaviour, by men who are co-respondents, are shown as routine male practice. Therefore, when Paul chooses to end his affair with Ella, his supportive male friend at work feels at liberty to sum her up as 'a pretty flighty piece'.[68]

Countering such male propaganda, Lessing's female characters approach sexual matters with brutal honesty. Ella and Julia are able to demystify their sexual encounters with remarks such as 'What's the matter, wasn't he any good in bed?' 'Not much.'[69] While exploring the tremendous freedom that sexual liberation can offer, Anna and Molly's lives also highlight the hazards of being free in the face of the double standards that are acceptable when it comes to men. As 'free women', Anna and Molly receive propositions from married men, who see them as sexually available. The various narratives reveal the 'double standard'[70] that men can exercise. The novel shows how this is also aided by the stereotypic cultural assumptions made about women. As an angry Julia remarks, 'What's the use of us being free if they aren't? I swear to God, that every one of them, even the best of them, have the old idea of good women and bad women.'[71]

In an important conversation in the novel, Paul talks to Ella of technological interventions like sperm banks which would allow women to do away with men altogether. A puzzled Ella wonders how that could be possible at all and demonstrates her unwillingness to replace the warmth of heterosexual relationships with the cold, sterile substitution of frozen sperm deposits. Paul's insistence that this will open up the war between the sexes needs to be understood as the insecurity and intimidation threatening older patriarchal assumptions. Patriarchy, having wrongly abrogated power and control despite its minimal contribution to the processes of creation, now faces disruption of the *status quo*. By allowing for the storage of the male sperm, scientific intervention seems to indicate the complete dispensability of the male.

Paul's anxieties are perhaps indicative of deep-rooted male insecurity. He cannot comprehend how an empirical discourse that was once so effective in establishing control and authority could now reduce man to a position of minimal relevance in the continuation of the human race. Paul's psychosis reflects deeply internalised male insecurity constructed by male cultural control and authority over female reproduction.

Another important demystification in *The Golden Notebook* pertains to the female body and its sexuality. The female body and its secretions of menstrual blood are recorded in explicit detail. The book describes the personal discomfort and pleasure that the body is subject to, and Ella attempts to break free of the disgust and taboo that religion and culture associates with these events. Thus, female bodily functions are seen as one aspect of a woman's life, not as an identity shaping experience.

A related subject that needs to be resolved is the accusation that Lessing chronicles 'institutional homophobia'[72] in *The Golden Notebook.* Indeed, Lessing does not present celebratory homosexual or lesbian relationships in the novel. What she does record, however, is Anna's repugnance at homosexuality and lesbianism. A great deal of irony is directed at this disgust of Anna's and her anxiety that her daughter will grow up without encountering any real men. This idiosyncrasy is matched by her assumption that lesbians are usually bitter women who unite due to their anger against men. Anna is also disturbed by the thought that Molly and she have been thought of as lesbians. Ella's observation that she 'ought to be like a man, caring more for [her] work than for people'[73] is meant to recall older identities demarcated for men and women.

Anna's notions of masculinity and femininity are shown as being limiting and outdated. Lessing treats Anna's limited definitions of sexuality ironically in the novel, as also Anna's dismissal of the restricted dimensions of human understanding posited by psychoanalysis. For instance, Anna is critical of Mother Sugar's psychoanalysis and describes it as 'old stuff issued so fresh and magisterial'.[74] Anna also quarrels with Mother Sugar's conviction that 'art is sacred'[75] in the face of the postmodern artist who remains unable to create or write at all. What the narrative repeatedly emphasises is the fact that it is no longer possible to use terms like 'real artist', 'real man' or 'real woman' without being ironic. *The Golden Notebook* draws attention to the existence of alternate sexualities despite its central protagonists' avowal of heterosexuality as the norm, thus stressing the off-centring of experience and the impossibility of a single point of focus.

Having shown how psychoanalytic readings tend to reconfirm stereotypes, the novel also examines the influence of Marxist ideology on women's issues in the twentieth century. The adoption of this ideology by Russian communists saw the beginnings of a world revolution that promised apocalyptic change. This system also promised to provide alternatives to bourgeois capitalism and cause a sea change in women's lives.

In her novel, Lessing documents events in the history of the communist struggle during the years of the Cold War and examines the impact of this global movement on women's lives. Anna's bedroom and her notebooks become the site from where this change is to be evaluated. This achieves two purposes. Firstly, through this juxtaposition, women become participants in the larger political and public upheavals in their lives—however mute. Also, the diary entries on all the countries where the socialist movement made inroads show the presence of great violence and oppression, be it Russia, China, Korea, Vietnam or Quemoy to name a few. The detailed accounts of the communist group in Central Africa, in the Black Notebook, also show how hierarchies of power remain in place irrespective of the system.

Looking back to the writing of *The Golden Notebook,* Lessing mentions that in those times a large number of sensitive, thinking people were either communist or had been communists. She goes on to add that:

> In the second half of the '50s, what I was observing with the 150 percenters was that they break down. Their entire beings were involved with communism, like a religion. And suddenly the whole thing turned out to be a dream.[76]

Lessing's awareness that communism, despite its mass appeal and its ability to reach out to a large multitude, still falls short of vitally addressing women's lives and plays back into traditional hierarchic structures is articulated through the Notebooks.

Despite rallying around the Communist Party and having a theoretical understanding of women's oppression, working-class men are unable to bridge the differences due to sexual/cultural division of labour in real life. When Anna campaigns for votes for the Communist Party, she finds extremely unhappy women—wives of working-class men who vote Labour every time. The wives of these men, hemmed in by domesticity and the confines of their homes, are 'going mad quietly by themselves, in spite of husband and children or rather because of them.'[77]

The hierarchy that exists between men and women and the perceptions of their sexual, social and cultural roles do not change within the so-called radical left group outlined in the Notebooks. George can feel very strongly about racial equality and at the same time father an illegitimate child upon the wife of a Black cook at the Mashopi hotel. While he romanticises the possibility of his illegitimate son asking him for a job in the distant future, George's exercise of his privileges of whiteness and maleness is made evident.

Difficult women, according to Willi, the leader of the group, need 'to be bullied' since their cure lies not in being understood but in a 'damned good hiding'.[78] It is by closely following the lives of people with an apparent Left orientation and their interaction with women or Black people that Lessing shows how—despite all its theoretical rigour—when it comes to practice, communism is as misogynistic as other systems of power have been. Nor are its practitioners free from vestiges of racism and sexism. Communism, Lessing emphasises, is very much part of the system of Eurocentric thought processes that have been subjected to criticism in *The Golden Notebook*.

Lenin and Gramsci: Notebooks as Experiments

It is also pertinent to draw attention to Lenin's *Philosophical Notebooks*[79] and Gramsci's *Prison Notebooks*[80] at this juncture. The idea of notebooks as an alternative space for the articulation of individual world views has been extant, particularly within the tradition of the Left. Lenin (1870–1924) and Gramsci (1891–1937), important theorists and analysts of Marxism, use the format of the notebook as a record of their negotiations with and assimilation and practise of philosophy and political ideology. Their notebooks were also translated into English and widely disseminated around the same time as Lessing's publication of *The Golden Notebook*. Lenin's and Gramsci's discourses on the nature of political and social reality invariably excluded women in matters of philosophical and political speculation.

It is plausible to see Lessing's inscribing of women's lives in *The Golden Notebook* as a response to their work. The format of the notebooks parallels official discourse and yet, by virtue of its separation from the main discourse, offers dissent. This parallel space provided by the notebooks continues to capture the imagination as a flexible form that lends itself to all kinds of experimental efforts.

The idea of using notebooks or *cahiers* as narrative strategies due to the inadequacy of extant forms fulfilled the need for experimentation. The need to present unofficial discourse was not confined solely to the written word. It extended to the visual medium of cinema as well. Experimentation in the film medium was an important topic of discussion in the film journal *Cahiers du Cinéma* that was very popular in the 1960s.[81]

The Golden Notebook's narrative strategy must be seen as part of a larger ethos of experimentation. This ethos extended to traditions outside of writing, spilling over into the visual arts. The Notebooks, in the context of the 1960s, thus become important signifiers in what is a pervasive questioning of extant discourses and a search for alternate strategies.

In bringing to the fore the hidden, subterranean lives of women, *The Golden Notebook* opens up new ways in which women can write and speak their lives. This brings us to the dilemma of women finding their voice, articulated by Anna in the Black Notebook. Anna's writer's block is not so much an inability to write as an inability to write in a particular way. She points out, 'Yet I am incapable of writing the only kind of novel which interests me: a book powered with an intellectual or moral passion strong enough to create order, to create a new way of looking at life.'[82]

Anna is freed her from her writing block by her breakdown. The breakdown symbolises a collapse of all the restrictions and taboos placed on Anna, the writer and participant of her life. At this point, the separate notebooks that she had been recording her experiences in are replaced by a 'Golden Notebook', which allows the co-existence of all subterranean and fragmented stories that the dictates of form, ideology and narrative had prevented Anna from voicing.

Saul Green and Anna exchange notebooks and write out the first lines of each other's new novel. This transaction becomes symbolic of the mutual inscribing that is carried out in the lives of men and women. This exchange of ideas of self-articulation between Anna and Saul is in marked contrast to the historic event where the Declaration of the Rights of Man and of the Citizen (1789) that erased women as a category altogether was openly challenged by the Declaration of the Rights of Woman and of the Female Citizen (1791), as well as *A Vindication of the Rights of Woman* (1792).[83] In their obscure personal identities, Saul and Anna set up a complementary exchange, stressing the mutuality and interdependence of male and female lives and rewriting history and narrative as it were. As Rowbotham points out 'The French Revolution made possible the idea of there being a common predicament of women that the transformation of state and society should affect.'[84] The need for societal transformation and a re-examination of restrictive stereotypes is what *The Golden Notebook* concludes with.

Lessing's novels after *The Golden Notebook* continue to tease out the significance of women's narratives. In *The Golden Notebook,* the disruption of the conventional linear form enables Lessing to work out the dilemmas of feminism, fiction and literary construction. In the same book, her experiment with the narrative form, characters, cultural relationships allotted to men and women and the role of art provide new ways of seeing. *The Golden Notebook* anticipates the incorporation of various narrative modes, personal narratives, myths, memoirs and science fiction as more politicised forms of women's writing in Lessing's subsequent fiction.

Endnotes

1. Doris Lessing, *The Golden Notebook* (New York: Simon & Schuster, 1962; London: Flamingo, 1993). All references to this novel are from the 1993 edition.
2. In her preface to the novel, Lessing emphasises the significance of its structure over that of its contents. While *The Golden Notebook*'s form stands out among other novels written in the late 1950s that focused on English social life, its structural virtuosity diminishes considerably when viewed alongside an earlier novel tradition. If one were to look back to the end of the First World War rather than the Second, one would have little hesitation in identifying the years after 1915 as the period in which major innovations in narrative structure can be seen in the novel written in English. Lessing was not unaware of the narrative tradition of the English novel, which assimilated the ruptures produced in narrative form in the experimental fiction of both Virginia Woolf (1882–1941) and James Joyce (1882–1941). Joyce and Woolf had signalled the limits of the conventional novel well before Lessing articulated her own dissatisfaction with it as a creative writer, through their delineation of the psychic lives of their characters and the fragmentation of both language and linear narrative when faced with the complexity of experience. *The Golden Notebook*'s technical innovations, when placed against those carried out by Woolf and Joyce, are minimal. A regular, conventional novel titled *Free Women* is divided into five sections, interspersed by sections from four notebooks variously coloured black, red, yellow and blue. At the end of the fourth block, the notebooks merge into a Golden Notebook. The *Free Women* sections of the novel lend themselves to a straightforward reading and one can recover the plot and configure the structure with very little effort.
3. Carey Kaplan and Ellen Cronan Rose, *The Canon and the Common Reader* (Knoxville: University of Tennessee Press, 1990).
4. Lessing, *The Golden Notebook*, 8.
5. The book is referred to as 'the first Tampax in world literature' by Rachel Blau DuPlessis, 'For the Etruscans,' in *The New Feminist Criticism: Essays on Women, Literature, and Theory*, ed. Elaine Showalter (New York: Pantheon, 1985), 279. If *The Golden Notebook* in its notebook form carries out the functions of Tampax, it becomes an important literal and literary symbol. It becomes both container and narrative tool, revealing/recording hitherto unmentioned essences of women. Also see Diana

Schemo's observation that 'if the Guggenheim were exhibiting not just Italian, but European, influences on the second half of the century, "The Golden Notebook" would surely be in a glass case, labeled perhaps, "Formative Work in Modern Feminism."' Diana Jean Schemo, 'At The Guggenheim With: Doris Lessing; A Portrait Unwinds, As in Life', *The New York Times Archive*, November 2, 1994, https://movies2.nytimes.com/books/99/01/10/specials/lessing-guggenheim.html.

6. Margaret Drabble remarks that *The Golden Notebook* is a transforming work. 'There is nothing at all like it. . . . [I]t was in a sense published too early. . . . In fact, what happened was that she got there first, once more prophetic. . . .' Margaret Drabble, 'Doris Lessing: Cassandra in a World Under Siege,' *Ramparts* 10 (February 1972): 50–53. Similar sentiments about *The Golden Notebook* having radically changed the consciousness of innumerable young women are voiced in Joyce Carol Oates, 'A Visit with Doris Lessing,' *The Southern Review* 9 (Autumn 1973): 873–882.
7. Lessing, *The Golden Notebook*, 13.
8. Lessing, *The Golden Notebook*, 415.
9. Lessing, *The Golden Notebook*, 415.
10. Louise Yelin, *From the Margins of Empire: Christina Stead, Doris Lessing, Nadine Gordimer* (Ithaca and London: Cornell University Press, 1998), 88.
11. Louise Yelin reads the novel as rooted in its times, and her analysis of Anna and Molly as women from communist groups disenchanted by the growing debacle within communism is reductive and dismissive of its transformative possibilities. Yelin, *From the Margins,* 71–91.
12. Lessing, *The Golden Notebook,* 11.
13. Lessing, *The Golden Notebook*, 13.
14. Lessing, *The Golden Notebook*, 11.
15. Marilyn French provides an extended account of the Red Revolution in the year 1917 and women's active participation at the onset of these revolutions, pointing out that subsequently women were relegated to secondary positions in all the areas where socialism prevailed as a political system. Marilyn French, *Beyond Power: On Women, Men, and Morals* (New York: Ballantine Books, 1985), 226–243.
16. Betsy Draine, 'Nostalgia and Irony: The Postmodern Order of "The Golden Notebook",' *Modern Fiction Studies* 26, no. 1 (Spring 1980): 31–34.
17. Shadia S. Fahim, *Doris Lessing: Sufi Equilibrium and the Evolving Form of the Novel* (New York: St. Martin's Press, 1994), 84.

18. Caryn Fuoroli, 'Doris Lessing's "Game": Referential Language and Fictional Form,' *Twentieth Century Literature* 27, no. 2 (Summer 1981): 146.
19. Lessing, *The Golden Notebook*, 210.
20. Joan B. Landes, *Women and The Public Sphere in the Age of the French Revolution* (Ithaca and London: Cornell University Press, 1988), 2–6.
21. Joan B. Landes documents how all women were affected by the dramatic alteration of public space in Landes, *Women and The Public Sphere*, 106 and 232. Joan Wallach Scott identifies the agenda of modern feminism as 'exposure of the ambiguities and repressions, the contradictions and silences in liberal political systems that present themselves as coherent, comprehensive, rational or just, because resting on natural, scientific, or universal principles'. Joan Wallach Scott, 'French Feminists and the Rights of "Man": Olympe de Gouges's Declarations,' in *The French Revolution: The Essential Readings*, ed. Ronald Schechter (Oxford and Massachusetts: Blackwell Publishing, 2001), 220.
22. Linda Kelly documents women's participation in the march to Versailles. She also draws attention to the mixed clubs where women were admitted on equal terms with men and provided a forum for political and legal questions in Linda Kelly, *Women of the French Revolution* (London: Hamish Hamilton, 1987), ix–x and 33–35.
23. Herbert Marder, 'The Paradox of Form in "The Golden Notebook",' *Modern Fiction Studies* 26, no. 1 (Spring 1980): 49–54.
24. Lessing, *The Golden Notebook*, 8.
25. Lessing, *The Golden Notebook*, 8.
26. Tests on the pill began in 1956 and it was approved in 1960. The pill became available in the early 1960s and white middle-class women, both in America and Europe, took to it enthusiastically. Women such as Barbara Seaman (1935–2008) raised objections to control over women's bodies by generic medicines and the dangers of the use of oestrogen. Rainey Horwitz, 'Barbara Seaman (1935–2008),' *The Embryo Project Encyclopedia*, May 25, 2018, https://embryo.asu.edu/pages/barbara-seaman-1935-2008.
27. Eric Hobsbawm, *The Age of Extremes: The Short Twentieth Century, 1914–1991* (London: Michael Joseph, 1994), 319. The rest of this paragraph is a paraphrasing of Hobsbawm's analysis.
28. 'The Four Demands' appeared first in issue no. 1 of the *Women's Newspaper*, on March 6, 1971. This is reproduced in Michelene Wandor, ed., *The Body Politic: Writings from the Women's Liberation Movement in Britain, 1969–1972* (London: Stage 1, 1972), 2.

29. Sheila Rowbotham, *A Century of Women: The History of Women in Britain and the United States* (London and New York: Viking Books, 1997; London and New York: Penguin Books, 1999), 338. All further references are from the 1999 edition.
30. Biographical Note by Lois Ames in Sylvia Plath, *The Bell Jar* (1963; New York: Harper and Row, 1971), 293. All further references are from the 1971 edition. Plath's novel is based on her own real-life experience of a breakdown that she lived through in 1953. All references to this novel are from this edition. Gayle Greene sees *The Bell Jar, The Golden Notebook*, Kaufman's *Diary of a Mad Housewife*, and Friedan's *The Feminine Mystique* as novels which explore the confinement of women in the family as citated in Yelin, *From the Margins*, 83. Drabble and Mortimer's writing in the 1960s chronicles the discomforts of housewives and mothers, before the actual emergence of the women's movement in Rowbotham, *A Century of Women*, 338.
31. Plath, *The Bell Jar*, 94.
32. Plath, *The Bell Jar*, 251.
33. Plath, *The Bell Jar*, 275.
34. Margaret Drabble, *The Millstone* (Harmondsworth: Penguin, 1965). All references to page numbers will be from this edition.
35. Drabble, *The Millstone*, 5.
36. Drabble, *The Millstone*, 170.
37. Drabble, *The Millstone*, 172.
38. Lessing, *The Golden Notebook*, 273.
39. Doris Lessing, *Martha Quest* (Great Britain: Michael Joseph, 1952; London and New York: Granada, 1966; repr., London and New York: Granada, 1982). All references to this novel are from the 1982 edition.
40. Doris Lessing, *A Proper Marriage* (London: Michael Joseph, 1954; London and New York: Granada, 1966). All references to this novel are from the 1966 edition.
41. Doris Lessing, *A Ripple from the Storm* (Great Britain: Michael Joseph, 1958; London and New York: Granada, 1966).
42. Naomi Mitchison's discomfort with her bodily processes as found in Rowbotham, *A Century of W*omen, 32. Lessing's account of the response of her mother's generation to sexuality is fictionalised in May Quest's distress at Martha's growing body and her need to confine it in Lessing, *Martha Quest*, 23–24. Mary Turner's squeamishness in sexual matters and Martha's own readings of Havelock Ellis, whose analysis of female

sexuality remains rooted in the hereditary sciences of the nineteenth century, set the tone for conventional and cultural responses to female sexuality. In providing Martha with an exuberant sexuality, Lessing is breaking new ground in this series. Besides there being very little discussion on the subject, such chronicling of women's lives is given short shrift in the context of enshrined social and cultural values. Clearly this was not the stuff that literature could present and if presented at, was to be viewed as irrelevant and tedious. For an account of how Lessing's documentation of the processes of pregnancy was received it is illuminating to look at how some of her contemporaries responded. The first account is by her contemporary, Kingsley Amis. Discussing *A Proper Marriage,* Amis remarks,

> Now it is always hard to summarise a story without seeming to be offensively implying that almost nothing happens, especially when, as here, almost nothing happens. Anyone with so little to narrate should, I feel, make more concessions to her readers than Mrs. Lessing does with her preference for description and . . . her thousand-word paragraphs, and her tissues of abstract commentary doing duty for characterisation.

In Claire Sprague and Virginia Tiger, eds., *Critical Essays on Doris Lessing* (Boston: G.K. Hall & Co., 1986), 174. Echoing Amis almost three decades later, James Gindin, at the end of a detailed analysis of Lessing's political beliefs and sociological inclinations, is critical of 'the long, dull, clinical study of discovering that one is pregnant which takes up about seventy pages of *A Proper Marriage*'. James Gindin, 'Doris Lessing's Intense Commitment,' in *Bloom's Modern Critical Views: Doris Lessing,* ed. Harold Bloom (New York: Chelsea House, 1986), 25.

43. Nancy Bazin finds similarities between *Martha Quest,* Lawrence's *Women in Love* and Joyce's *A Portrait of the Artist as a Young Man.* Nancy Topping Bazin, 'The Moment of Revelation in "Martha Quest" And Comparable Moments by Two Modernists,' *Modern Fiction Studies* 26, no. 1 (Spring 1980): 87–98.
44. Doris Lessing, *Under My Skin: Volume One of My Autobiography, to 1949* (Great Britain: HarperCollins, 1994), 160–161.
45. For a detailed analysis on the insularity of the novel in English, see Gilbert Phelps, 'The Novel Today,' in *The Pelican Guide to English Literature,* ed. Boris Ford, vol. 7, *The Modern Age* (Harmondsworth: Penguin Books,

1961), 475–495. Among Lessing's female contemporaries, Muriel Spark (1918–2006)—who sailed to Southern Rhodesia looking forward to not having to do any housework in that country—states in her autobiography: 'Just about the time I was born society was changing rapidly'. In Muriel Spark, *Curriculum Vitae: A Volume of Autobiography* (Harmondsworth: Penguin Books, 1992), 40. Yet Spark's early work, while reflecting the cultural rootedness of her middle-class life and accomplishments in Edinburgh, does not incorporate any sense of this changing world of which England is no longer the centre. See also Randall Stevenson, *The British Novel Since the Thirties: An Introduction* (London: Batsford, 1986), 123–160.

46. Doris Lessing complains of the xenophobia and small-mindedness of the British, and identifies this attitude as one her father defined as the 'parish pump mentality' in Doris Lessing, *Walking in the Shade: Volume Two of My Autobiography, 1949 to 1962* (New York: HarperCollins,1997), 234.
47. Lessing, *Martha Quest*, 14–15.
48. Lessing, *Under My Skin,* 8.
49. Lessing, *Martha Quest*, 16–17.
50. Lessing, *A Proper Marriage*, 73.
51. Lessing, *A Proper Marriage*, 229.
52. Virginia Woolf, *The Pargiters: The Novel-Essay Portion of THE YEARS*, ed. Mitchell A. Leaska (New York: Harcourt Brace Jovanovich, 1978), xxxviii–xxxix.
53. Large-scale access to education became a reality for women in Britain in the 1920s. In *Mrs Dalloway*, Clarissa's young daughter, Elizabeth, is shown to have more access to career options than her mother could have ever dreamed of.
54. 'Tradition and Individual Talent' can be found in T.S. Eliot, *Selected Essays 1917–1932* (London: Faber & Faber, 1932).
55. Roberta Rubenstein, 'Fixing the Past: Yearning and Nostalgia in Woolf and Lessing,' in *Woolf and Lessing: Breaking the Mold*, eds. Ruth Saxton and Jean Tobin (New York: St. Martin's Press, 1994), 16. Woolf's words 'we think back through our mothers if we are women' are from Virginia Woolf, *A Room of One's Own* (London: Hogarth Press, 1929; London: Panther Books, 1977), 72–73.
56. The references to Karenina and Woolf are also made by Jocelyn Harris, 'Doris Lessing's Beautiful Impossible Blueprints', in *The British and Irish Novel since 1960,* ed. James Acheson (New York: St. Martin's Press, 1991), 36.

57. Lessing, *The Golden Notebook*, 28.
58. Lessing, *The Golden Notebook*, 30.
59. Lessing, *The Golden Notebook*, 396.
60. Lessing, *The Golden Notebook*, 397.
61. Lessing, *The Golden Notebook*, 298.
62. Claire Sprague, 'Multipersonal and Dialogic Modes in *Mrs. Dalloway* and *The Golden Notebook*', in Saxton and Tobin, *Woolf and Lessing*, 8.
63. Lessing, *The Golden Notebook*, 557.
64. Lessing, *The Golden Notebook*, 557.
65. Freud's reading of penis envy was supplanted by Lacan's reading of phallic envy in what is a fascinating amalgamation of psychosexuality and linguistics.
66. Lessing, *The Golden Notebook*, 37.
67. Lessing, *The Golden Notebook*, 398.
68. Lessing, *The Golden Notebook*, 207.
69. Lessing, *The Golden Notebook*, 296.
70. Lessing, *The Golden Notebook*, 400.
71. Lessing, *The Golden Notebook*, 404.
72. While analysing Anna and Molly's sexually free lives as a reaction to the domestication of women that was part of the ideology of 'companionate marriage' in the late 1940s and 1950s, Louise Yelin takes exception to Anna's homophobia and sees it as 'implicating her in invidious patriarchal constructions of the feminine' while vitiating 'her critique of misogyny', adding that even historicising the novel does not 'change the way homophobia infects its critique of gender' in Yelin, *From the Margins*, 84–86.
73. Lessing, *The Golden Notebook*, 283.
74. Lessing, *The Golden Notebook*, 76.
75. Lessing, *The Golden Notebook*, 214.
76. Doris Lessing, 'Doris Lessing: Hot Dawns,' interview by Harvey Blume, *The Boston Book Review*, 1998, http://mural.uv.es/vemivein/dorisinterviews.html. Lessing, in *The Golden Notebook*, is also making a journey out of and away from communism. She had, as a matter of fact, resigned from the Communist Party in 1956. Yet, it is through the narrative of this novel that she traces the dilemmas of communism and pinpoints its limitations as a tool for further development or positive change. *A Ripple from the Storm* and *Landlocked*, novels that are semi-autobiographical, also capture some of the intense fascination and anger

generated from Lessing's own experience within the party. It is, of course, in a much later text called *The Good Terrorist*—published in 1985—that Lessing offers a brilliant and penetrating critique of the subculture of the many Marxist groups in contemporary Britain. Lessing takes this up again in *The Sweetest Dream,* a novel written over fifteen years after *The Good Terrorist,* wherein she goes back to the 1960s, looking ironically at the antics of a diehard communist while locating strong generations of women who raise families and run households.

Lessing's rejoinder to E.P. Thompson's observations on *The Golden Notebook* indicates what the standard Marxist male response to the novel has been and also spells out Lessing's own position very effectively: 'I think to say that I am something that wandered out of the bush dazzled by bright lights is perhaps an easy way out of thinking about the kind of outsider's view someone with my kind of upbringing is bound to have about Europe'. In Lessing, *Walking in the Shade,* 344.

77. Lessing, *The Golden Notebook,* 161.
78. Lessing, *The Golden Notebook,* 107.
79. From 1900, Lenin's illegal newspaper called *Iskra* played a decisive role in the formation of a revolutionary Marxist Party of the working class in Russia. Lenin's work was originally published in the Lenin Miscellany 1929–1930. *Philosophical Notebooks* were published in a collected volume in the years 1933–1947. They were later translated into English and published in 1961. See Vladimir Lenin, *Philosophical Notebooks,* trans. Clemens Dutt, vol. 38 (Moscow: Progress Publishers, 1961).
80. Antonio Gramsci (1891–1937) was a major figure in the Italian Communist Party. Under the Fascist regime, he was arrested and sentenced to prison for twenty years. In prison, he obtained permission to write and kept many notebooks on a variety of subjects. Written between 1928 and 1937, *The Prison Notebooks* were first published in 1948. Translations into the English language began in 1957 and the text was more widely disseminated in the 1960s.
81. *Cahiers du cinéma,* a film review freshly launched in 1951, began to function as a 'manifesto for the French New Wave' cinema of the 1960s. Showing that the film is also 'a text and a play of tensions, silences and repressions', *Cahiers du cinéma* challenged the notion of a single film theory or a single point of view and emphasised that film required by virtue of its polyvalent production, to be about multiple theory. For more

details, see Susan Hayward, *Cinema Studies: The Key Concepts* (London and New York: Routledge, 2000), 19–27.

82. Lessing, *The Golden Notebook*, 76.
83. The Declaration of the Rights of Man and Citizen was written by the Marquis de Lafayette, with help from Thomas Jefferson in 1789 and approved by the National Assembly of France in August 1789. See 'Declaration of the Rights of Man – 178,' The Avalon Project, accessed 13 September 2020, https://avalon.law.yale.edu/18th_century/rightsof.asp. Protesting against the invisibility of women in this version, Olympe de Gouges (1748–1793) drafted The Declaration of the Rights of Woman and Citizen in September 1791, modelling it on the earlier draft of 1789 that had left out all mention of women. See a discussion on Gouges' draft on the web at 'Déclaration des Droits de la Femme et de la Citoyenne,' Towards Emancipation? Women in Modern European History, accessed 13 September 2020, http://hist259.web.unc.edu/declaration-of-the-rights-of-woman/. In the following year of 1792, Mary Wollstonecraft's longer tract questioning the erasure of women, *Vindication*, was published.
84. Sheila Rowbotham, *Women in Movement: Feminism and Social Action* (New York and London: Routledge, 1992), 28.

IV

Science Fiction: Lessing's Forays into Alternative Space

Lessing's experiments with the novel form continue after *The Golden Notebook*. With the exception of *Landlocked* (1965), the fourth book in the Children of Violence series, Lessing's novels written after *The Golden Notebook* into the early 1980s reveal her ongoing innovations with narrative form, and her use of newer strategies to explicate and uncover women's experience. Lessing's narrative techniques reveal the use of memoirs, medical records and science fiction (SF) landscapes as well as the creation of new cosmologies in her main corpus of science fiction writing in this period, the five-volume series called *Canopus in Argos: Archives* (1979–1983).

This chapter will look at three of her novels predating Canopus in Argos—namely, *The Four-Gated City* (1969),[1] *Briefing for a Descent into Hell* (1971)[2] and *Memoirs of a Survivor* (1974).[3] These novels underline Lessing's dramatic shift from the realistic tradition of the novel so familiar to aficionados of her work. Lessing herself had earlier validated the realist tradition of the novel, calling it the 'highest point of literature'.[4] She had also used it effectively to document women's lives and to draw attention to the silencing of women within cultural practice. How does one then respond to this new format and perspective? What do we make of Lessing's leap into the fantastic, using non-realistic modes of narration?

Lessing's increasing interest in non-realistic modes of narration is noticeable in her fiction as early as the 1960s. In the novels under discussion, Lessing stretches the boundaries of fiction and of the thought process itself to explore new modes of existence. Alert to the changes taking place in the world around her, Lessing adopts a critical perspective on extant empirical realities and consciously locates value outside of this dimension. The three novels under discussion extend

Lessing's enquiry into the retrieval of women's lives—this time, by being sharply critical of the extant tradition of science and scientific progress. Written and published over five years, these novels share a commonality of themes and interests. Collectively, all three novels map out new directions for feminism. In these novels, Lessing consciously locates value outside realist dimensions.

Lessing explains this writing as being about 'Inner-space fiction. For there is never anywhere to go but in'.[5] Lessing's explication charts for us the unique nature of the voyage that her protagonist is about to embark on. This experience is like a quest but unlike Martha's journey, it no longer involves a young individual's search for self-identity. Instead, circumstances direct an older protagonist to re-examine his/her world minutely. All earlier presuppositions come under review. As a result, it makes the protagonist and the reader contemplate the world afresh. At the end of this 'inner space' journey, the consequent insights and orientations provide a resolution.

The three novels highlight Lessing's deliberate shift from a focus on individual trajectories to a detailed examination of an entire community. She questions at length tacit assumptions about scientific progress and advancement in parts of the technologically developed West. The critical reading of the value attached to science in her fiction benefits from criticism made by articulate contemporary women scientists. One can surmise that Rachel Carson's *Silent Spring* (1962), for instance, was a major influence in this period. Further, Lessing's own eclectic reading of milestones in the scientific world contributes to the argument developed in her novels. Lessing represents a tradition of women's writing which questions masculine science and asks new questions about the human being and the cosmos. Lessing's novels draw attention to the darker side of a technologically advanced and developed society. In doing so, the novels contest notions regarding the Golden Age of Europe that is seen as having commenced around the 1950s with the revival of Western capitalism at the end of the wars.[6] *The Four-Gated City* is critical of the values posited by scientific advancement, rationality and progress in a post-Second World War scenario. This gloomy and stark perception is reiterated in *Briefing* and *Memoirs* as well.

A brief synopsis of each of the novels at this juncture will be useful in highlighting the common themes that Lessing explores through them. *The Four-Gated City*, published in 1969, is chronologically the first in this group and covers a period of a little over fifty years. Beginning in the late 1940s with Martha in London, the novel quickly abandons its early naturalist mode to highlight the anguish and horror that forms the substratum of life in London. Martha's amble through the city of the 1940s and 1950s precedes a quick account of the 1960s, followed by a glimpse into the futuristic Britain of the 1970s. We are given details of a poisoned city with its teeming residents constantly under pressure. The world maps in Mark's study chart out the continual pollution of the world's scarce soil and water resources. London is destroyed as a result of a nerve-gas leak and the last section of the novel, its appendix, updates us on the life of the survivors who continued to live in distant outposts up to the year 2000.

Briefing, published in 1971, deals with the journeys of amnesiac professor Charles Watkins—found wandering by the embankment and placed under medical treatment at a city hospital. Doctors X and Y, who attend on him, prescribe two different sets of medications, interpret his condition and proceed to treat him from diametrically opposed positions. The patient himself resists their diagnosis and their attempts to pinpoint his condition through the greater part of the narrative. Watkins' journeys and the experiences he recounts may be the wanderings of a delirious mind, but they are far more thought-provoking than the sedated state the hospital authorities would like to maintain him in. His insights during a so-called delirious state—as he stumbles upon a city at the moment of its inception and its subsequent growth and decay—make for more stimulating reading than his post-electric shock return to a 'sane, normal world'.

Memoirs, published in 1974, records life in a city whose administrative machinery and daily infrastructural needs exist in a state of collapse. The survivor in *Memoirs* offers a detailed study of the events taking place in the city from the vantage point of a bystander at the window of a flat. The narrative is punctuated with remarks on the breakdown of the machinery of the city and of city life itself:

> I went about the streets . . . wondering how long this city would stand, eroded as it was in every way, its supplies going and gone, its people fleeing, its food supplies worsening, its law and order consisting more and more of what citizens imposed on themselves.[7]

The central movement in this novel revolves around an elderly narrator who watches, waits, records and wanders in and out of the city, in and out of several walls. The narrator is also entrusted with the guardianship of Emily, who grows very rapidly from a young girl to a middle-aged woman. Of great significance is the narrator's eventual escape to a better world, along with Emily, Gerald, the tribe of children they are responsible for and their half-dog, half-cat Hugo.

Lessing's interchangeable use of the male and female protagonists as primary narrators in all three novels is noteworthy. Martha and Mark voice the core ideas in *The Four-Gated City*. While Watkins is the chief narrator in *Briefing*, Rosemary Baines and Violet also raise significant issues. The female identity of the narrator in *Memoirs* is made known to us quite late in the novel, when Emily takes permission from Gerald to invite her guardian to their house: 'I asked him, you see? I said to him, *can she come*'[8] [emphasis added]. This disclosure of the narrator's sex almost at the end of the narrative suggests that her gender is of minimal significance within the narrative. Outside of the text, the narrator's underplayed gender throws open for speculation the androgynous nature of human experience.

Lessing's interchangeable use of narrators echoes the insight of feminist theory in the social sciences that 'behaviors that mark masculinity and femininity are socially constructed, neither innate nor determined once and for all by a biological substratum.'[9] Lessing's refusal to read gender as based simplistically on biology does not deter her from the scrutiny of gender relations that are hierarchical and reductive in their perception of women. The entrenchment of such hierarchies in scientific practice and their percolation to the empirical level remain an important site of investigation. It would be useful at this juncture to establish how Lessing's novels share common grounds with feminist analyses, both in the questioning of hegemonies erected by the world of science and in being sceptical of the notions of development postulated as its achievement.

Materialist Utopias and Counterculture: Shifting Perceptions of the 1960s

The growth in agriculture, industry and trade in the 1950s, along with the economic boom at the end of the world wars, continued into the 1960s and was accepted as part of the upward graph of development and progress among the developed industrial nations of the world. As Hobsbawm takes pains to point out, by the end of the 1950s the 'dominant ideology of progress took it for granted that the growing domination of nature by man was the very measure of humanity's advance.'[10]

This 'dominant ideology of progress' can be seen as a tacit reiteration of attitudes that can be traced back to the emergence of science as a system of empirical knowledge. Scientific study, central to Western patriarchal belief and practice, can be traced back to its origins in the sixteenth century when it was made popular by Francis Bacon—popularly termed the father of modern science.[11] Baconian science played an integral role in furthering rapid industrialisation and the subsequent imperial and colonial expansion of the West. It was implicitly sexist and gendered in its association of reason with the male and nature with the female. The subsequent dissemination of scientific knowledge followed this pattern and systematically disparaged, if not excluded, women's participation in the world of scientific and technological innovation.

Consequently, science effectively established itself as an empirical system of analysis and control, influencing more and more aspects of human life. Women as practitioners and active participants occupied marginal points of entry into the world of science. They remained on the fringes of the scientific community despite the presence of sporadic female scientists.[12] Science's sphere of influence in social, cultural, economic and technological activities has been significant, particularly in the twentieth century, and the resources invested in scientific and technological activities all over the world have been on the increase.

The assumption that the singular progress of science and technology represented the onward march of Western civilisation faced little resistance or scepticism before the Second World War. After Hiroshima and the Vietnam War, the naïve belief in the advancements made by science was supplanted by a growing awareness of its destructive capability and its foreclosure of all other modes of perception. Increasingly, the potential of science to use knowledge and technology in collusion with institutionalised political power—to dominate, exclude and dismiss as detrimental everything that was part of 'nature'—came under scrutiny. Ashis Nandy points out that the successful incorporation of Western empirical science further reinforces its centrality as a power available to the state.[13]

This vision excluded not only greater parts of the non-European world, but also reinforced the assumptions of Baconian science that 'masculinity' and 'science' existed in a category far superior to 'women' and 'nature'. As Mary Evans points out, it was as late as the 1970s when feminist historians began to warn 'that the rise of science in Europe shifted the understanding of our human relationship to Nature.'[14] Recognising that science was not value-free, a host of women such as Anne Sayre, Alice Rossi, Hilary Rose, Sandra Harding and Donna Haraway turned their attention to a study of the dissemination of scientific knowledge.

Lessing's writing reveals a keen interest in scientific developments and interventions. She recognises its mind-altering potential and asserts that the most exciting things are happening in the realm of science today. 'Scientific ideas permeate our thinking and our vocabulary. Everyone knows science has made our world. It is for the next scientific discovery that we all wait, as once they did for the last chapter of a Dickens novel.'[15]

Yet, Lessing's astute sense of political reality does not blind her to the fact that science also functions as a double-edged tool, and that it is too often used by the modern state to chart hegemonic discourse. As one of the founder members of The Campaign for Nuclear Disarmament (CND), she also featured among the organisers and participants of the Aldermaston Marches against nuclear weapons in the late 1950s. Lessing is sharply critical of the furthering of science for the production of weapons of mass destruction. Her activism concerning scientific issues stemmed from her scepticism about the linear progress associated with the advent of science and technology. Her work reveals her disillusionment with scientific progress, especially in the backdrop of the new wave of personal and social liberation that characterised the late 1960s.

These were the years of counterculture—characterised by the erosion of familial and social bonds, and general dissent against the state, power, authority, law and convention. Small wonder then, that the late 1960s saw the rise of a whole host of movements: the youth movements, the peace movements, the women's movements, the civil rights movements, the anti-Vietnam war movements, the hippie movements, the years of the flower children, the gay movements, drugs and a search for solutions in Eastern spiritual beliefs are some of the events that characterised this period. This cultural internationalism that was the high point of the late 1960s and early 1970s in Europe and America posed a challenge to authority and the state in its search for alternatives and generated 'much radical and popular optimism about the dawn of a new order.'[16]

This sense of looking for directions can be seen in *The Four-Gated City*, *Briefings* and *Memoirs*. In each of these novels, Eurocentric authority represented by a fictionalised London is under threat and on a course of irretrievable ruin. Lessing's emphasis regarding her non-Eurocentric focus needs to be cited here:

> I'm glad that I was not educated in literature and history and philosophy, which means that I did not have this Eurocentered thing driven into me, which I think is the single biggest hang-up Europe has got. It's almost impossible for anyone in the West not to see the West as the God-given gift to the world.[17]

Lessing's disavowal of her Western inheritance and her search for alternate beliefs and philosophies at this stage finds expression in her fascination with the work of C.S. Jung and R.D. Laing and absorption with the philosophy of Sufism. Her writing, impacted by the dissent of counterculture, reveals her distancing from communism as she explores other alternatives.

It is pertinent now to delve into the issues of women's involvement with the sciences and clarify a few points. In the prominence assumed by science in the shaping of modern Western societies, what is the nature of the space that has been available to women? How are women implicated in scientific advancements? Do they have access to the scientific disciplines? Does women's intervention provide for dissent or alternate theorising within scientific practice?

Despite the rise of the women's movements in the late 1960s, women's participation and engagement with scientific ideology had been minimal. As Lynda Birke and Marsha Henry point out, in the late 1960s, women involved with 'second-wave feminism' were often hostile to the study of science.[18] Although there were representative women scientists who worked within the discipline of science, they were not really in a position to engage with the ideology that governed the sciences.

The historical and cultural relativity of modern science has only been recognised in the last thirty years or so. As Sandra Harding, one of the feminist theorists analysing scientific practice, says,

> men's experiences and activities on which Western knowledge has been based are only partial; they represent only masculine experience and activity, not the distinctively and admirably human, as men perennially claim.[19]

Harding also takes issue with the marginalisation of women in scientific studies. She locates women's absence as a patriarchal ploy and draws attention to the lack of multiculturalism in science's delineation of its roots as essentially Euro-American. Modern science is seen as doubly guilty, both in its silencing of women and its unwillingness to acknowledge its borrowings from non-European sources.[20]

Stressing the fact that women's exclusion from science is not simply an oversight of history, science's continued sustenance of older patriarchal constructs and its reiteration of older cultural constructs of women has been highlighted. As Evelyn Keller succinctly points out '[t]he same cultural tradition that names rational, objective and transcendent as male, and irrational, subjective, and immanent as female, also, simultaneously names the scientific mind as male and material nature as female. . . . '[21] Veronica Stolte-Heiskanen explains that such essentialist constructions have not only lead to a distortion of knowledge but also contributed to substantive gaps in women's knowledge of the world they inhabit.[22]

Women scientists are now aware that they must play a proactive role in the technology that affects their lives. Women's intervention in the scientific arena has highlighted the role played by the state in the furthering of science and technology. The participation of women scientists at the levels of data collection, examination and presentation is one of the most significant aspects of feminist inputs in the area of scientific study. Women scientists have drawn attention to the short-term agendas of most scientific projects and questioned the premises behind scientific control and conquest of the environment. Their work indicts the exploitative nature of scientific study and draws our attention to the consequences of such an approach by highlighting the environmental dangers posed by the relentless pursuit of technological advancement.

Rachel Carson's work[23] was the earliest feminist critique of the pollution of air, water and land resources in the 1960s. Helen Caldicott's[24] warning regarding the grave dangers of nuclear power reverberated through the 1970s. The coining of the phrase 'ecofeminism' by Francoise d'Eaubonne in 1974 is an etymological reassertion of women's sensitivity to the ravages inflicted on the environment and resistance to aggressive development.[25]

Lessing acknowledges her fascination for scientific data by featuring excerpts culled from school textbooks at the beginning of the various sections of *The Four-Gated City*. The citations at the beginning of Lessing's novels also record her familiarity with the work of contemporary women scientists. Citations from marine biologist Rachel Carson's work *The Edge of the Sea* feature prominently both in *The Four-Gated City* and in *Briefing*. Lessing approaches the question of science's intervention in human life from her vantage position as a creative writer. She incorporates suggestions from Carson into her fiction and throws in a whole range of eclectic discourses for discussion—from the interpretation of schizophrenia as a sane response to an insane world by R.D. Laing to antipsychiatry movements supported by Jung, as well as the aspiring to cosmic levels of consciousness recommended by Sufi wisdom.[26]

The placing of Carson's picturesque account of marine life from *The Edge of the Sea* beneath an extract from a fourteenth-century mystical text by sage Mahmoud Shabistari in *Briefing*[27] highlights the shared similarities in the world view of the mystic and the eco-scientist. Both offer descriptions of the incredible and unfathomable beauty of the natural world governed by its own set of laws. It is this more nebulous, more open-ended space—free from mechanistic constructions and conceptions of science—that Lessing chooses to move towards in the three novels under discussion.

The Four-Gated City, Briefing and *Memoirs*—novels written around the time that feminist scientists articulated their dissent with the pedagogy of scientific progress—can be seen as offering an overlapping criticism of the rational epistemology of Western civilisation. This is heightened by the connections that Lessing herself makes in all the novels, at the level of subject matter, theme and intent. In the novels, life in the real world leads towards experiences in an imagined world that defies assimilation. The nature of the experience and its effect upon the character defies evaluation through linear notions of time and space. Lessing draws upon the mythic, the imaginary, the unconscious, the fantastic and the world of dreams to document this experience. By bringing to fore this new dimension and seeking to validate it, Lessing reworks her way through existing binary oppositions that have hitherto devalued such accounts. She situates meaning in her narratives, outside of the structures of rationality and empirical truths that Western science has sought to ratify in alignment with other master discourses.

In *The Four-Gated City*, Martha voices Lessing's concern while she searches for explanations that will confer meaning upon her experience. Ploughing through literature and books, Martha eventually identifies this space:

> There were books on Rosicrucianism and the old Alchemists; Buddhist books and the dozen or so varieties of Yoga; here were Zoroastrianism and esoteric Christianity; tracts on the I Ching; Zen, witchcraft, magic, astrology and vampirism; scholarly treatises on Sufism; the works of the Christian mystics. Here in short, was a kind of potted library representing everything rejected by official culture and scholarship.[28]

The defining principle behind this 'potted library' or motley group is that it falls outside of established models of mainstream knowledge. All these references call for readings and perspectives that situate themselves within the counterculture movements. This point of view is 'anti-rational' and 'non-scientific'. It is also culturally associated with the female or feminine modes of apprehension. This space which Martha first hesitantly approaches in *The Four-Gated City* also forms part of the new landscape of *Briefing* and *Memoirs*, where Watkins and the unnamed narrator strive towards a similar understanding.

The various influences that feed into Lessing's work at this time are her engagement with perspectives and philosophies outside of the Occident, her scientific activism, her scepticism about the technological and rational thrust of her times, as well as the concerted impact of counterculture and her gleanings from Sufism. All of these contribute to unexamined and radical alternatives that emerge through the very act of fiction's engagement with the ideas of its time.

Women and Science: Structuring Dialogue through Literature?

Reactions to scientific and rational premises in the 1960s also find expression in the form of fictional outpourings. A vast amount of imaginative writing proliferated as a result of easy access to scientific ideas. Yet, this was not the first time that creative writers were provoked into writing as a response to the scientific temper of their age. If one were to trace older links, there has always been an extant tradition of fiction that lent itself to exploring dimensions of the psyche outside the pale of the material and rational and highlighted the significance of non-rational modes of enquiry.

This tradition of fiction writing incorporated the devices of myth and fantasy as alternate modes of seeing. In different historical epochs, this has resulted in the creation of imaginative and imaginary worlds with the actual world and its problems as the point of reference. While this can be seen in Butler's *Erehwon* or even Swift's *Gulliver's Travels*, it is the Gothic narratives of the eighteenth century and their influence upon the nineteenth-century English novel and prose fiction that contributed significantly to an entire school of imaginative writing termed 'science fiction'.[29] Mary Shelley's *Frankenstein* (1818) is an example of one of the earliest SF novels that draws from the tradition of the Gothic narratives and engages with the debates of its times about the dangers inherent in scientific pursuit.

Adam Roberts places the origins of SF between 1780 and 1830 and sees it as having developed into 'a meaningful category in its own right' with the work of Jules Verne (1828–1905) and H.G. Wells (1866–1946). He highlights 'Wellsian fascination with encountering difference embodied in material form' and concurs with Patrick Parrinder in seeing Wells as 'the pivotal figure in the evolution of scientific romance into modern science fiction'.[30] Despite the existence of a fictional tradition that offered resistance to the advancing juggernaut of science in the work of Mary Shelley, Jules Verne and H.G. Wells, Adams sees the proliferation in the genre of SF as having taken place in the late 1930s, continuing into the 1960s.

Originating in the United States and then extending to Europe, SF in the decades of the 1940s and early 1950s echoed the excitement and tumult that characterised scientific research and advancement itself. It is in the subsequent decades that this genre began to mirror an increasing scepticism about 'technological solutions to social and environmental problems.'[31] Around the same time, SF also became an increasingly popular medium for creative expression among women writers. Women's appropriation of this literary form is significant in the light of the connections that can be made between science fiction, women's writing and feminist interventions.

Adam Roberts points out that this genre celebrated scientific culture and catered predominantly to 'a fan culture of young white males' in the 1930s and 1940s.[32] The academies, traditional centres of literary canon formation, frowned upon this narrative form. SF's location vis-à-vis the academies, it is possible to stress, replicated on an average the inferior status occupied by women in their cultural location. Women's adoption of this disparaged genre often paralleled SF's location in the fictional hierarchy. Gary Westfahl refers to this as the 'feminine aura'[33] of SF.

SF's older association with the Gothic tradition also draws attention to this feminine aura. Both Gothic and dystopic traditions commonly emerge as the underside of cultural dominants—namely, reason and rationality in the context of the Gothic tradition, and scientific progress in the context of SF. Both genres lend themselves to a recording of the deviant and the different at various points in history and culture. They provide critical insights into the dominant traditions in which they choose to intervene. The use of dreamlike states, visions and nightmares is part of the repertoire of both genres. The imaginative faculty and heightened sensibility due to which such visions are apprehended also play a prominent role in the envisioning of non-rational worlds which exist outside of the normative everyday world.

Women writers who adopted the genre of SF and were at ease in it challenged archaic notions about the absence of scientific temperament in women by virtue of their gender. A significant aspect of the SF written by women was the tendency towards dystopic narratives. Women retrieved this disparaged genre and made use of it to address the lacunae in mainstream perspectives relating to science. Women's experiences and those articulated by SF also share parallels. Both SF and women's experience continue to inhabit less privileged spaces in the linguistic registers of culture. Facets of women's experience have routinely been jettisoned without discussion or examined minimally. Therefore, it made perfect sense to explore new avenues for women's utterances through the genre of SF.

Lessing's account of SF's slow rise to popularity enables us to register the shifts in response to this particular genre:

> At first the readers of science fiction were few, and they were aficionados of the ideas and not the writing, which was crude. . . . Yet, while large numbers of people everywhere read science fiction, some are still furtively addicted because of the unrespectability of the genre.[34]

Is the recent use of this genre a possible forum for the articulation of women's authentic voices? Does the incorporation of science fiction as a new narrative strategy provide women writers with sites for experimentation that are not available within realist traditions? As a narrative strategy that tries to hone in on women's experience, does this genre enhance our understanding of how women view the world? *The Four-Gated City* addresses the issue of women's point of view, where Martha Quest reflects on Joe's mother, an older woman, as she strolls through bombed-out London streets:

> Put her brain, together with the other million brains, women's brains, that recorded in such tiny loving anxious detail the histories of window sills, skins of paint, replaced curtains and salvaged baulks of timber, there would be a recording instrument, a sort of six-dimensional map which included the histories and lives and loves of people, London—a section map in depth.[35]

The reference to the 'six-dimensional map' is intriguing. What precisely are these six dimensions? Are we to identify a dimension outside of those documented by the five organs of sense perception? Is this a reference to intuitive faculties that science does not address? How do millions of women's brains contribute to this? Is Martha's use of the term 'women's brains' a reading of women's capabilities that have survived outside of the perimeters set by science and the systems of constricting cultural codes? Or does one read the metonymic use of brains to signify women's cognitive memories, thereby suggesting that such interventions can offer valuable insights overlooked by scientific systems in place?

This is a question that Martha addresses to Jimmy Wood:

> Do you think that at some point three, four hundred years ago, science threw out a very important baby with the bath water? What do you think of those capacities you write about called telepathy, second sight, levitation, and the rest?[36]

All these systems of intuition, it must be remembered, were dismissed as pseudosciences since empirical means of documenting them did not exist. In *The Four-Gated City*, by postulating that there is a six-dimensional map that women's perception can create, Lessing foregrounds those aspects of experience that have been overlooked because of the prioritisation of scientific value in human life. *The Four-Gated City*, *Briefing for a Descent into Hell* and *The Memoirs of a Survivor* raise questions about the nature of science and progress and are also prescient about the directions feminist philosophy will take.

SF, using the devices of the fantastic and focusing on the non rational, becomes an important feminist vehicle in posing paradigms for science. The genre delineates fantastic and futuristic scenarios which function outside of the empirical certainties offered by science. As a dystopic medium, it undercuts the notion of progressive linear development that science has sought to arrogate to itself. Sharing affinities with the imaginative faculties, the Gothic and the fantastic, rather than the rational, SF operates as a grey area providing suitable ground to articulate women's voices. SF records the underside of cultural, political and historical processes. Women have forever occupied this territory. The genre's attempt to demystify and directly address all the hidden and oblique facets of empirical data echoes feminist concerns. Both SF and feminism share a common platform in their concerns about the creation of a better or equal world.

SF thus provided a new literary and imaginative space for the woman writer, from where she could articulate her viewpoint. Ursula K. Le Guin (1929–2018), Marion Zimmer Bradley (1930–1999) and Octavia Butler (1947–2006), prolific writers associated with the success of the genre, raised troubling questions related to the onrush of science and technology.[37] Women's SF in the 1960s is characterised by the self-conscious use of the genre. Le Guin describes her writing of SF as 'based on "social science, psychology, anthropology [and] history"'.[38] Octavia Butler voices similar sentiment when she describes herself 'merely as a chronicler of the human heart using science fiction as a tool of revelation'.[39] Lessing, in a recent interview, also points out that 'in science fiction is some of the best social fiction of our time.'[40] Although currently there is far greater awareness of women writers of science fiction and far more credibility extended to the genre itself, this was not the case in the late 1960s when Le Guin, Bradley, Butler and Lessing produced work in this genre. Lessing's novels belonging to this period were viewed ambiguously, both from the standpoint of feminism as well as that of SF. When interviewer Susan Stamberg asked Lessing in 1984 if she had now shifted from 'realistic writing to fantasy writing or visionary writing,' Lessing responded with, '[w]hy do you make it 'or, or, or? It could be and, and, and.'[41] Lessing's retort failed to convince individual admirers such as Nicole Ward Jouve, who is critical of Lessing's technique in *The Four-Gated City* and states categorically that 'one mode cannot be used to establish another,' and that 'one cannot move from the particular to the universal as Lessing does without contradictions.'[42]

Lessing's work has attracted minimal attention in commentaries on SF as well. A recent reader called *Science Fiction* that traces the genesis of this narrative form and charts its history and numerous practitioners does not refer to Lessing.[43] This is in spite of the fact that Lessing has around seven books to her credit which fall indisputably into this category. The three novels under discussion, however, are very much a part of Lessing's redefinition of feminism, which works as an insistent questioning of ground realities.

Within each novel, Lessing unravels space that feminists have now begun to rightly claim as their own. Lessing's way of drawing attention to woman-centred perspectives in these novels is to focus persistently on communities and groups rather than on the individual. This emphasis on the collective instead of the solitary protagonist of patriarchal traditions marks Lessing's search for new possibilities. Lessing's engagement with ongoing women's issues along with a shift in focus from individual narratives to an entire community as the site of articulation for new feminist perceptions is significant.[44] It enables her to speak for a larger group and draw attention to a perspective that is not confined to a single, arbitrary individual.

It becomes relevant to draw attention to Lessing's treatment of madness in her fiction. Central figures in Lessing's novels often act contrary to conventional expectations. They seem to be on a different wavelength when viewed alongside other members of their world. Lessing emphasises that the state of mind of her protagonists is one of heightened awareness. Within the framework of the novel, Lessing's characters resist definition as dysfunctional or abnormal. This is of significance, as the perceptions gleaned by her characters challenge the convictions and assumptions of sane persons. Madness or delusion in Lessing's novel comes full circle and moves closer to older notions of 'vision' and 'inspiration,' eluding the confined, repressive space it occupied in the nineteenth century. Madness works in opposition to the rational world that Lessing shows herself to be deeply critical of.[45]

Reverberations and Current Trends: Feminist Prognosis for the Future

All three novels situate women amidst a technological age gone awry. Pinpointing the reasons for this, the novels also engage with the world through the eyes of women and suggest possibilities that emerge from their experiences. *The Four-Gated City* chronicles Martha's struggle for personal, sexual and economic independence, from the late 1940s to the 1970s with literary reverberations from the past.

The Coldridge household in Bloomsbury where Martha resides operates as a many-splendoured symbol. This household functions as a microscopic representation of London. Bloomsbury is also meant to evoke older literary associations that date back to the eclectic and articulate group of young intellectuals surrounding the Stephen and Woolf households. This was the cultural and literary heart of England in the first four decades of the twentieth century. Ensuring that her readers do not miss these connections, Lessing takes the trouble to spell them out through an uninitiated May Quest, Martha's mother, for whom Bloomsbury's literary connections do not exist:

> Mrs. Quest planned to live in this house, as Martha's mother, and to participate in some kind of imagined life. Bloomsbury. For Mrs. Quest this did not mean literature, she would not have that kind of association. It meant trips to the British Museum.[46]

For May Quest, the British Museum recalls older and more glorious associations with the empire. The novel also documents the end of this tradition through the changes taking place in the Coldridge house, drawing attention to Britain's peripheral role in geopolitical hierarchies. The eventual collapse of the Coldridge house indicates the complete shift in British life, from the epicentre of the world to a minimal role in the new configuration. This erasure of what it meant to be British is traced alongside the deliberate reduction of interest in individuals.

Martha's job as secretary and housekeeper in a household where her employer has a wife who is mentally ill evokes associations with *Jane Eyre*. It also 'draws attention to the difference between the nineteenth century and the present and the inadequacy of the conventions of the past to contemporary situations.'[47] There is a significant shift in Lessing's treatment of the nineteenth-century theme of the madwoman in the attic. Lynda, the New Age madwoman, is very different from her literary predecessor Bertha Mason. Martha's intimacy with Mark does not disturb her relationship with Lynda. Martha's entry into the Coldridge household sets new precedents which rewrite older literary connections. Mark had married Lynda for love. He lives in an age of easy access to sexual and emotional gratification and does not wish to either keep Lynda's existence a secret or do away with her. Nor is he constricted by religious or civic protocols. Martha's identification with Lynda, unlike Jane's ambiguous recognition of Bertha Mason, is very lucid:

> And here it was that a closed secret nerve ached and nagged in Martha: she had not met Lynda, save through improbably beautiful photographs, but she knew her, oh yes, very well, though she and Martha were not alike, and could not be, since Martha was not 'ill' and in the hand of doctors. But for a variety of reasons, Lynda Coldridge, who was in a very expensive mental hospital because she could not stand being Mark's wife, and Francis' mother, came too close to Martha.[48]

Lessing presciently voices several agendas of the early 1970s in *The Four-Gated City.* Women's associations in the West demanded remuneration within the household and emphasised the need for the state to fix appropriate wages for such activity.[49] The need to compute domestic labour and the organising of night marches by large groups of women—to assuage women's anxieties about lack of mobility and safety at night—were some of the significant features of women's activism in the early 1970s.[50] Martha Quest's drawing of a salary as a housekeeper as well as her long walks at night, in the dark and rather threatening parts of London, anticipate events that are scheduled to happen.

The Four-Gated City also deals with the epochal lives of women. Lessing achieved this by the continued depersonalisation of Martha in the novel, even as she takes on the multiple roles of active co-author, secretary, housekeeper and nurturer, catering to different age groups in the Coldridge household. Watching the younger girls in the household walk into her room to borrow her clothes and accessories, Martha reflects that 'the rejuvenation a young girl gives her mother or an older woman is a setting free into impersonality, a setting free, also, from her personal past.'[51]

Deliberately shifting focus from the central protagonist Martha, the novel charts the lives of several women over a few generations: May Quest, Margaret, Lynda, Iris, Stella, Sarah-Sally, Nanny Butts, Patty, Phoebe, Jill, Gwen, Zena and Rita Maynard. The novel shows how individual lives are punctuated by the larger world of scientific discoveries, technological exploits, increasing global pollution, development of nuclear arsenals and the side effects of the poisoning of air and water—all of which become an increasing collection of graphs and statistics on maps in Mark Coldridge's study.

Given the context of hapless residents in an inhospitable world, Lessing then draws attention to how certain individuals respond by detailing their breakdown in *The Four-Gated City* and *Briefing*. Exploring their psyches which fall outside the definition of conventional normalcy, Lessing's fiction echoes R.D. Laing's thesis that, 'insanity is not an abandonment of the real but a potentially intelligible attempt to achieve ontological security through the expression of a self fragmented by the pressures and violences of a competitive and exploitative society'.[52]

We find the earliest exploration of this condition in Anna's breakdown in *The Golden Notebook*. Lessing traces this idea further through the character of Lynda in *The Four-Gated City*. Martha's intuitive identification with Lynda marks the beginning of a long relationship with the latter and both of them undertake journeys together, from the basement. Their journeys consist of similar thought processes as they plug into new frequencies of experience beyond the comprehension of sane persons. Lynda's illness requires her continued stay in mental hospitals. She draws the reader's attention to the impersonal and mechanical dispensation of medical treatment and the exercise of efficient control over the patient. *Briefing* is sharply critical of the system of medication and the coercive sedation of the patient, and the authorial voice indicates its disapproval when Charles Watkins begins a regimen of compulsory medication.[53]

Watkins' spells of delirium perform the same function as Lynda's in providing critical insights and altering perceptions. A system of empirical knowledge certifies Lynda's insanity. This system is ratified by its machines and practitioners such as Dr Lamb. This world, despite its systems of checks and restraints, is responsible for unending acts of violence and control upon people and places.

Lynda's madness eludes conventional diagnosis. Medical science and psychotherapy can only provide limited analysis of her condition. Pained by her illness and unable to handle the situation, Lynda's well-meaning family always falls back on conventional systems of diagnosis. Normal people and sane society find it difficult to accept that Lynda has a very different point of view.

The medical diagnosis of Watkins' illness by the doctors attending to him displays a near-identical world view. Watkin's story, in many ways, becomes a replaying of Lynda's predicament. The theme of breakdown which began with Anna Wulf in *The Golden Notebook* and continued with Lynda and Martha in *The Four-Gated City* extends into *Briefing* as well. In these novels, a breakdown in the medical sense of the term becomes an enabling experience for the reader. The reader arrives at new insights on personal and social issues due to the altered subject position of the narrator. As the authorial voice remarks in *The Four-Gated City*, this

> was because if society is so organized, or rather has so grown, that it will not admit what one knows to be true, will not admit it, that is, except as it comes out perverted, through madness, then it is through madness and its variants it must be sought after.[54]

Madness becomes a metaphor for a system of beliefs that seem to be of little value. The thought processes of Lynda, Martha and Joe's mother become valuable aids in such a world. Through such mind instruments, it is possible to tune into other frequencies of experience and understanding not necessarily available to a person who is 'normal' or certifiably sane.

In *The Four-Gated City,* Lessing uses the geographical space of the basement and the psychic space of madness to highlight a perspective that is seemingly at variance with the rhythms of routine life in London. Martha and Lynda's experiences in the basement challenge the empirical reality of the world outside and provide fresh insights to it. Their madness enables them to critique the limited empirical view that seems to be inexorably pushing all the inhabitants of Britain towards the great 'catastrophe'.

Lynda and Martha provide insights deeply critical of the values and beliefs of their age. They indict the city and humans inhabiting it. We also observe Martha's recoil from the grey, war-bogged city of London and its incredible ugliness. Martha wonders 'what race was this that filled their river with garbage and excrement and let it run so evilly between the building that crystallized their pride, their history.'[55] The city whose ugliness and contamination Martha notices in the late 1940s is subject to all kinds of cataclysmic experiences up to the very end. Damaged first in the bombing during the First World War and marred by subsequent events such as the Korean War, nuclear disarmament protests and finally the chemical disaster that triggers the catastrophe—all of these take their toll. All these events become symptomatic of a certain moral disorder and Lessing suggests that the strife and environmental pollution is indicative of the more insidious damage occurring within individual psyches.

Martha's disgust at London, years after settling down there, is not very different from the previously quoted outburst that marks her arrival. This time, armed with an inner vision as she ventures out of the house, she evinces disgust and records details of the ugly, littered city streets with an objectivity that is reminiscent of Swift:

> for these people walked in their fouled and disgusting streets full of ordure and bits of refuse and paper as if they were not conscious of their existence here, were somewhere else. . . .
>
> For their eyes were half-useless: many wore bits of corrective glass over these spoilt or ill-grown organs; their ears were defective; many wore machines to help them hear even much as the sounds made by their fellows: and their mouths were full of metal and foreign substances to assist teeth that were rotting, if not equipped entirely with artificial teeth ... their guts were full of drugs because they could not defecate normally; and their nervous systems were numbed by the drugs they took to alleviate the damage done by the din they had chosen to live in, the fear and anxiety and tension of their lives. And they stank. . . . They lived in an air which was like a thick soup of petrol and fumes

> and stink of sweat and bad air from lungs full of the smoke they used as a narcotic, and filthy air from their bowels.[56]

This description of modern humans living in a world of technological debris and refuse is a telling indictment. Lessing's dystopic vision recalls for us the savage disgust of Jonathan Swift. Like Swift in *Gulliver's Travels*, Martha's disgust at the human body and the self-absorbed and short-sighted activity of clothing, feeding and sheltering 'a tiny favoured few' at the expense of 'nine-tenths of the world's population'[57] communicates itself to the reader. Only Martha and a few others seem to possess such levels of discomfort. This mode of perception is unavailable to countless normal people everywhere. However, Martha and Mark spend their entire lives observing and documenting this experience. The world maps inside Mark's study reiterate their vision by providing visual data on arms and arsenals, the polluted and poisoned sites of the world, as well as the stretches of the globe dogged by poverty and adverse living conditions. Increasingly, the external landscape of the city and the inscape of Mark's study highlight the costs of the self-serving agendas of scientific and technological progress.

This brings us to the conclusion of *The Four-Gated City* set futuristically in the decade of the 1990s—which has come and gone without leading up to the impending doom that Lessing prophesied. Yet, the alternatives chosen by some of the friends and inmates of the Coldridge household to escape the pollution of London and seek a holistic life in remote places are not lost on the reader. The catastrophe expected to finish off Britain warns against the naïve optimism invested in a limited empirical technology such as science. The prognosis for science and technology and the future promised by its unrelenting advance remains grave and bleak.

In *Briefing*, it is from the geographical space of a modern hospital—from the diagnostic systems of modern medicine confident in its skills in treating all manner of ailments—that the narrative moves into less charted territory. Madness or delirium is the state in which Watkins' perception is at its most lucid; in his sane moments before and after his delirious phase is over, Watkins' persona is easy to dislike. Watkins' enhanced sensitivity with regard to the world he inhabits in his delirious state is in marked contrast to his indifference and self-centredness in everyday life, as documented by his close friend and colleague of many years—Jeremy Thorne.

Briefing and *Memoirs* extend further the attack upon Western systems that pride themselves upon their rational and scientific approach. Contesting the limitations of this approach and seeing it as constricting in the human context, *Briefing* and *Memoirs* capture the sense of a Europe in decline and display intense anguish over the failure of civilisation. Following the precedent set by *The Four-Gated City*, *Briefing* and *Memoirs* also record innumerable shifts from the material details of the city to its psychological, metaphysical, mythical and dystopic dimensions.

The image of the city under siege, a predominant feature in all three novels, is the signifier of the failure of post-Enlightenment notions of the rational and scientific base of Western civilisation. Mary Evans identifies this as part of 'the chronology of the developments of a feminist critique of science and rational/objective inquiry that emerged in the late 1970s'.[58]

In *Briefing*, amnesia wrenches Watkins away from the everyday and the familiar and places him as an observer and participant in an altogether pristine and idyllic prelapsarian world. Tossed over various seas, he rides on the back of a porpoise that deposits him near a shore. His long walk away from the seashore brings him to a lush, verdant landscape that is magnificent and imposing. Here he finds powerful animals, all manner of delicious fruit to eat and a habitation unspoiled by humans. In the centre of this country are the remains of an old city, where two separate tribes—the Rat-dogs and the monkeys—arrive and establish parallel settlements. Through these tribes, we relive the familiar history of the world—the drama of racial strife and territorial conquests, all over again.

Parodying and paralleling Western civilisation's rapid expansion and control of greater parts of the world, the Rat-dogs kill off many of the monkeys. The wars between these two tribes result in the general despoiling of the whole city and country, its eventual rapine, pollution of land and water and the callous treatment of the weak and the vulnerable. Unable to stop any of this, the narrator can only lament:

> I cried out to them, 'No, No, No,' not to foul the clean river and then the sea, but remembered how men had poisoned all the oceans and rivers so that the beasts and fish were dying there, and so, feeling sick and hopeless, I went away, thinking that what corpses succeeded in making their way from out the dark riverine channels through the earth, and out to the waterfalls and cataracts, and from there to the wide level river, and at last to the sea—these corpses would at least be cleaner offal than the lethal filth men feed to sea currents.[59]

The déjà vu situation that the narrator and the reader find themselves in is accentuated by this horrific description of the amatory and reproductive encounters of the Rat-dogs in a state of war:

> I saw a female Rat-dog, with its sleek brown hide all bloodied and gashed, sitting up with its back to a wall, snapping at a couple of male Rat-dogs, and at the same time she was giving birth. Puppies tumbled out of her scarlet slit in a spout of blood and tissue, while she fought for her life. The two round mounds on her chest, which were her breasts, were swollen and had been torn, so that blood and milk poured out together. Her sharp muzzle had hairy flesh hanging from her teeth, and as she snapped and bit at the two tall staggering males who menaced her, she became so crazed with fear and the need to help her puppies' birth, that even as she fought, she would give a deadly snap in front, at an antagonist, and then snap downwards at her young, and perhaps wound or kill one . . . the two males who were as mad with long fighting as she was, for notwithstanding they were trying to kill her (or at least acting in such a way that she had to defend herself) and indeed succeeding, for she sank down in her own blood as we swept past the groups, their sexual organs were swollen with excitement, and one of them attempted to mate with her even as she died. She died in a spasm that was as much a birth-as a death-spasm.[60]

How does one respond to this gruesome episode? It refuses dismissal as a fantastic account. The ground realities of horror and violence visited upon hapless victims in the context of war or ethnic conflicts now furnish us with data on similar incidents.[61] This episode, appalling as an instance of human behaviour, is the culmination of extreme forms of individualistic and competitive aggression—leading to violence, assault and mutual self-destruction. In the realm of science fiction, such encounters shorn of the trappings of custom and culture force us to encounter the raw brutality of human relationships. This savage encounter described at close range shocks and dislocates all attempts to read male and female identity in a societal context.[62] We realise that the vocabulary to explain such aspects of our psyche is woefully inadequate. Also, human potential for brutality and violence, which stretches interminably, remains to be mapped.

From violent close-ups, the narrative shifts next to a bird's-eye view. Watching the city ravaged by war atop a white flying bird, a delirious Charles Watkins enables the reader to view human progress on earth from the point of Western civilisation.

At a cosmic level, the gods too offer an analysis. Mercury—the God of communication and intelligence—alias Merk Ury diagnoses that human beings have not understood that they are parts of a larger cosmic harmony and are only motivated by their own drives or functions.[63]

> Each individual of this species is locked up inside his own skull, his own personal experience—or believes he is—and while a great part of their ethical systems, religious systems, etc., state the Unity of Life, even the most recent religion, which being the most recent, is the most powerful, called Science, has only very fitful and inadequate gleams of insights into the fact that life is One. In fact, the distinguishing feature of this new religion, and why it has proved so inadequate, is its insistence on dividing off, compartmenting, pigeon-holing, and one of the most lamentable of these symptoms is its suspicion of and clumsiness with words.[64]

Almost identical observations form part of the preface to *The Golden Notebook*, published in the same year as *Briefing*. The criticism voiced by Anna about unidimensional perception also surfaces in *Briefing*. It examines the entire history of Western civilisation and charts the inadequacies of language, reason and science in mapping the world. Rosemary Baines and Frederick Larson's analysis in *Briefing* is a moot point to consider as it draws attention to dimensions within human existence that a material culture tends to overlook. They conclude:

> that our society was dominated by things, artefacts, possessions, machines, objects, and that we judged previous societies by artefacts—things. There was no way of knowing an ancient society's ideas except through the barrier of our own.[65]

Watkins' journey alludes to Jonah and Jason, heroes from Christian and classical myth. This allusion highlights the allegorical nature of Watkins' journey. The descent into hell or the human condition is also a reference to Dante's *Divine Commedia.*[66]

Yet, despite the enormity of this undertaking, Watkins is not transformed by his experience. At his most lucid, Watkins' experiences are not recognised or accepted by sane society at large. The only two exceptions to this are Violet, a fellow patient at the hospital, and Rosemary Baines, a schoolteacher. Eventually, when he must choose between the two worlds, Watkins' denies his newfound awareness and voluntarily submits to cure by electric shock after which he is gradually resocialised into his earlier, pre-amnesiac life. At this stage, he cannot recall his earlier interactions with either Rosemary or Larson. Nor does he wish to renew his acquaintance with them. The novel ends with Watkins' return to his opaque, normal self, with all its implications of a self-centred, complacent and insular identity. Dystopic though the nature of Watkins' voyage has been, it has left him with little or no new insight. His unwillingness to grow from his experience is also a telling comment on the socialising experience. He prefers to remain sexist, focused and self-absorbed. Watkins' reversion to the *status quo* is a realistic estimation of the difficulties in changing older patterns of thinking. Lessing's afterword in *Briefing* is in the form of a reminiscence. It draws our attention to the fact that organised societies can only 'favour the conforming, the average, the obedient' and become handicapped by the presence of 'extra sensitivity and perception'.[67]

Characters such as Violet, Rosemary and her friend Frederick Larson—archaeologist and teacher of history whose experience parallels that of Watkins—provide pointers. They retain their newer perception of the world. Frederick's expedition to various sites and his close reading of archaeology allows him a window into the plurality of cultures, making him question extant theories around origins and influences in Western civilisation:

> That 'Greece was the mother of western civilization and Rome its daddy' directed archaeology and excavation for a long time—yet he, Frederick, would be able to make out a case that the Arabs, Moors and

> Saracens were parents to 'western' civilization, sources of its ideas, its literature, its science, a case based on the same kind of evidence that made us legitimate heirs to Greece and Rome . . . this case wouldn't necessarily be more true, but its bases would be as powerful.[68]

Frederick Larson's viewpoint is one that Lessing endorses. By making him voice the possibility of alternate, unacknowledged sources which fostered 'Western civilization,' Lessing signals her disenchantment with prevailing ideologies. Larson's perspective is offered only to the initiated, very few in number. One can count the interested reader among them, pushed into the abyss beneath the veneer of a sane society. The reader is in a more conducive frame of mind, recognising the precarious nature of logic in constructing social structures. Unlike Watkins who recovers from his breakdown and moves into comfortable amnesia, the reader is in no real danger of being allowed to forget. By positing this awareness with the reader, Lessing stretches the fragile nature of this understanding and the difficulties inherent in nurturing it in a world that has shut itself into complacency. Violet, Rosemary and Larson's perceptions, like those of Martha and Lynda in *The Four-Gated City*, evolve through roads less travelled by.

Lessing's Feminist Interventions

What then are the new parameters that Lessing asks us to recognise? 'Inner-space fiction', a term that Lessing uses to describe this writing, is useful and explicatory since the nature of the journeys focuses on the realm of intimate, inward dimensions. In all three novels, a structured and explicable world—recognisably Western—becomes limited and confining. While most characters seem to go about their everyday concerns, Lessing invests her energy in introducing us to a few characters who are disturbed by the world they inhabit. They are acutely aware of something it shuts out, and they try to work their way towards this hidden, unrecognised value. The realms that these characters discover, through strange journeys, seem to suggest a far greater possibility. The Inner-space journeys that Lessing provides in the three novels engage with the exploration of the depths of the human mind. This transformative journey enables both the character in question, as well as the reader, to transcend the decrepit boundaries and disintegrating cities portrayed in the novels.

Lessing first draws our attention to the discontent of her characters. Subsequently, she introduces the reader to the heightened and expansive nature of their experiences. In this way, she alerts us to the significance of values hitherto marginalised in a society built on material progress. Rejecting the values propagated in an individualistic and male-centred world, Lessing works at creating an alternate set of values that open up new possibilities. This is Lessing's feminist intervention, whereby she provides alternate ways of seeing.

The question of alternate values and the scope for their implementation is addressed in *Memoirs,* which begins with a central narrator looking back upon an odd time: '[w]e were still in the stage of generalized unease. Things weren't too good, they were even pretty bad. A great many things were bad, breaking down, giving up, or "giving cause for alarm", as the newscasts might put it.'[69] These lines echo the feelings expressed by Martha at various points in *The Four-Gated City*. 'It was already a bad time. All muddle and misery and suspicion and doubt.'[70] 'A bad time is announced by an event. . . . When a bad time starts, it is as if on a smooth green lawn a toad appears'.[71] 'When a very bad time is over there is no moment when one can say: this is it, now it's finished.'[72]

Published six years after *The Four-Gated City, Memoirs* carries over Lessing's re-examination of the same issues that repeatedly perplexed Martha—this time from an entirely different angle. While *The Four-Gated City* embarked upon a depersonalising of Martha's experience, setting it against an epoch, *Memoirs* begins on a more dismal note. The city in *Memoirs* has disintegrated completely. The cities in *The Four-Gated City* and *Briefing* revealed some semblance of order. London in *The Four-Gated City* is in a state of disrepair after the war. We see it in the beginning as a solid structure harking back to an older time. London in *Briefing* also shares some of these aspects.

In *Memoirs,* the collapse is something that we register almost at once. A bewildering change that is the result of a systemic collapse replaces an earlier epoch and a way of life that is over. The collapse of major systems of civic society, the breakdown of authority, shortages of various kinds, the drifting hordes, the redundancy of all the gadgets of technology and the inefficacy of most socially prescribed forms of conduct blot the world of *Memoirs*.

The shift from the external world to the internal in *Memoirs* is far more emphatic than compared to the two earlier novels. A middle-aged person, possibly bordering on elderly, chronicles life in this city. The protagonist's account is largely about what is visible through a window facing the street. The protagonist has a secret life. She stumbles upon this while moving through walls that lead to an unknown set of rooms which, in their turn, present new experiences and lives. The movement that is taking place here is an alteration in perspective, from the continuities of external life to the disjunctions that exist within.

The attempt in all three novels discussed here is to find those aspects of the individual's psyche that contribute not so much to the lived material nature of their lives, but to a shared collectivity of ideas. Martha's interrogation of Western forms of analysis and interpretation is examined by Lessing and found wanting in *The Four-Gated City*. It is examined next through Watkins' delirium in *Briefing* and is further questioned in *Memoirs*. The collapse of the external world in all three novels shows the ecological deterioration of the city due to its pursuance of aggressive technological development.

Of greater significance is the schism between the external and the internal worlds and the directions they seem to be taking. While the external world heads to the point of no return in all the three novels, endless possibilities are invested in the journeys of the inner worlds. Where then is hope to be found? Certainly not in notions of progress that have been shown as inadequate and ineffective in successive novels. The answer to this is in the alternatives provided by feminist philosophy. Rejecting the individualistic and aggressive onrush of technocracy, this involves a close look at the values of connectivity fostered by characters in all three novels.

This brings us to the question of women's writing and its associations with both madness and autobiography. Lessing calls *Memoirs* 'An Attempt at an Autobiography'.[73] In reference to the earlier Martha Quest narratives, she acknowledged that she had tried to take 'the story out of the personal into the general' and that her 'interest in the series was a historical one'.[74] Lessing's observations enable us to see the vital connections between women's writing, autobiography and fiction.

The act of writing fiction creates a space in which personal experience can be reworked. In the first four books of the Children of Violence series, Lessing attempts to transform Martha's personal narrative into history by fictionalising it. In the three novels examined here, she pulls her characters out of linear time and space and locates them in the realms of the fantastic—making an altogether different point. The element of autobiography here lies not in narrating the development of a unitary and distinct identity, but in locating a central philosophy or belief within the contradictions of an age. Lessing's convictions fuel the element of autobiography in these three novels. What is narrated is her vision, which she sees as the central principle feeding into the pulse of the age itself. *Memoirs* is an autobiographical account of life in the decade of the 1970s, recounting not so much the substance of an individual life but a summing up of an epoch of human history.[75]

The internal life portrayed in *Memoirs* becomes significant in terms of the directions that it envisages for feminism. It harks back to a long tradition in women's writing. Indicative of women's confinement and silencing by society, the world behind the wall has remained a secret space—occasionally displaying its potential for disruption. Charlotte Perkins Gilman's story 'The Yellow Wallpaper' (1892) is one example that comes immediately to mind.[76] The protagonist, a convalescent woman, is forced to rest by the doubled authority of husband and doctor so that she may not strain her creative faculties. She begins noticing the patterns on the wallpaper and identifies with a whole life trapped in the wallpaper pattern. The design on the wall becomes the site of resistance to the oppressive and deadening prescriptions of the patriarchal structure that controls her. Sending her husband into a state of shock, she escapes this world by stepping out of the human form and taking on a subhuman shape—crawling on all fours. This is the only space from where she can subvert patriarchal norms.

The woman in 'The Yellow Wallpaper' is an important prototype, recording the experience of restrictions and oppressions within patriarchal societies. Her story is part of the layered prehistory rewritten in Lessing's *Memoirs*. Looking into the past, the survivor of *Memoirs* records the silencing and restrictions in a woman's world. Emily's mother, the woman behind the walls, felt trapped by her marriage and her children. The narrative voice tells us that she 'sat looking inward into the demands of her days and nights. No one else was there for her, because she felt she was talking to herself: they could not hear, or would not.'[77]

This existence, part of women's lives for a very long time, undergoes a change. Instead of binding herself to the confining world outside, the elderly woman in *Memoirs* discovers a world outside the walls and a new life. By moving into this world at the end of the novel, she also suggests infinite hope. A search for alternatives seems to be the affirmative leap that we are being asked to make at the end of *Memoirs*.

What precisely are the points of affirmation in the three novels? In Lessing's narratives, the inner world of madness is set up in opposition to an external order in a state of collapse. All three novels show the disintegration of the conventional family. The family as a primary unit of the state—so familiar as a structural unit, particularly in fiction—was under attack from socialist and feminist ideologies in the late 1960s. While socialist analysis saw the family unit as a prop of the capitalist system, feminists saw the family as the primary location of women's oppression as women.[78]

The state of disarray within the family is recorded in all the three novels discussed here. In the Coldridge household, interpersonal relationships are scarred, frozen or marred; the novel records the collapse of traditional systems of authority within the family. There are generations of missing parents in *The Four-Gated City* and the erosion of the family as a social unit suggests the diminishing of patriarchal power and control. *Briefing* and *Memoirs* also reveal families in a more advanced state of disintegration. The family as an integral unit is replaced by smaller units of nurture, interaction and care in all three narratives, which replicate personal and domestic activity but no longer endorse older systems. This is highlighted in the case of interpersonal relationships in all three novels.

In *Memoirs*, among the ruins of a crumbling city, the only activities that seem to go on are the continuingly humane acts of connectivity and care. We see this quality first in the narrator who is responsible for nurturing young Emily. Subsequently, Emily, June and Gerald manage a tribe of little children on their own. It is such acts to which our attention is repeatedly drawn and it is such activity that sustains our interest and hope. The small gestures of nurture and care that the narrator, Emily and Emily's mother display in *Memoirs* remain invested with promise. Emily's mother is shown as belonging to another dimension altogether, her life and its concerns being placed in a different geographical realm behind the wall.

Lessing's many women characters reveal the overlapping and repetitive nature of their lives as chroniclers of women's time. June and Emily replay at various levels the lives lived by the narrator or Emily's mother. The momentum of these lives parallels the city's movement from bad to worse, eventually leading to a total collapse. Contrary to records and indicators of progress and development, visibly little has changed concerning the isolation felt by each of the characters. Each one of them has to start from scratch to establish a niche. The overwhelming change the novel records is the death of the city as an efficient machine and the collapse of systems of control. There is an urgent need to search for new systems and balances.

One positive way of identifying these new systems is to examine the significance of the realm of private, personal experience, intimately experienced by the narrator, Emily's mother and several other women. This would perhaps explain why the narrator can effortlessly enter a world, access to which is normally so difficult. This low-key world is the highlight of the novel's conclusion. The narrator, Emily, her dog–cat Hugo, Gerald and a motley group of children escape the collapse of their city by venturing into a new dimension. They are led out of the material world they inhabit, Pied Piper fashion, by 'that One who went ahead showing the way out of this collapsed little world into another order of world altogether.'[79]

This sudden and unexpected assistance provides new bearings. Leading them out of this world is a mysterious woman whose presence the narrator is unable to explain to the reader:

> But the one person I had been looking for all this time was there: there she was. No, I am not able to say clearly what she was like. She was beautiful: it is a word that will do. I only saw her for a moment, in a time like the fading of a spark on dark air—a glimpse: she turned her face just once to me, and all I can say is . . . nothing at all.[80]

Memoirs concludes enigmatically and leaves us wondering about the nature and intent of the mysterious leader and the promised land she is taking her new-found subjects to.

The escape from the external world and its systems, which Lessing impresses upon the reader as imperative in all three novels, is concluded with *Memoirs*. This new world which is intuitively apprehended by the narrator places value on connectivity, care and nurture—all of which have been activities associated with the uneconomic, private sphere inhabited by women.

It is possible to posit 'another order of world' as that of personal relationships invested in by women who remain unnamed and indefinable due to the cultural invisibility permeating their lives? Increasingly, it is this hidden world and its strengths that Lessing's narratives uncover. The beautiful, mysterious woman we meet at the end of *Memoirs* is indescribable, as she falls outside of the linguistic and experiential vocabulary available to the narrator. What do we make of Lessing's evocation of this quasi-mystical woman figure who represents tremendous energy and possibilities for transformation? In the realm of inner space fiction, recording the anguish of a generation that despaired of patriarchal systems, this could be a simple exercise in wish fulfilment—namely, a shout out to the Goddess, instead of an anthropomorphic God. A more useful exercise would be to turn to the work of feminist theologians in the 1970s such as Mary Daly, Rosemary Ruether and Elisabeth Schussler Fiorenza, whose critique of patriarchal religion provided the basis for the creation 'of new ways for women to find their religious power, autonomy, and identity'.[81]

This does not imply that *Memoirs* must be read as the beginnings of Lessing's journey into theological fields. There is now a major body of work that engages with 'Lessing's spiritual vision' and clarifies that to 'draw near Lessing's spirituality . . . requires sensitivity to its use in individual texts.'[82] My engagement with Lessing's work lies primarily with what I see as her contribution to women's lives within the dimensions of the material world.

Lessing places this mysterious woman figure as pivotal to the change in *Memoirs*. Why does Lessing endow her with great power and authority? I would argue that Lessing's woman figure is of great significance. Her presence underscores the need to create a theology for women, in place of the patriarchal version of God as the father or God in man's image. What Lessing offers her readers is the Goddess as a woman, creating possibilities for sharper images of self-construction. The shift in perspective gained thereby is from the idea of the mythic Goddess to the remaking of women in the image of the Goddess. This construction reconceptualises women's lives within political and social territories and endows them with far more meaning and value.

As Carol P. Christ points out, the affirmation of female power contained in the Goddess symbol psychologically defeats the patriarchal view of women's power as inferior and dangerous. Politically, the assertion of female power 'supports and undergirds women's trust in their power and the power of other women in family and society.'[83] It is an unending project. A decade after the writing of these novels, Lessing continues to seek feminist alternatives. Her explorations continue to extend to mixed genres, mythologies and current events.

Endnotes

1. Doris Lessing, *The Four-Gated City* (Great Britain: MacGibbon & Kee Ltd, 1969; London and New York: Granada, 1972). All further references to this novel are from the 1972 edition.
2. Doris Lessing, *Briefing for a Descent into Hell* (Great Britain: Jonathan Cape, 1971; London: Grafton Books, 1972). All further references to this novel are from the 1972 edition. The abbreviation Briefing will be used to refer to this title.
3. Doris Lessing, The *Memoirs of a Survivor* (Great Britain: Octagon, 1974; London: Picador/Pan Books, 1976). All further references to this novel are from the 1976 edition. The abbreviation Memoirs will be used to refer to this title.

4. Doris Lessing, 'The Small Personal Voice,' in *A Small Personal Voice: Essays, Reviews, Interviews*, ed. Paul Schlueter (United States: Alfred A. Knopf, 1974; New York: Vintage Books, 1975), 4. The reference corresponds to the 1975 edition. This was a viewpoint that Lessing voiced in the 1950s and in less than a decade, her work had undergone a sea change in terms of the directions it could be seen as taking.
5. Lessing, *Briefing*, 9.
6. Eric Hobsbawm attributes the coinage of the term 'The Golden Age' to Marglin and Schor, 1990, to describe this period in Anglo-American progress. His chapter 'The Golden Years' is alternatively interleaved as 'The Golden Age' in Eric Hobsbawm, *The Age of Extremes: The Short Twentieth Century, 1914–1991* (London: Michael Joseph, 1994), 257–286.
7. Lessing, *Memoirs*, 75–76.
8. Lessing, *Memoirs*, 113.
9. Micheline R. Malson, Jean F. O'Barr, Sarah Westphal-Wihl and Mary Wyer, eds., introduction to *Feminist Theory in Practice and Process* (Chicago and London: University of Chicago Press, 1989), 4.
10. Hobsbawm, *The Age of Extremes*, 261.
11. In Bacon's cosmology of science, science was pitted as an extremely rational and analytical tool to be employed by the male in order to study and exploit nature—which was presented as female. Under Francis Bacon (1561–1626) was created the binary opposition between scientific temperaments and the natural world, the latter being under the command of the former. This distribution eventually accentuated and reinforced the differences between men and women in a manner that replicated the views advocated in other facets of primarily patriarchal societies. Extending the categories of rational and analytical science, which would be used to study and exploit a passive nature, Bacon's definition and prescription of science lead to a reinforcement of patriarchal cultural codes. Science and male rationality were seen as aligned together in this scheme of things while at the opposite end, woman and nature were grouped together on the basis of a perceived affinity. Jatinder K. Bajaj, 'Francis Bacon, the first philosopher of modern science: A non-western view', in *Science, Hegemony and Violence: A Requiem for Modernity*, ed. Ashis Nandy (Delhi and Bombay: Oxford University Press, 1988), 24–67.
12. See Veronica Stolte-Heiskanen, ed., introduction to *Women in Science: Token Women or Gender Equality?* (New York: St. Martin's Press, 1991), 1–8.

13. Ashis Nandy sees this as a shift in the role played by science and technology as a civilising mission to occupying a central role in national agendas for development in Nandy, *Science, Hegemony and Violence,* 23.
14. Mary Evans, *Introducing Contemporary Feminist Thought* (Oxford, Cambridge and Malden: Polity Press, 1997), 52–53.
15. Doris Lessing, 'Between the fax and the fiction,' *The Guardian*, December 13, 1991.
16. Patricia Waugh, *Harvest of the Sixties: English Literature and its Background, 1960 to 1990* (Oxford and New York: Oxford University Press, 1995), 5. For a succinct discussion on counterculture, see 1–21.
17. Doris Lessing, 'Doris Lessing on Feminism, Communism and 'Space Fiction,' interview by Lesley Hazelton, *The New York Times,* July 25, 1982, https://archive.nytimes.com/www.nytimes.com/books/99/01/10/specials/lessing-space.html?_r=1.
18. See Lynda Birke and Marsha Henry, 'The Black Hole: Women's Studies, Science and Technology,' in *Introducing Women's Studies: Feminist Theory and Practice*, eds. Victoria Robinson and Diane Richardson (Basingstoke and London: Macmillan, 1993), 220–238.
19. Sandra Harding, 'How the Women's Movement Benefits Science: Two Views', in *Inventing Women: Science, Technology and Gender*, eds. Gill Kirkup and Laurie S. Keller (Oxford: Polity Press, 1992), 61.
20. See the thought-provoking essay, Sandra Harding, 'Is Science Multicultural? Challenges, Resources, Opportunities, Uncertainties,' in *The Gender and Science Reader*, eds. Muriel Lederman and Ingrid Bartsch (London and New York: Routledge, 2001), 189–212.
21. Evelyn Fox Keller, 'How gender matters, or, why it's so hard for us to count past two', in *Inventing Women: Science, Technology and Gender*, eds. Gill Kirkup and Laurie S. Keller (Oxford: Polity Press, 1992), 47.
22. This is a paraphrasing of Veronica Stolte-Heiskanen's ideas in her introduction. Stolte-Heiskanen, introduction to *Women in Science,* 8.
23. Rachel Carson (1907–1964) was an American marine biologist and a prominent woman in the history of modern science. Her book *Silent Spring* (1962) documented the loss of bird and fish life as a result of water contamination due to the use of pesticides. More importantly, it launched the American and global environmental movements by speaking of the connection of humanity to the earth and the fragile balance in nature that makes human existence possible—contesting prevailing perceptions of man as the controller of a world created to satisfy his needs.

24. Helen Caldicott, an Australian-born paediatrician who worked in America, was the leading figure behind Australia's protest against French nuclear testing in the Pacific in 1971. She published *Nuclear Madness: What You Can Do!* in 1978 and founded the Physicians for Social Responsibility between 1977 and 1978. She continues to campaign on the dangers of nuclear weapons, nuclear power and nuclear war.
25. See Gill Kirkup and Laurie S. Keller, eds., *Inventing Women: Science, Technology and Gender* (Oxford: Polity Press, 1992), 282.
26. For a reading that sees Sufi philosophy as a central influence on Lessing's fiction, see Shadia S. Fahim, *Doris Lessing and Sufi Equilibrium: The Evolving Form of The Novel* (New York: St. Martin's Press, 1994).
27. Lessing, *Briefing*, 7.
28. Lessing, *The Four-Gated City*, 528.
29. Science fiction will be referred to as SF from here onwards.
30. In his comprehensive guide, Adam Roberts suggests that the starting point of SF can be traced as far back as Thomas More's Latin version of Utopia (1516). However, his personal preference for locating the genre falls in the period between 1780 and 1830 which he terms as the post-Romantic era. The rest of the paragraph is a paraphrasing of his ideas regarding influences on SF. Adam Roberts, *Science Fiction* (London and New York: Routledge, 2000), 53–67.
31. John Huntington, *Rationalizing Genius: Ideological Strategies in the Classic American Science Fiction Short Story* (New Brunswick: Rutgers University Press, 1989), 2.
32. Roberts, *Science Fiction*, 28–29.
33. Gary Westfahl, 'Janeways and Thaneways; the Better Half, and Worse Half, of Science Fiction Television,' *Interzone*, no. 140 (February 1999): 31–33.
34. Lessing, 'fax and the fiction'. Ellipsis in original.
35. Lessing, *The Four-Gated City*, 20.
36. Lessing, *The Four-Gated City*, 529.
37. Roberts, *Science Fiction*, 90.
38. See Keith N. Hull, 'What is Human? Ursula Leguin and Science Fiction's Great Theme,' *Modern Fiction Studies* 32, no. 1 (Spring 1986): 69.
39. J. Douglas Allen Taylor, 'Novelist and short-story writer Octavia Butler defies categories,' *Metro,* January 4–10, 1996, http://www.metroactive.com/papers/metro/01.04.96/books-9601.html.

40. Doris Lessing, 'Doris Lessing: Hot Dawns', interview by Harvey Blume, *The Boston Book Review*, 1998, http://mural.uv.es/vemivein/dorisinterviews.html.
41. This section of the interview from Carey Kaplan and Ellen Cronan Rose, eds., 'Lessing and Her Readers: Celebrating Difference,' in *Doris Lessing: The Alchemy of Survival* (Ohio: Ohio University Press, 1988), 3. Also see Clare Hanson, 'Doris Lessing in Pursuit of the English, or, No Small, Personal Voice,' in *In Pursuit of Doris Lessing: Nine Nations Reading*, ed. Claire Sprague (London: Palgrave Macmillan, 1990), 61–73.
42. Nicole Ward Jouve, *White Woman Speaks with Forked Tongue: Criticism as Autobiography* (London and New York: Routledge, 1991), 137.
43. See Roberts, *Science Fiction*, 91–115.
44. Katherine Fishburn draws attention to Lessing's shift from individual characters to narrator figures who espouse authorial intention in Katherine Fishburn, *The Unexpected Universe of Doris Lessing: A Study in Narrative Technique* (Westport: Greenwood Press, 1985), 11.
45. Lessing's deliberate construction of madness as a means for heightened perception is discussed by Barbara Hill Rigney, '"A Rehearsal for Madness": Hysteria as Sanity in the Four-Gated City,' in Bloom's *Modern Critical Views: Doris Lessing*, ed. Harold Bloom (New York: Chelsea House, 1986), 133–150.
46. Lessing, *The Four-Gated City*, 228.
47. This observation is made by Gayle Greene, *Doris Lessing: The Poetics of Change* (Ann Arbor: University of Michigan Press, 1994), 76. She also identifies Jane Eyre as the literary precedent for Martha's position as governess-secretary in a household in which there also exists a mad wife.
48. Lessing, *The Four-Gated City*, 125.
49. Women's concern about economic returns for unpaid housework became a subject for theoretical debate. See Rose-Marie Lagrave, 'A Supervised Emancipation', in *A History of Women in the West: Toward a Cultural Identity in the Twentieth Century*, ed. Françoise Thébaud, trans. Arthur Goldhammer (1994; Cambridge, Massachusetts and London: Harvard University Press, 1996), 5: 452–489. The reference is from the 1996 edition.
50. Articulating the dangers of the dark or recognising the fears that women faced in walking alone in the cities, the first 'Take Back the Night' demonstration was held in Edinburgh in 1977. Sheila Rowbotham, *A Century of Women: The History of Women in Britain and the United States* (London and New York: Viking Books, 1997; London and

New York: Penguin Books, 1999), 407. All further references are from the 1999 edition. Robin Morgan has a chapter which details the terror and trauma inherent in the simple act of a woman walking alone. See Robin Morgan, *The Demon Lover: On the Sexuality of Terrorism* (New York and London: W.W. Norton & Company, 1989), 23–50.

51. Lessing, *The Four-Gated City*, 401.
52. Laing cited by Patricia Waugh who emphasises that his were the most powerful ideas that emerged out of the radical movements of the 1960s, in Waugh, *Harvest of the Sixties*, 6.
53. Laing's observations of the inhuman treatment of mental patients in asylums during the 1950s recorded by Rowbotham, *A Century of Women*, 345.
54. Lessing, *The Four-Gated City*, 389.
55. Lessing, *The Four-Gated City*, 27.
56. Lessing, *The Four-Gated City*, 521–522.
57. Lessing, *The Four-Gated City*, 361.
58. Evans, *Introducing Contemporary Feminist Thought*, 57.
59. Lessing, *Briefing*, 79.
60. Lessing, *Briefing*, 85.
61. This act of brutality and violence directed at a 'creature in labour' in Briefings remained a hideous possibility till newspaper reports began providing accounts of the violence practiced on one community by members of another community. In Gujarat state's capital Ahmedabad, during the communal violence that was unleashed there in March 2002, a gruesome account of a pregnant woman who was raped and then had her unborn baby ripped out of her womb before being killed herself was carried by many newspapers and periodicals. See Arundhati Roy, 'Democracy: Who's she when she's at home?' *Outlook*, May 6, 2002, 20–30. There she highlights several acts of violence visited on hapless women.
62. For a compelling psychoanalytic reading of this novel, see Jeanette King, 'Inner-Space Fiction: Briefing for a Descent into Hell,' in *Doris Lessing* (London and New York: Edward Arnold, 1989), 55 onwards.
63. Betsy Draine finds the entire pastiche involving a dialogue between the gods rather offensive though she never really explains why. Betsy Draine, *Substance Under Pressure: Artistic Coherence and Evolving Form in the Novels of Doris Lessing* (Wisconsin: University of Wisconsin Press, 1983), 91. While there is an element of sheer comedy in Lessing's creation of the gods in the humans' image and this style of narration is

also part of an older tradition, gods in the Hindu pantheon—like their Greek counterparts—also engaged with mortals. Hindu mythology is full of anecdotal narratives of this kind. Already located within Watkins' delirium, this theological space is threatened by disbelief from rational, historical, scientific and medical quarters.

64. Lessing, *Briefing*, 121.
65. Lessing, *Briefing*, 165.
66. King, *Doris Lessing*, 56.
67. Lessing, *Briefing*, 251.
68. Lessing, *Briefing*, 167. Ellipsis in original.
69. Lessing, *Memoirs*, 9.
70. Lessing, *The Four-Gated City*, 164.
71. Lessing, *The Four-Gated City*, 167.
72. Lessing, *The Four-Gated City*, 304.
73. Doris Lessing, *Under My Skin: Volume One of My Autobiography, to 1949* (Great Britain: HarperCollins, 1994), 28.
74. Lessing, *Under My Skin*, 160–161.
75. The name Emily, given to the young girl who is left at the narrator's flat, echoes that of Lessing's mother and grandmother who had the same name. In her autobiography, Lessing acknowledges that the memories of her childhood in Kermanshah provide the setting for the dream world of Memoirs and that the adults in this world are exaggerated versions of her own parents. See Lessing, *Under My Skin*, 29–31 and 241.
76. 'The Yellow Wallpaper' is a short story by Charlotte Perkins Gilman (1860–1935). This story can be seen as part of a tradition of women's writing which sought to uncover the oppressive nature of patriarchal authority and its impact on women. It is significant for its representation of woman-as-victim and its evocation suggests the distances that feminist fiction and theory have travelled—where over and above the recognition of women's oppression is the attempt to formulate new perspectives and new itineraries.
77. Lessing, *Memoirs*, 64.
78. For a detailed discussion on the socialist and feminist debates on the family, see Mary McIntosh, 'The Family in Socialist-Feminist Politics,' in *Feminism, Culture and Politics*, eds. Rosalind Brunt and Caroline Rowan (London: Lawrence and Wishart, 1982), 109–130.
79. Lessing, *Memoirs*, 190.
80. Lessing, *Memoirs*, 190. Ellipsis in original.

81. Marie Tulip, introduction to 'Part VIII: Religion', in *A Reader in Feminist Knowledge*, ed. Sneja Gunew (London and New York: Routledge, 1991), 259.
82. See Phyllis Sternberg Perrakis, ed., introduction to *Spiritual Exploration in the Works of Doris Lessing* (Westport, CT: Greenwood Press, 1999), xi. Divided into three parts, this book has nine essays that explore theological and spiritual insights into Lessing's fiction.
83. Carol P. Christ, 'Why Women Need the Goddess', in *A Reader in Feminist Knowledge*, ed. Sneja Gunew (London and New York: Routledge, 1991), 290–302.

V

Eschewing Violence: Lessing's Feminist Formulations of the 1980s

Lessing's fictional output after the 1960s is characterised by increasing experimentation with form, indicating her innovation with narrative techniques. Using a whole range of genres, Lessing articulates an insistent questioning of older patriarchal structures of authority and knowledge. Her earlier work revealed its critical distance from Eurocentric belief in technological progress and the making of 'computer man'[1] and also registered how accelerating violence characterised most human activity—the wars of conquest, territorial and national disputes, bombs, the stockpiling of weapons and the existence of nuclear arsenals being some immediate examples that come to mind.

All of Lessing's early novels explore violence in some form or the other. However, in her work written in the 1980s, she examines in minute detail the structures of violence that have been built into contemporary social and political life. Three novels written by Lessing which focus on the issue of violence are *The Marriages Between Zones Three, Four, and Five* (1980),[2] *The Good Terrorist* (1985)[3] and *The Wind Blows Away Our Words* (1987).[4] There are obvious generic differences among the three novels and the nature of political struggles charted in them is extremely diverse, yet all three texts focus on extant violence.

Marriages, the second novel in Lessing's science fiction series Canopus in Argos, is written in the format of 'fable or myth'.[5] It looks at the possibilities of growth in magical intergalactic space, in the absence of the violence and control exerted by different kinds of institutions. Although it is part of a series, *Marriages* also works as a self-contained unit—providing a significant point of reference for two other novels.

The Good Terrorist, placed in a First World country, provides an acerbic critique of radical left politics in Britain in the 1980s. Written in the realist tradition, it portrays the unmitigated disaster caused due to the adoption of violence by a Left commune in contemporary London. Chronologically the last novel in this discussion, *The Wind* is in part a travelogue—put together after Lessing's survey of ground realities among dissident Afghan refugees in Islamabad. Although the travelogue documents the condition of the Afghan refugees—both civilians and the *mujahidin*—actively resisting Russian invasion, Lessing begins this account by invoking an ancient myth. She invokes the legend of sisters Helen and Cassandra, the daughters born of the mating of Leda and Zeus—which is supposed to have ushered in the very beginnings of European civilisation.

As adult women implicated in the war by belonging to one of the tribes at war, both of them wait for Troy to be vanquished. Helen, whose elopement with Paris triggers the invasion of Troy, is shown as excitedly anticipating the thrill promised by the event, to say nothing of meeting the men fighting in the war. Her sister Cassandra, whose response is very different, shudders as she prophesies its horrors. We are made to recognise that Helen and Cassandra are also in a sense 'children of violence', as they have witnessed and been subject to incessant warfare—from the very moment of their conception to their adult years. Violence, Lessing would have us remember, has run through the very veins of human society for innumerable ages.

Through varying genres, Lessing reworks an old preoccupation of hers—namely, the mapping out of the various destinies of 'the children of violence'.[6] Born at the end of the First World War and having lived through the Second, Lessing identifies violence as endemic to human society and forces us to recognise that it is a pivotal ideology structuring human activity. Tracing its roots far back to the mythic war of Troy, Lessing takes a hard look at the politics of aggression and its subsequent development. In each of the novels under discussion, Lessing examines the percolation and ramifications of social processes deeply imbued with the ideology of violence. Lessing's narratives document the nature of this antagonism, its distribution in social space and its implications. All three novels ask for a radical re-examination of prevalent methods of political dissent. Lessing's analysis of violence in modern society gains greater relevance in the face of increasingly ruthless means used to redress social, political, religious and personal grievances. A global escalation of acts of violence, one may recall, was a predominant feature of the 1970s.[7]

An overview of the period reveals that the revolutions of the 1970s, despite being 'a geographically and politically ill-assorted ensemble', erupted in parts of Europe, the Third World, Central America, the Caribbean and Iran. These were completely dissimilar to the mass movements in 1917 or in the 1930s. The movements of the 1970s were based on smaller group identities, tended to be ideological and were fought by activist minorities. The modus operandi of terrorism became the distinguishing feature of the minority protests with terrorists operating as rural or urban guerrillas. An increase in the number of attacks and death toll was the result of acts of violence 'in the developed world', 'parts of South Asia and the Islamic zone'.[8]

The nature of violence became the subject of significant discussions among activists and women's groups at this juncture. One important factor that must be mentioned here is the tremendous acrimony witnessed regarding the issue of inherent masculine violence at the Women's Liberation conference held in 1978. The participants were so divided in opinion that a similar conference was never subsequently convened.[9] Nevertheless, the whole issue of violence, the reasons for its use and the continued participation of both men and women in perpetrating violent acts needs to be closely examined. Hobbesian analyses of violence as a mode of existence in man's pre-social, natural state, outside of the structures of civil society, are no longer relevant in the context of the state-of-the-art technology that is now available to assist violence targeted at governments, unsuspecting civilians and public property. How, then, does one deal with violence in modern society? Can it be seen as endemic to men and entrenched in prescriptive systems of patriarchy as the separatist women's groups of the late 1960s and 1970s pointed out?[10] Does violence become the last resort for splinter groups or the marginalised when faced with the need to assert their own identity and freedom against oppressive political, religious or patriarchal majorities?

This chapter will explore Lessing's treatment of this theme and its implications for women by analysing the way women characters in her novels are made to address this particular issue. This is significant since violence seems to be a continuous part of everyday life. Before examining and analysing the political context of these novels, it would be fruitful to briefly go over the stand of women's movements and feminist theorists on the subject.

Women and Violence: Structured through the Personal and the Political

Physically weaker and socially conditioned to be economically dependent upon men, women have often been subjected to physical and sexual aggression within the private sphere of the family. Quite often, such aggression receives the tacit approval of religious and cultural authority. Fieldwork, data collection and subsequent public awareness raising and protests have drawn attention to the nature of this oppression in the course of everyday interpersonal relationships. Women's groups have campaigned vociferously to draw public attention to violence perpetrated upon women and highlighted the need for intervention on their behalf of in situations of rape, wife-beating, assault, battery, molestation, verbal and mental cruelty and so on. Feminism has sought to analyse the structures of power and domination that exist within the once-sanctified private space of the family. The agenda of the consciousness-raising groups in the 1960s, in both Europe and America, was to urge women to openly speak about the extent and nature of the oppression faced by them.[11] Robin Morgan describes the violence that women are subjected to in their personal lives and in societal terms as a 'continuum of violence . . . internal as well as external . . . across the world and across time'.[12]

Outside of their personal lives, women have invariably been involved with various forms of protests—such as nationalist movements and anti-colonial movements—and have been part of terrorist and separatist groups. While women have associated themselves with anti-militarism since the time of the First World War,[13] it is possible to look back at the early years of the twentieth century and locate a large number of women who identified with violence as a possible means of achieving their political objective. The history of women's ideological support for warfare, their participation in violence and the incorporation of women into armed sedition is fairly well-documented. In England, even a suffragist of Emmeline Pankhurst's stature rallied around the First World War and was inspired by acts of martial valour. She readily prioritised the claims of the soldiers at war over the rights of women to campaign for the vote.[14] Both Maud Gonne and Constance Markievicz fought against the British, actively engaging with strategies of violence for Ireland's independence.[15] Frantz Fanon, in Algiers, who spoke eloquently for the wretched of the earth, displayed little or no interest in the Black woman[16] although Black women furthered militant struggle in Algiers. Women's difference from men in terms of their traditional clothing of veils and loose gowns provided excellent camouflage for smuggling essential weapons and secret communications. Quite often, men escaped to safety in women's costumes. In the communist countries and the Third World, women were part of new political uprisings. Ironically, despite new coalitions and a change in the old guard, women were effectively sidelined since newer power structures were not inclusive of women. As Hobsbawm points out, invariably what got forgotten was 'the major part played by women in war, resistance and liberation.'[17]

Other than the fact that women's contributory role has been systematically overlooked, there remains the vexed question of women's active participation in terrorism. How does feminism view women's involvement with such groups? One must remember that the participation of women in political movements has often imploded in violence.

Take, for instance, the involvement of Leila Khaled[18] and Dhanu[19] in two different liberation struggles taking place in two different parts of the world. Khaled, a Palestinian militant, participated in plane hijackings in 1969 and 1970 to draw world attention to the Palestinian cause. Dhanu—a member of the Tamil Tigers Liberation Front in Sri Lanka—transformed herself into a human bomb in 1991 to ensure the death of India's ex-prime minister, Rajiv Gandhi. To date, Palestine remains troubled and the rights of the Palestinian people have been rendered irrelevant. Meanwhile, Tamil terrorists have been wiped off the map in Sri Lanka.

Given this context, how do feminists view the role of women as terrorists and human bombs or in suicide squads? Answers to this question are not easy. What is available to us is the knowledge that violence has played a significant role in shaping modern national identities.[20] Violence continues to be used to shape and safeguard modern societies to date, from the building up of arsenals of weapons worldwide to the policing of civilian lives by different governments. The recourse to violence as a recurring pattern is a disquieting feature of our times.

Every time the question of the freedom of a smaller group is raised, it is threatened by oppressive structures such as the state, religious institutions or majoritarian politics. This larger oppressive structure then becomes the site against which personal freedoms are asserted. When we look at resistance movements fought by small groups against the state itself, it becomes difficult to ignore their struggle for freedom and self-determination. Recognising the validity of this struggle and the fact that people have minority identities which ought not to be erased makes for complex responses.

If feminism does deal with the rights and freedom of women in the context of oppressive patriarchy—which is how we initially defined it in an earlier chapter—how do feminists view the violence practised by fringe groups that are engaged in an assertion of their particular rights and identities? In the context of the escalating violence and terror that has been a worldwide phenomenon over the last two decades, what is the perspective on violence that can be garnered from feminists? What do we make of the women who participate in acts of violence and terrorism?

The revolutions of the 1970s—which grew out of the responses shaped by European and Third World nationalisms that were asserted earlier in the twentieth century—incorporated the idea of violence as part of the politics of inevitable confrontation. In most of these revolutions, violence was directed at the state. The recurrence of such instances across the world highlights the commonality of intent in the choice of violence to further the cause of greater freedom and group identity.

Norwegian feminist Berit As describes the use of violence as a distinctive feature of a patriarchal state which she defines as 'one which is either rehabilitating from war, is presently at war, or is preparing for war.'[21] War, as pointed out earlier in this discussion, has been an underlying aspect of political and national definition throughout the twentieth century. Women's participation in the process then needs to be understood as a corollary springing from their internalisation of the violence inherent in their socialising.

Thanatos and *Eros*

In a very incisive analysis of 'patriarchal violence', Robin Morgan draws attention to its operation in 'multiple contexts—national, international, cultural, historical, philosophical, religious, aesthetic, psychological, economic etc.—'as terrorism.[22] Morgan sees the practice of terrorism as 'the logical incarnation of patriarchal politics in a technological world'[23], stemming from the 'politics of *Thanatos*'; she feels the need to replace this with *Eros. Thanatos* implies the force of hostility and the magnetism of death in Greek. Counterposed to the politics of *Thanatos,* which has been ruling the world for a considerable time, is the politics of *Eros*—representing the power of desire, the life force. The power of *Eros*, according to Morgan, is what feminism and women are beginning to reclaim. Representing within themselves the capacity to give life, women's affirmation of the desire for life is the only way that the politics of *Thanatos* can be effectively countered. Lessing's novels, as subsequent analyses will show, direct us towards a similar conclusion.

Marriages, the first of the three novels under discussion, is an imaginative rendering of possibilities in a world where *Thanatos* is not always the presiding deity. *Marriages* is located in a magical land—in Zone Three, far away from the harsh realities of life on planet Earth. The reader is introduced to an intergalactic terrain which is the country of Al • Ith. Falling into the genre of science fiction and tracing its action through imaginary and imagined realms, *Marriages*—despite being written years before *The Good Terrorist* and *The Wind*—serves as a referral point for the questions raised in the latter texts. Zones Four and Five in *Marriages* anticipate the worlds of *The Good Terrorist* and *The Wind* and while it is difficult to attribute this either to coincidence or intention, Lessing's position on violence and its impact on human life is made quite clear.

The format of *Marriages* allows Lessing free play with ideas that she suggests, traces and develops, unhindered by the pressures of historical placement. Although she does describe the novel as 'a fable, or myth' she goes on to admit that it has turned out 'oddly enough, to be more realistic'.[24] Zones Three, Four and Five and their inhabitants are an effective reworking of gender stereotypes and political struggle. Lessing creates a mythical landscape with both utopic and dystopic aspects that provide the 'frame work . . . to tell . . . a beguiling tale or two; to put questions, both to myself and to others; to explore ideas and sociological possibilities'.[25]

Zones Four and Five are dystopic and are depicted as civil societies that are hierarchical and tyrannical in the treatment of their inhabitants. Of the two, Zone Five offers a study of a society that is primitive and feudal. Controlled by a powerful chieftain's daughter, it is 'a place of deserts and thin scrub, where a few nomad tribes moved.'[26] Here rule Queen Vahshi and her army, 'bands of ragged men who could live for weeks off the milk of their mares and a few handfuls of dried provisions.'[27] 'Each tribe, or even group of aligned tribes, owed to the members of it a fanatical and fantastic loyalty, even to death.'[28] This group feeds off the produce of the lands lying to their east, looting and plundering and exhorting whatever they desire. This zone, with its hardy inhabitants, suggests the real world of *The Wind* while its landscape evokes associations of Afghanistan with its warriors caught in a time warp. Vahshi, the female ruler of Zone Five, embodies physical prowess and martial authority, using her strength to loot and maraud those less strong than she. Zone Five is a very poor country with most of its populace living at subsistence level despite its powerful, militant chieftain and her horde of warriors.

Zone Four is more developed and prosperous than Zone Five and evokes the world of *The Good Terrorist*. In its preoccupation with military readiness and its gendered structuring of men and women's roles, it recalls a developing modern nation. Zone Four's investment of its wealth largely in building up its huge army is a familiar feature. So is the wide discrepancy between the upper echelons and the poor. '[I]f you are poor and barbaric, it is because all your wealth goes into war—a needless, stupid, senseless war'[29]—this is an observation that could have been made by any of our pacifists, drawing attention to the enormous money invested in defending borders and the war industry that keeps it all well oiled. The division of people into hierarchies based on their social position is not alien to our understanding. The same can be said of the distinctions observed between the social classes by the emphasis on different modes of dress and conduct that accentuate and perpetuate these differences: 'of course a queen would have to wear one richness of garment and the wife of a soldier another.'[30]

This shared similarity with contemporary nations extends to other aspects of life in Zone Four. An emphasis on individualism and competitiveness exists in all aspects of life, be it in the army or the peasantry or in the segregation of the roles undertaken by men and women. Al • Ith diagnoses this segregation and offers new interpretations of identity formation.[31] She pinpoints the reasons as to why Zone Four is full of men 'without softness for women, only contempt for them, and hardness.'[32] This, she clarifies, is because of the

> boys brought up by women. Then when they are ten or eleven they are put into the boys' companies, and turn against their mothers and sisters. . . . Boys have to turn against women when they have known nothing but women, in order to become men at all.[33]

Lessing allows Al • Ith to shift the focus of Freudian and Lacanian arguments of identity formation, wherein the dominant identity is that of the male child whose yardsticks of selection remain all that is prioritised in a patriarchal world. Feminist theorist Nancy Chodorow, in her work, arrives at conclusions that reiterate Lessing's views. Chodorow points out that because the mother plays a significant role in the boy's early life and 'because of the absence of concrete, real, available male figures of identification and love who are as salient for him as female figures, learning what it is to be masculine comes to mean learning to be not-feminine, or not-womanly'.[34]

Measuring the anomalies between Zone Four and Zone Three, his own more evolved territory, the narrator Lusik yearns wistfully for the time it would 'take Zone Four to learn this absolute equality, individual to individual, when divisions and classes and rank and respect for these—servility—had been stamped so long into its deepest substance.'[35] Lusik's criticism of Zone Four highlights inequities and anomalies that exist within our political and social structures. This extends to the monetary allocations for war and territorial protection, as well as the conviction that war is a normal state of existence. When the soldiers are sent back to rebuild their homes and immediate surroundings, Jarnti—their general—misses the glory associated with war and works at the household chores 'with a baffled and incredulous air that said he could not believe in himself in this role.'[36] Feeling that his whole 'life has gone for nothing', Jarnti takes considerable time to adjust to peace.[37]

The intimate relationships between men and women in Zone Four follow the patterns of conventional society. The men go to fight, while the women bear and rear children in the domestic sphere. Women's expectations and aspirations are voiced amongst themselves in secret conclaves. The heavy metal helmets they are made to wear as punishment highlight the restrictions imposed upon them. These prevent the women from stretching their necks and looking up to see the mountain ranges and the sky and the clouds stretching above and around them. They are instruments of control, functioning as the bit, bridle and harness do for horses. Their physical restriction symbolises the denial of abilities to think and visualise. Men and women in this zone are perceived as very different from each other and this is further reiterated by the demarcation of roles allotted to them. The tremendous hostility and suspicion on either side recalls the conventional role-playing that men and women adopt in patriarchal societies.

The marriage between Al • Ith and Ben Ata, the queen of Zone Three and the ruler of Zone Four respectively, is ordained to showcase the differences between both territories and to bring amelioration. Ben Ata's relationship with Al • Ith pushes him to discover the possibility of a different way of feeling, thinking and being. He examines his aggressive sexuality, his violent and war-oriented kingdom, the waste of talent and the hidden costs of war. He is also made to reconsider his attitude towards women. From a man who never thought of women, except as objects to be ravished, he begins to puzzle about them: '[i]t seemed to him that half his realm, the female half, was a dark dangerous marsh from which monsters might suddenly appear'.[38] Reacting at first with contempt to the new ideas offered to him, Ben Ata is forced to acknowledge within himself 'this emotion of doing-down, of superiority,' which 'was the fuel for his energy.'[39] His initiation to this new plane of knowledge allows him to function more sensitively as ruler, king and man. Consequently, Ben Ata plays a catalytic role similar to the one played by Al • Ith in Zone Four. Ben Ata's subsequent marriage to Vahshi of Zone Five sets in motion a continuing process of evolvement and growth.

Zone Three, perhaps, comes closest to achieving an ideal balance in terms of political structures and equally shared spaces for men and women. Here, Lessing creates a modern-day feminist utopia. We are shown a community of people who have achieved a very high level of development. It is characterised by an absence of war, equality of status between the rulers and the ruled, prosperous land and livestock, egalitarian relationships between men and women with tremendous care and affection extended to every living thing. Work is not categorised and prescriptively allocated according to gender. A whole host of activities exist, both primary and secondary, and are carried out without any gender bias. Exchanges between men and women are marked by respect for women. Relationships are not centred on ownership and possessiveness but seem to be communitarian in their inclusion of physicality, emotion, intellect and communion of thought. In this regard, Al • Ith and her sister Murti •, Zone Three's women rulers, are unusual. Their responsibility as mothers provides inputs into their roles as rulers. Control of their kingdom requires of them an extension of the function of care, sympathy and nurture, which remain essential ingredients for mothering.

Through Al • Ith's fascinating rumination on how babies are made in Zone Three, Lessing offers her critique of the self-limiting nature of this enterprise in Zone Four and by analogy, in our world. Instead of treating the birth of a child as the result of a sexual union that ensures for the parent the ownership of the child, Zone Three recognises the presence of the biological mother and father and several mind fathers and mothers. In place of a monogamous heterosexual unit as the starting point of a family, Lessing suggests the need for more people to participate in order to nourish the child with ideas and thoughts from the moment of conception. The notion that the child imbibes influences from the womb has been part of folklore wisdom and has recently been supplemented by scientific study. Zone Three's childbearing and rearing practices take the drudgery out of childcare and locate it as an invaluable community responsibility. What is on offer here is a radical restructuring of the single-unit family, an idea that Lessing has been advancing as the corollary to social change. Lessing's dissatisfaction with the traditional nuclear family and conventional child-rearing options has also been communicated earlier in *The Four-Gated City, Briefing* and *Memoirs*. This extended family unit is a reinvention that harks back to an older pattern in cultures worldwide that began going out of fashion in the twentieth century—namely, the joint family.

Zone Three seems to be a glorious world to live in. Its inhabitants enjoy great happiness and endless possibilities, their existence approximating those very futures that feminist agendas have begun to envisage. Roberta Rubenstein records the following observation made by Lessing on *Marriages*.

> It's been my experience again and again . . .
> that you only have to write something and what you write starts coming true in all kinds of direct and indirect ways. It's as if you bring something towards you if you imagine it and then write it.[40]

Zone Three represents an imaginative rendering of infinite possibilities available to human beings, free from control and domination. The distancing of Zone Three from chronological history and time makes for a very effective strategy. It makes the narrative function at the level of myth, tracing mankind's deepest desires, and magically shapes this world through language. Lusik, the narrator who is part chronicler and part visionary, contributes simultaneously to our sense of the strange and the unchangingly familiar. Zone Three is an incredibly beautiful world; it represents infinite possibility and enacts our innermost dreams, those of living an ideal life in an ideal community with equitable sharing, distribution and development of resources and people. As Gayle Greene points out,

> we are given some space to pause and remember what we loved about life—a scene of humans living in harmony with one another in an unspoiled natural landscape, an ambience of 'olden times' than of 'space fiction'. We are allowed to rest awhile and breathe easily.[41]

Zone Three's idyllic personal and community life is a feminist utopia where creativity, the rearing and nurture of children and manual labour are seen as celebratory. It is shown as existing without the desire to control and dominate in the absence of hierarchies and violence. The splendour of Zone Three is reinforced by the contrast provided by the politics of violence and hierarchy in Zone Four and Zone Five that has cumulatively contributed to impoverishment and an embattled existence. The reader's return to the real world is a wrenching away from the idyllic world of Zone Three in *Marriages. The Good Terrorist* and *The Wind,* the two other novels forming part of this discussion, examine violence in real life, in situations mired in the real world. However, in both novels, arguments continue to be made against *Thanatos* and both texts reassert the need for a cult of *Eros.*

The Good Terrorist and *The Wind Blows Away Our Words*

Lessing offers a feminist critique of the dilemma posed by political acts of violence and its long-term implications by drawing from the history of violent political events in these two novels. The politics of the Irish Republican Army (IRA) and that of the Afghan *mujahidin* provide the context for *The Good Terrorist* and *The Wind* respectively. *The Good Terrorist,* located in contemporary London, examines the workings of a splinter Left group that is violently anti-establishment. *The Wind* hones in on the real story of human lives in the aftermath of the Kabul uprising in 1978 that had initially enthused the entire Western world with the possibility of a transformed society in Afghanistan.[42] This euphoria in the West was short-lived and was replaced by growing anger and cynicism on account of the subsequent Russian intervention.

The political activism of the IRA and political change and tumult in Afghanistan is illustrative of the growing violence, both individual and state-sponsored, that occupied centre stage at the end of the 1970s and has continued to do so. The activism of a violent nature and justification of violence as a method of settling political grievances that became part of the global political scene in the late 1970s continue to be a part of our lives to date. The aftermath of the revolution in Afghanistan in 1978 and repeated acts of violence perpetrated by the IRA from 1979 to 1984 are pertinent issues discussed in the two novels.

The IRA's entrenched history dates back to Ireland's religious and political self-formation, and its association with violence has been legion. In the year 1979, Lord Mountbatten—a 'soft civilian target' on holiday, years after he ceased to be politically active—was murdered.[43] Subsequently, in 1984, Margaret Thatcher—then Prime Minister of England—escaped an 'almost disastrously successful bombing' while she was on an official visit to Brighton.[44] The IRA claimed responsibility for both catastrophes. These acts of violence were presumed to have their origins in left-wing perception in Ireland that the continued occupation of Northern Ireland by British troops since 1969 was creating a sectarian state. The absence of legal and political safeguards for voicing anti-British opinions and the continued hostility on the part of British political authority towards Irish demands was seen as the provocation for continuing acts of terrorism.[45]

In the context of Afghanistan, violence operated very differently. It came on the heels of a revolution that had promised to transform the country as it then existed. Instead of a transformation, the newly formed regime alienated the 'local landlords, Moslem clergy and other believers in the status quo by such godless activities as land reform and rights for women.'[46] When the reforms were resisted, the new regime took to coercion and repression tactics resulting in unrest. Russia, with its centuries-old imperial interest in Afghanistan, marched in its troops under the pretext of providing aid. Russia's move outraged vestigial imperial sentiment in Europe and America from where strong protests were lodged.

In both narratives, two examples of state oppression are made visible—one practised by the British government in Northern Ireland

and the other in the Russian invasion of Afghanistan. This brings us to the most disturbing aspect of the politics of violence—namely, how does one resolve the issue of violence arising from a committed core group that is itself protesting against the violence of the state, based on small but extremely important markers of identity? The contradictory nature of the direction this self-expression takes in the case of small groups, who are disenchanted with existing power distribution and implementation, is relevant for our consideration.

One must remember that the IRA had ancient origins and its choice of the use of violence in protests dates back to the time of Britain's imperialist policies in Ireland. Similarly, the coup in Afghanistan was envisaged as heralding the creation of a more equitable society that would thereafter correct extant imbalances and inequities. The fact that both struggles focused on changing hostile and discriminatory situations into more equal conditions for an otherwise oppressed people spurred the imagination and aroused sympathy worldwide. Despite such laudatory aims, both movements record the presence of large-scale violence, the wanton destruction of life and property and the hardship and deprivation faced, ironically, by those very people who were to be the beneficiaries.

How, then, does one understand this violence? On the one hand, violence as a modus operandi seems to be antithetical to any of the goals these revolutions promised. Yet, such violence seems to be a source of strength and sustenance for these groups that were formed as a response to the tyranny and unfair policies of existing systems of power. This is both paradoxical and ironical since the revolutionary groups themselves evolved in reaction to the existing system's apathy and insensitivity to their distinct, separate entity.

In the accounts in *The Good Terrorist* and *The Wind*, it is the small groups that are shown as unleashing an extreme form of violence. The nature of this violence is destructive, directed sharply at existing structures and is far removed from and detrimental to the values originally espoused by the movements themselves. What we have, then, is a division of sympathies—pro-cause and anti-violence. Is it possible to see this continuing propensity for violence as showing up the state of impoverishment and the dead end that Western political theory and practice seem to have reached? This seems to be a logical conclusion to notions of individual and national self-assertion that have always been based on a degree of aggression. This is also perhaps the reason why, historically, the struggle against any hegemony has always manifested itself in some form of violence. Protest for smaller freedoms against a larger oppressive force has invariably followed a rather flawed pattern of valid causes being asserted through wrong means.

This possibly accounts for the common factor that features prominently in any political struggle—namely, the desire for freedom and self-determination, coupled with great anger and resentment directed at political authority, which is always viewed as the perpetrator of injustice. This holds for the IRA's demand for Northern Ireland's right to self-governance and identification of centralised power in the British government as the source of Northern Ireland's oppression; it is also true for the IRA's use of violence to sabotage the functioning of the British government. The *mujahidin* fighting the Soviet Union for what they saw as their religious and national identity also chose armed struggle despite the power of the Soviet state. Both the IRA and the *mujahidin*, despite the differences in cultural and geographical locations and the kinds of oppression, share similarities in the manner of their reaction to continued political tyranny. The interaction between the smaller protesting party and the larger power ranged against it in both *The Good Terrorist* and *The Wind* only manifests in recurring acts of violence, both at the individual and group level. Dealing with the question of recurring violence in both novels, Lessing explores the roles played by women in two entirely different contexts.

Self-definitions in Patriarchal Society: Afghan Women Refugees in *The Wind*

In *The Wind*, Lessing documents women's lives as war refugees in peacetime within religious and cultural formations. Women's roles in war and in times of peace, at the level of active participation or incorporation, reinforce her reading of violence as deeply imbedded within patriarchal structures. The change in guard in Afghanistan's politics was a predominantly male affair. However, the idea of the loss of ethnic and religious identities was fiercely resisted by the whole of Afghanistan. What were the circumstances created for women in this context? Women's traditional identities that were sought to be reinstated by the new regime underwent further modification as the Russian intervention changed the nature of the civil war in Afghanistan into a *jihad* or a fight for spiritual liberation. Alongside this was the trauma of the Afghan peoples' dispossession from their land and their refugee status.

Women in this situation in Afghanistan were caught in a double bind—they were now required to frame their identities within the cultural space sanctioned to them by religious practice and, at the same time, they needed to bolster their men in a tribal war largely fought by Afghan males against the Russian invaders. Thus, women's rights in Afghanistan at this point had to be worked out very differently from, say, the struggles of middle-class women in European society in peacetime. This implies a definite ideological distancing from their sisters in the West and a more culture-specific definition of themselves and their rights. What are the interventions that feminism can make in such a scenario, where there is no longer any uniform position that can be taken? Lessing's accounts of women in *The Wind* provide fresh insights.

The Wind is a semi-travelogue, detailing Lessing's trip to Pakistan to hear at first hand the experiences of the refugees pouring in from Afghanistan. The imaginary country Lessing visits is part of an underdeveloped Asia where a ragtag army of Afghans with little other than primitive weapons of war fight against a technologically superior Russia.

What she finds is a far cry from the change anticipated by the Western media in 1978. This is no promised land transformed by a band of inspired revolutionaries in power but a war-torn and exhausted country—depleted of its resources, its heritage pilloried and destroyed and its people living at bare subsistence levels, unsure of any reprieve. The graphic accounts of fleeing women carrying babies who were the first casualties of the fallout is a chilling and sobering indictment of war.

Outside of their promised land and among the dispossessed, the accounts of the Afghan refugee villages that Lessing visits at Peshawar show up social formations that are a throwback to an earlier time rather than an indication of a forward march. First-person accounts of refugees 'streaming out from newly bombed areas because irrigation systems have been deliberately destroyed and the crops burned'[47] draw our attention to the large-scale destruction caused by the Russian invasion in the name of 'civilizing and modernizing'.[48]

Lessing's record of the conditions of the Afghan refugees, the militancy of the Afghans against the Russians and the slowly played-out war shows how such conditions have only further entrenched social demarcations between men and women. Men are involved in fighting the war while the women huddle in small mud structures bearing and rearing children, as 'upholders of the private foundation of the political world of men.'[49]

Documenting her first-hand experience within a household, Lessing emphasises the vulnerability of the young Afghan women—'hung about with infants'—who seemed to be in need of protection. Lessing describes this as a 'stage of family life long gone in the West, blown into the past by birth control and Women's Liberation.' Our attention is also drawn to the 'possessive, angry, jailer husband . . . as good a husband as he was a father, in the old style: uxorial, jealous, sexual, demanding, all-encompassing.'[50] Coming especially after a reading of *Marriages,* the heightened emphasis provided here highlights the restrictive nature of gendered roles and boundaries.

It is not only women who are shown as conforming to certain stereotypes. The men too are constrained within the roles formulated for them. The men operate within the framework of war-weary but determined fighters, 'because it is their convention to present themselves as intrepid and heroic.'[51] The women, however, are shown as more communicative of their experience.

> They tell you at once what it was like, how terrible, how frightening, how they suffered, how they suffer now. They weep; they tell you all the details that journalists long to hear and which it is so hard to get from the men.[52]

Lessing supplements this picture of women as victims of a war they did not want or make by recording personal accounts of the mobility, exposure and freedom enjoyed by women in Afghanistan before the invasion. We are told of a woman accountant who had travelled to different countries and her daughter, a qualified doctor, who asserts that she was 'free in Kabul, wore western dress, studied and worked as she liked. Now she is in Purdah, has to be veiled the moment she shows her face out of doors.'[53] This is a picture of a society caught in a time warp as women and men are thrown back into older cultural roles—over and above the hardships and deprivations that they are obliged to face.

It is, of course, possible to accuse Lessing of evaluating the experiences of Afghan men and women from a Western viewpoint. It is correct to assume that the wearing of Western clothing by Afghan women is not necessarily a marker of progress or emancipation by itself. Also, feminist scholars such as Fatima Mernissi and Fadwa El Guindi see the act of observing *purdah,* through the wearing of hijabs and burkhas, as an important political statement—that of women asserting their cultural and ethnic identities against oppressive hegemonies.[54] While their work makes it very clear that it is no longer possible to equate the wearing of the burkha with social backwardness, as a Third World inhabitant myself, I would like to stress that the burkha as a garment comes into use in contexts that remain prescriptive. Whether women wear it under social or religious pressure or to make a political statement, it remains a very visible marker of its wearer's identity as a woman. In this case, observing *purdah* emphasises a literal and metaphorical shutting out of women and a systematic regulation of their lives. In *The Wind*, registering the absence of women on the streets and in decision-making bodies along with the fear and deprivation they live under, Lessing shows how the veil seals off or shuts out alternatives.

Observing *purdah* also distinguishes between men and women based on biological difference and reiterates the existing processes of social stratification. Even if it is a politically expedient tool, since men can disguise themselves as women or carry ammunition, it still evokes associations of concealment. The conscious decision to wear the burkha as a traditional costume or as an assertion of ethnic identity is rather limited and does not necessarily translate into a symbol of empowering feminist space.[55] The notion that less irksome garments could be worn in sultry or heatwave conditions, providing greater comfort to the wearer, is by no means far-fetched.

In fact, the hijab, burkha and the *chador* are very often prescribed as clothing for Muslim women by fundamentalist regimes. Evidence of this can be found in the implementation of religious strictures whereby dress codes for women are enforced by mullahs in Islamic countries or by power groups of orthodox women in Iran or by the Taliban—the new religious and political regime which oversaw women's destinies in Afghanistan till October 2001. Amir Mohamedi's statement that 'Islam has improved the situation of women' and 'is a good basis to build on' must be viewed alongside his acceptance that 'there are, and have been abuses.'[56]

His thesis that '[i]t is one thing to say that Islam oppresses women, another to say that men oppress women'[57] shows us how the structures of imposition and abuse are built into prescriptive codes, irrespective of their religious or political origin. Both religious heads and heads of families, one must remember, tend to be men. This situation, as Lessing points out, is not confined to Islam. 'Somewhere in the early history of Islam there must have been an obsessive authoritarian like Saint Paul who imposed himself on Christianity, tormenting and humiliating women with centuries of prohibitions that could never have emanated from Christ.'[58] The structures of religious practice worldwide have always subjected women to special supervision on account of their gender. Women have remained at the receiving end of the backlash from extremist or fundamentalist groups, irrespective of the religion.[59]

Lessing mentions that her group had hoped to set up meetings with 'educated or professional Afghan women refugees' to hear from any one of them 'that in spite of suffering in Pakistan from all the disadvantages of Purdah, of being veiled, she nevertheless was protesting against the invasion of her country by the Russians, who were claiming to have freed women.'[60] None of the women the group met could be placed in this category. On the contrary, most of them seemed to have been pushed into an acceptance of the extreme situation they were placed in by factors outside their control.

Given the later history of Afghanistan, well over a decade after Lessing's book was published, it is not difficult to surmise that expressions of independence on the part of women would have invariably been crushed by militant, nationalist and fundamentalist agendas.[61] Clearly, Afghan women have had a minimal role to play in the actual decision-making process. Significantly, the question of the mullahs in Pakistan imposing their orthodoxy on Afghan women is not challenged within the framework of *The Wind*. Territorial boundaries, one can only assume, become fluid in the context of religious prescriptions for women—no matter how fixed they might be in the course of assertions about a nation-state formulated by men.

The Wind also engages with women who are not victims of their circumstances and who have not been caught in a double bind. They are not like their other sisters who have reconciled themselves to domestic containment despite having enjoyed liberal freedom before the war. These martial women who eagerly adopt the institutions of war and violence bring to mind the character Vahshi from *Marriages*. Both *The Good Terrorist* and *The Wind* make references to women who readily adapt and equip themselves for violence. The first section of *The Wind* frames the context of a society at war by echoing Cassandra's unheeded warnings about impending battle. It also provides a close-up of Helen—the desired and coveted sister for whom the Battle of Troy was fought. Unlike her contrary sister, Helen is shown as relishing the prospect of victory and accepting violence as an unfortunate but necessary by-product of the war.

Lessing imaginatively links contemporary political happenings by foregrounding her account of the Afghan refugees with a scene from Greek mythology, showing them as resonant with reverberations from ancient paradigms. Pre-empting queries about the juxtaposition of two very different wars Lessing observes, '[w]hy do we have to worry about what was said so many centuries ago? Obviously there is something in the mechanism of the human mind that demands it.'[62] Lessing draws attention to the way in which notions of violence are absorbed and internalised in cultural practice. This process seems to hold when we view the assimilation of the principles of violence in so-called civil societies across history. Such notions continue to reverberate to this day.

Helen's persona is open to multiple interpretations. At one level she can be seen as exercising active and willing agency, accepting the war as a necessary intervention. At another level, Helen is also the objective behind the war; she is the ultimate prize that Menelaus and his men will reclaim as the outcome of their victory. The myth thus leaves Helen with little choice but to be implicated in the politics of war which is made to correspond to her desire. In the context of Afghanistan, the struggle for control and power over the land replaces Helen as the object of desire. It, however, continues to be underwritten by the bodies of innumerable Helens. The female body itself continues to remain a site for contestation, carrying with it all the accretions of the Helen myth.

Women within the ideology of war can only function within limited counters; either as advocates of the war or by providing a second line of support and reinforcement. The only other option available to them is to allow monitoring by proprietary males as potential mothers of the next generation of soldiers, although they cook, keep house, help and continue to provide sexual release.

Lessing captures Helen's excitement over the war. We are given graphic descriptions of how 'the smell of blood will be making her heart beat' and 'her blood race.'[63] Women in *The Good Terrorist* also feel a similar emotion. Such excitement is supposedly characteristic of the brave Afghan women actively engaged in battle. Very early in *The Wind*, we are informed of the Western journalists' quest for the all-female groups into which women had organised themselves to make important military contributions to the war. In the modern war in Afghanistan, much searching yields information about one intrepid woman commander—as chronicled in Part Three. Mrs Tajwar Kakar shows herself capable of tremendous resilience and recounts her long struggle against the Russians, enduring severe and excruciating torture. Details abound concerning women's participation in the war, their seducing and leading Russian men to their death, carrying messages and munitions and spying under the protection of the veil. All these activities carried out by women, it needs to be emphasised, merely replicate and endorse patriarchal ideology. Lessing does not intend us to see them as indicative of alternatives. The roles available to women or chosen by them in an advanced modern state seldom fall outside of the prescriptive and limited patriarchal ideologies of violence and control.

Women and Violence: Reiterating Patriarchal Goals in *The Good Terrorist*

The Good Terrorist looks at the operations of a left-wing group and its compulsive gravitation towards violence. It provides us with a story from another side, that of middle-class, free and emancipated women in London—the capital of an ostensibly advanced nation. These women, unlike the women in Afghanistan, have personal lives that are largely free from the confines of religious and familial power structures. The dissatisfaction that these women exhibit stems from anger at their insular bourgeois lives and at the state which has remained insensitive to the situation of the poor and the impoverished. Somewhere along the line, their anger at the system and their desire for change pushes this group towards openly espousing violence. Beginning with protests that demonstrate their anger at the political establishment, the women eventually begin to take part in planned violence—somewhat aware of its death-dealing potential. They assemble a bomb fully aware of its capacity to destroy. How do we analyse this chosen path of violence? The argument that Lessing puts forward in *The Good Terrorist* seems to be that when women are allowed access to the same hegemonic spaces that men wield power from, they equal if not excel men in adopting violence as a means of achieving their ends. *The Wind* and *The Good Terrorist* show that violence as a means of self-expression is not limited to men alone. It is as easily and effectively appropriated by women. The roots of this violence originate within the predominant system of politics and culture. This pattern of violence, intrinsic and internalised, is present at both ends of the political spectrum, irrespective of whether the Afghan *mujahidin* espouse it or members of the ultra-left.

In *The Good Terrorist*, Alice—a product of a cushioned, middle-class family—breaks away from the world of 'rich, selfish bourgeoisie'.[64] She aims to work towards a new world of shared values purportedly based on principles very different from the despicable world that she has opted out of. She becomes part of the Communist Central

Union (CCU) because her lover Jasper is aligned with the group. The torchbearers of the CCU, who eventually offer their services to the IRA, are easily identified by their hatred for the system. Nevertheless, they are willing to pillage plunder and live off all the benefits the system can offer. Their grudging acceptance of these benefits as a given is overshadowed by their strong sense of superiority and correctness. This self-righteousness attaches itself to all the causes they support. Another characteristic of the CCU and its members is that, within their so-called commune, older, private patterns of subordination prevail despite their professed contempt for the existing system. All the women play roles secondary to those played by men. Most of them are involved with the group because their men friends are.

Alice's emotional dependence on Jasper mimics older patterns. It is through the small pairings and single members of the commune that Lessing shows us the continuation of hierarchies of power in interpersonal relationships. Each member of the commune is capable of inflicting violence and does so gratuitously despite personally having been subjected to physical or mental violence. Jasper, who exploits Alice's emotional need for him and feels little compunction in living off her resources, subjects her to physical, mental and emotional violence not very different from that found in conventional marriages. Faye, with a battered childhood behind her, displays capacity for tremendous cruelty. One of the early demonstrations of Faye's potential for cruelty is revealed in the episode involving a young girl with small children, who is brusquely pushed out of House No. 43. Ironically, both Faye and the young woman's claim to a place in House No. 43 are hypothetically equal. What settles the issue is not any moral or ethical choice, but Faye's aggression—backed by the presence of other acquiescent members of the CCU. This incident occurs shortly after Faye's animated statement about the atrocities of her childhood and how she wishes to give children a better world to live in. Lessing's juxtaposition of the stated intent and the contrary action clarifies for the reader the tremendous gap between theory and action.

Pat, impelled by the break-up of her relationship with Bert, wants to leave the group and eventually does so. She is fragile in build and soft-spoken; yet, she thinks nothing of wanton and gratuitous destruction.

While helping to fix broken slats on the rooftop, she stumbles upon a pigeon's nest with eggs in it and hurls the eggs down one by one insisting that these were merely birds' eggs and not people. Alice, who displays self-righteous anger against any authority figure, has few qualms about stealing money from her father's home or office. Worse, she indulges in unprovoked acts of arson. She throws a stone smashing her father's drawing room windows on one occasion and, on another, she steals her mother's curtains from the flat the latter had put up for sale. Despite all the violence she directs against her family, she still feels that she can morally demand their help as and when the occasion demands it.

Each person living at No. 43, an abandoned house likely to be pulled down by the council, fits very easily into the slot of being either victim or oppressor. What holds the group together is a hatred of the system they pretend to repudiate. They are fuelled by the conviction that 'when [they] have abolished fascist imperialism'[65] and 'capitalism that was so hard and hurtful and did not care about the pain of its victims',[66] the world would be a different place to live in. Each character is motivated by a strong sense of injustice—both personal and general. The prevailing sentiment that each one of them nurses is that none of them have received what is their rightful due. This sense of injustice sustains deeply ingrained anger but finds its outlet in sporadic violence.

Lessing highlights the handicaps inherent in dreams of social and political justice when not accompanied by change at the individual level. Unless the belief in power and violence that motivates these characters can be transformed, Lessing observes, all programmes of change will only replicate structures of domination and subordination. The CCU's vision of the end of the reign of 'fascist, imperialist'[67] structures and its replacement by more equitable systems is doomed to fail since their perception of a new social order does not involve any modification in the older system of values. Their critique of the *status quo* is individualistic. Since they see themselves as outside the pale of all laws and rules, they show themselves to be extremely anarchic by complying only with those rules that they deem necessary. Everything outside of the blueprint of change that they envision is treated with scant respect—be it rules, laws, state machinery, property or people.

The Good Terrorist is a story of whimsical individualists whose steady graduation from the capacity for personal violence to terrorism is fuelled by anger directed against the state and its people. Highlighting the gap between the haves and have-nots in London, a cosmopolitan First World capital, Lessing records the rage within the people protesting against the system. Through them, Lessing warns of the dangers of unchecked individualism. Alice's rejection of a personal life to fight for an ideal larger than herself is not propelled by any shifts in patterns of thinking or strategy. Changes in the system, Lessing makes very clear, cannot come about without a corresponding transformation in individual perceptions about ethical values. This, she emphasises, calls for recognition and extensive analysis of deeply ingrained patterns of domination, subordination and control. The absence of such analysis in *The Good Terrorist* slowly but surely pushes the main figures from wanton appropriation and destruction towards planned and ruthlessly executed damage.

The suggestion that Lessing makes several times in the narrative about the pleasure, excitement and thrill of inflicting damage and escaping the consequences is significant. By placing on record the deeply felt instinct for and enjoyment of such acts of vandalism and violence, she shows us how women can be co-opted into seeking and accepting violence as a modus operandi. Alice, who participates in acts of violence and derives pleasure out of them, is not the only woman to do so. Jocelin, the maker of the bomb, is a woman and so is Faye, the woman who sets the bomb's timer incorrectly and is unfortunately blown up. By creating women who respond so excitedly to violence,[68] Lessing is dispensing with the mythology of violence as an activity valorised only by men.

Violence, as Lessing shows us, is something that is imbibed culturally and then manifested through the actions of both men and women. Women's participation in political structures can, therefore, be seen as a continuation and furthering of male ideology. Even women who are unhappy with an existing power structure are drawn into accepting the ideology of violence as an effective weapon upon joining extant modes of protest. What we see in *The Good Terrorist* is the logical working out of this thesis. Peddling an aggressive individualism in their personal lives, the women are unable to counter or offer any alternate systems of political formation and the same aggression overshadows the visions of the new world they hope to build.

Gayle Greene, in her reading of *The Good Terrorist,* remarks on Lessing's excremental vision and identifies Lessing with Alice—thereby summing up the novel's conclusion as one that places us 'in a dark pit, with no glimmer of an elsewhere'.[69] While Alice is a satirical reworking of Martha Quest, following similar patterns of breaking away from extant family ties to create a new social revolution, Lessing makes it very clear—both within and outside of the novel—that she has very little sympathy with Alice's views.[70] As readers, we are never left in doubt about the criticism directed at Alice. Yet the novel does have moments in which Lessing keeps pushing for alternative perceptions, which emerge even at catastrophic movements, offering a glimmer of hope. One such glimmer is provided by Alice herself, minutes before the bomb is about to explode.

Alice awakens suddenly to the realisation of the damaging and death-delivering properties of the bomb. In terror, she telephones the Samaritans, 'while the little whimpering yelping cries came out of her, uncontrollably, as though the animal lodged inside her were being beaten.'[71] This anguish of conscience is one that has so far been buried under the instinct of herd mentality. Alice's constant alternation between disgust at the system and the nature of her protest against it has been aggressive and violent. At the same time, Alice has provided shelter, nurture, care and housekeeping and cooking services for the commune that she has adopted as her own. This reveals an aspect of her personality outside of the embryonic aggression that she directs against her bourgeois family and the state. Alice is hampered by having to choose between two very flawed systems. Her rejection of ordinary middle-class life and her visualisation of a life outside of conventional structures are in themselves noteworthy. Her intentions are to be seen as springing from a misplaced idealism, rather than from the kind of motivated self-interest shown by Mary and her beau who intend to use House No. 43 as a transit accommodation till they can buy their own.

The novel does not place us 'in a dark pit', at the point of no return, but in a context that provides sufficient illumination for the way out.

Louise Yelin sees *The Good Terrorist* as a distortion of 'the political landscape of Britain in the 1980s by ignoring or discrediting the new social movements of gays, blacks, and women that arose during this period in opposition to policies identified with Thatcher' and in its erasure of 'once significant distinctions—between the Left and the Right, anarchist and communist, middle class and working class'.[72] While Lessing does conflate different kinds of politics, it would be more fruitful to read *The Good Terrorist* outside of the topical context of British politics and British identity within which Yelin's reading seeks to confine Lessing's novel. In *The Good Terrorist*, Lessing is far more engrossed in drawing attention to the commonality of violence adopted by diverse movements. Lessing's diagnosis that violence is not a justifiable means to any kind of end is further reiterated, in my view, by her extended analysis of violence in *The Wind*.

It would be fruitful at this juncture to look at the situation in Afghanistan post-1987, where Lessing's narrative ends. From the time of the revolution, different political groups who came to power lost little time in prescribing codes of dress and conduct for women. Larger political forces with vested interests mobilised the local groups exercising control in Afghanistan. The *mujahidin,* who offered resistance to the Russian army, were aided in their struggle by an American supply of weapons and ammunitions—enabling a proxy war between the two superpowers. Russia's withdrawal from superpower status in the 1980s and subsequently from Afghanistan in 1989 saw the beginnings of civil war among the *mujahidin* of different ethnic groups and the declaration of an Islamic State in 1992 by the Tajik *mujahidin.* By 1994, the Taliban—Islamic extremist fighters—took over Kandahar in the south and over four years, established their regime in the north. The condition of women in Afghanistan throughout this time has been one of continued oppression and deprivation.[73] Given such a context, no one can argue that the practice of violence by any group, however impeccable its political credentials, is viable or justifiable.

The conclusion to *The Good Terrorist* shows Alice readying unwittingly for a meeting with an intelligence agent. It also highlights the possibility of reprisal from angry Russian ultras whose orders she has disobeyed. It is chilling in its assertion that individual and collective acts of aggression can only elicit similar responses. Alice's walk towards the future that she has mapped out evokes memories of an earlier final journey made by Mary Turner in *The Grass is Singing*. Lessing, in *The Good Terrorist*, signals very clearly that transformation cannot be effected through a bloody coup or intimations of violence. Such actions can never change the inequities in the system or usher in a hopeful future. Instead, she provides a close, hard look at the ruthlessness and power wielded by individual participants in the political process and the consequences they must subsequently come to terms with.

Lessing's fiction seems to be making larger connections and addressing itself to new, evolving formulations in feminist ethics. The care, nurture and 'mothering' that Alice provides are not, as Yelin suggests, 'an extreme case of psychological regression'[74] but an instance of other deep-rooted instincts that are seen as being of little or no value in a hostile environment. Except for Alice, most of the commune's inhabitants see these activities as irrelevant to their grand purposes. This viewpoint, I would like to emphasise, echoes a long-standing patriarchal tradition wherein domestic work has always occupied a diminished stature.

It is in this connection that the activities of caring, cooking and housekeeping present in Lessing's narratives gain priority as essential acts of nurture and growth in any society. This is a theme explored at great length in *Marriages* and highlighted in *The Wind* when women articulate the deprivations they face under the war's onslaught. Care and nurture are alternative human values that remain constricted in *The Good Terrorist* and *The Wind*. In this context, Lessing's substitution of a far more heterogeneous community in place of the conventional family based on blood ties and kinship, not taken note of by Yelin, suggests important possibilities—especially if one recalls the Coldridge house in *The Four-Gated City* and the new household formations in *Memoirs*. Does Lessing posit hope and possibilities for the future in this new familial structure? Does her recording of the disintegration of kinship and her creation of more heterogeneous groups suggest a new format in which interpersonal connections can be made?

New Feminist Agendas: Self-expression, Creativity, Care and Nurture

In the three novels discussed above, Lessing looks closely at violent political activity, traces its practice and nurture in social and personal relationships and examines the impact this has on roles allotted to men and women. Examining these roles, she locates their origins in much older systems of political and philosophical thought. Tracing the idea of violence in the everyday world of her characters, Lessing highlights the inevitable path taken by political movements towards violence—given the contexts in which they emerge. This is perhaps why movements based on the ideals of equality and fair play display in their operational strategies the potential for so much destruction and an utter lack of sensitivity to anything that is outside of their scheduled agendas. It is no longer possible either to explain away the violence generated by small groups or to sympathise with the desperation that turns them into 'extremists'.

The three novels discussed above provide a complex analysis and critique of Western political systems of power and oppression. They also offer a detailed study of the nature of violence that is unleashed on a hapless, unsuspecting people. A possible blueprint towards the creation of an ideal world is offered by Zone Three in *Marriages*. Lessing's alternatives, I would like to argue, move away from patriarchal notions of control and subjugation towards the larger idea of nurture and reciprocity as fundamental civilisational values. Her relocation of the emphasis on power and authority to care and nurture must be seen as important pointers towards a new feminist agenda. Lessing's focus on these as primary to civil lives possibly echoes a rather conservative idea from the late 1950s which suggests that men and women are different from each other in their approach to politics and society.[75]

Autodidactic and eclectic, Lessing is influenced by these ideas and uses them in her work. However, as her novels reveal, she is opposed to readings of 'male' and 'female' based on any kind of essentialism. Her fiction—which from the 1960s has increasingly paid attention to political and social structures from the woman's point of view—now dwells on newly formed communities. Communities such as the one set up in Zone Three in *Marriages* demonstrate the possibilities of new group formations based on mutual trust and shared values. This is very different from the squat in *The Good Terrorist* which is based on older patriarchal assumptions of abstract individualism.[76] Unlike the women huddled in refugee camps in *The Wind*—confined within strict codes—Lessing's idea of community, in this work, explores notions of choice and shared value.

Within this new community, the positives are the 'relational associations' between individuals. Thus, values that have been traditionally associated with women and the domestic sphere they have occupied gain significance and there is a focus on the relevance of these activities for the continuation of civilisation. Lessing's shift from activities associated with or part of the values of a patriarchal system shares common ground with radical feminism's critique[77] of essentially male structures of power that breed individualism and violence; also, it speaks for the need to critically examine the crisis in existing systems. Lessing, with remarkable prescience, seems in agreement with new feminist theories that challenge traditional, moral choices and offer far-reaching, innovative possibilities.[78] Envisaging a move away from the entire value system associated with the male world and dismissing power structures and hegemonies of rank as essentially patriarchal constructs, Lessing's fiction makes out a case for a very different feminist politics. These embryonic perceptions form the premise of Lessing's subsequent novels.

Endnotes

1. Doris Lessing, *Briefing for a Descent into Hell* (Great Britain: Jonathan Cape, 1971; London: Grafton Books, 1972).
2. Doris Lessing, *The Marriages Between Zones Three, Four and Five, Canopus In Argos: Archives* (Great Britain: Jonathan Cape, 1980; New York: Vintage International, 1992). All references to the book are from the 1992 edition. Further references to this book will be abbreviated as *Marriages.*

3. Doris Lessing, *The Good Terrorist* (Great Britain: Jonathan Cape, 1985; London: Grafton Books, 1986). All references to this book are from the 1986 edition.
4. Doris Lessing, *The Wind Blows Away Our Words* (London: Picador/Pan Books, 1987). All references to this book are from this edition. Further references to the book will be abbreviated as *The Wind.*
5. See the 'Some Remarks' section of Doris Lessing, *Canopus in Argos: Archives* (New York: Vintage International, 1992).
6. The expression 'children of violence' is used first by Lessing as a title to her five-volume series beginning with *Martha Quest.* In her autobiography, she also refers specifically to her generation as the children of violence.
7. To provide an exhaustive catalogue of the violent events in world history is beyond the possibilities of this discussion. Hobsbawm refers to 'the rise of autonomist and separatist movements mainly after 1970' and identifies this as a peculiarly Western phenomenon. At the same time, he notes the rise of identity groups seeking collective separatism in various parts of the world in Eric Hobsbawm, *The Age of Extremes: The Short Twentieth Century, 1914–1991* (London: Michael Joseph, 1994), 425–428.
8. This entire paragraph is a paraphrasing of the account of the rise of urban terrorism and the escalating casualties in Hobsbawm, *Age of Extremes,* 452–460.
9. This is a paraphrasing of the accounts of women's lives in Britain and the United States in the late 1970s in Sheila Rowbotham, *A Century of Women: The History of Women in Britain and the United States* (London and New York: Viking Books, 1997; London and New York: Penguin Books, 1999), 407. All further references are from the 1999 edition.
10. Radical feminists and socialist feminists aimed to create a separate female space. Separatist groups like the Leeds Revolutionary Feminist Group argued 'that men should be avoided . . . as a political duty'. Rowbotham, *A Century of Women,* 431.
11. The term 'consciousness-raising' was coined by Kathie Sarachild in 1964 and 'consciousness-raising groups created a context where women could draw on their own experiences and interpret them', as mentioned in Rowbotham, *A Century of Women,* 378. See also her account of the consciousness-raising groups emerging out of the women's liberation groups in Britain in the early 1970s, in Rowbotham, *A Century of Women,* 404.
12. Robin Morgan, *The Demon Lover: On the Sexuality of Terrorism* (New York and London: W.W. Norton and Company, 1989), 17.

13. Virginia Woolf's *Three Guineas* (1938) is one of the earliest anti-war tracts of this century.
14. Emmeline Pankhurst, it must be remembered, was one of the founding members of the Women's Social and Political Union in 1903. Yet, her own understanding of women's rights echoes conventional patriarchal perceptions of women's issues as one more item in a larger agenda. Rowbotham, *A Century of Women,* 67.
15. Rowbotham, *A Century of Women,* 69–70. The subject of the damage done to themselves by the two women appears time and again in the poetry of W.B. Yeats. Particularly in 'No Second Troy' and 'A Prayer for My Daughter', the choice of violence on the part of both women is indicted and held up as a terrible example to follow.
16. Fanon speaks eloquently of the psyche of the Black man and the need to restructure the world but his restructuring concerns itself entirely with the world of the Black man and is silent about the Black woman in Frantz Fanon, *Black Skins, White Masks,* trans. Charles Lam Markmann (New York: Grove Press, 1967), 82.
17. Hobsbawm, *Age of Extremes,* 176. Carole Pateman and Mary Lyndon Shanley point out that despite the occasional reference to powerful women, Western political thought has been conceived and built through the exclusion of women and all that is represented by 'femininity'. Mary Lyndon Shanley and Carole Pateman, eds., *Feminist Interpretations and Political Theory* (Oxford: Polity Press, 1991), 3.
18. Rajeswari Mohan observes that Leila Khaled's autobiography My People Shall Live (1975) 'heightens our uncertainty about the tensions likely to rise between . . . Khaled's investments in revolutionary (self)-fashioning, notwithstanding the crosscurrents set up by Khaled's avowed commitment to the emancipation of Palestinian women', in Rajeswari Mohan, 'Loving Palestine: Nationalist activism and feminist agency in Leila Khaled's subversive bodily acts', *Interventions* 1, no. 1 (1998): 52–80.
19. Dhanu, in the guise of 'an innocent looking woman offering . . . a garland', was actually part of a diabolical plot of assassination, 'Rajiv Gandhi', last modified 20 May 1991, www.rediff.com/news.
20. With the exception of Mahatma Gandhi's philosophy of non-violence implemented in the course of India's struggle for independence, one cannot really think of any other nationalist movement which was organised around the ethics of non-violence. Partition, which was a corollary to India's independence, was bloody and brutal. Subsequent

hostilities between India and Pakistan have also been marked by violent and bloody encounters. The other campaigner for non-violence as an ethical choice was Martin Luther King Jr during the civil rights movements in the United States.

21. Berit As, 'More Power To Women,' in *Sisterhood Is Global: The International Women's Movement Anthology,* ed. Robin Morgan (Garden City and New York: Anchor Press/Doubleday, 1984), 514.
22. Morgan, *The Demon Lover,* 16.
23. Morgan, *The Demon Lover*, 33 and 84. Morgan's analysis frames my own readings of Lessing's treatment of violence in the three novels under discussion.
24. Doris Lessing, introduction to *Canopus in Argos: Archives,* xi.
25. Doris Lessing, preface to *The Sirian Experiments*, in *Canopus in Argos: Archives,* 617.
26. Lessing, *Marriages*, 576.
27. Lessing, *Marriages*, 577.
28. Lessing, *Marriages*, 581.
29. Lessing, *Marriages*, 442.
30. Lessing, *Marriages*, 441.
31. Lessing addresses debates originating in the 1940s in Britain that laid the onus of childcare entirely on mothers. Donald Winnicott's broadcasts in the 1950s and 1960s, and John Bowlby—author of *Child Care and Growth of Love* (1953) and *Can I Leave My Baby?* (1958)—were challenged in the late 1960s by works such as *The Captive Wife* (1966) by Hannah Gavron. Sheila Rowbotham, *A Century of Women,* 292–294 and 352–353.
32. Lessing, *Marriages*, 570.
33. Lessing, *Marriages*, 569.
34. Nancy Julia Chodorow, 'Gender, Relation, and Difference in Psychoanalytic Perspective', *Feminist Social Thought: A Reader,* ed. Diana Tietjens Meyers (New York and London: Routledge, 1997), 15.
35. Lessing, *Marriages*, 589.
36. Lessing, *Marriages*, 600.
37. Lessing, *Marriages*, 601.
38. Lessing, *Marriages*, 544.
39. Lessing, *Marriages*, 523.
40. Doris Lessing in a letter to Rubenstein. Roberta Rubenstein, *The Novelistic Vision of Doris Lessing: Breaking the Forms of Consciousness* (Urbana: University of Illinois Press, 1979), 198.

41. Gayle Greene, *Doris Lessing: The Poetics of Change* (Ann Arbor: University of Michigan Press, 1994), 177.
42. Halliday's piece hailed the April 1978 uprising in Kabul as a 'revolutionary process of some description' with the formation of a new regime that had 'committed itself to land reform, to equality of the nationalities, to emancipating women, to a solution of the nomadic question'. Fred Halliday, 'Revolution in Afghanistan,' *New Left Review*, no. 112 (November–December 1978): 4–5, https://newleftreview.org/issues/I112/articles/fred-halliday-revolution-in-afghanistan.
43. Malcolm Pearce and Geoffrey Stewart, *British Political History, 1867–1990: Democracy and Decline* (London and New York: Routledge, 1992), 506.
44. Pearce and Stewart, *British Political History,* 507.
45. Pearce and Stewart, 'Ireland in the Thatcher Years', in *British Political History,* 506–508.
46. Hobsbawm, *Age of Extremes*, 479. This prompted Thatcher's government to lodge a strong protest against the Russian intervention in December 1979.
47. Lessing, *The Wind,* 74.
48. Lessing, *The Wind,* 56.
49. This expression is used to describe the space granted to women in patriarchal societies in both private and the public sphere by Shanley and Pateman, *Feminist Interpretations and Political Theory,* 3.
50. Lessing, *The Wind,* 79.
51. Lessing, *The Wind,* 77.
52. Lessing, *The Wind,* 77.
53. Lessing, *The Wind,* 82.
54. Fatima Mernissi, *Beyond the Veil: Male–Female Dynamics in Muslim Society* (Cambridge, Massachusetts: Schenkman Publishing Company, 1975; London: Al Saqi Books, 1985), 7–24 and 165–179. Also see Fadwa El Guindi, *Veil: Modesty, Privacy and Resistance* (New York and Oxford: Berg Publishers, 1999), 1–49. Both Mernissi and Guindi stress that the underlying concepts of female sexuality in Christian society and Muslim traditions are very different.
55. I refer in particular to feminist-poet Kamala Das who recently converted to Islam and spoke with pleasure and relief of the *chador* and *purdah*, which she said made her feel protected and safe from prying male eyes. See Kamala Das, 'Love is the Only Ritual I Believe in,' interview by Priya

Pathiyan, *The Times of India*, April 1, 2001. Das's need to protect herself from male rapacity and her conviction that being draped from head to toe in a veiled costume would provide such safety can only be located in the context of personal choice. Accounts of women being molested or violated despite being similarly dressed could not have escaped her notice.

56. Lessing, *The Wind*, 66–67.
57. Lessing, *The Wind*, 67.
58. Lessing, *The Wind*, 103.
59. Outside of this novel, one can locate such a position adopted by the Hindu right wing in its codes for women. The other significant example that comes to mind is that of Nawal el Saadawi, the Egyptian feminist who faced charges of apostasy in May 2001 for restating her 'opposition to the veil' and emphasising that women 'are oppressed in all religions. The problem is not Islam, it is the political systems that use Islam and religion'. Saadawi as quoted in Kalpana Sharma, 'Egypt's face of courage', *The Hindu Magazine*, Sunday, June 3, 2001, 2.
60. Lessing, *The Wind*, 116.
61. A moving account of women's lives in Afghanistan is provided by Latifa, *My Forbidden Face: Growing Up Under the Taliban; A Young Woman's Story*, trans. Lisa Appignanesi (2001; London: Virago, 2002). Documenting her mother's life and her own, Latifa describes the continuing constrictions placed on women's lives from the time of the Soviet invasion.
62. Lessing, *The Wind*, 103.
63. Lessing, *The Wind*, 29.
64. Lessing, *The Good Terrorist*, 19.
65. Lessing, *The Good Terrorist*, 54.
66. Lessing, *The Good Terrorist*, 110.
67. Lessing, *The Good Terrorist*, 85.
68. Robin Morgan speaks of the powerful compulsion that violence as an ideology provides in Morgan, *The Demon Lover*, 17–18.
69. Greene, *The Poetics of Change*, 218.
70. Virginia Tiger recounts Lessing's remark at the end of her second lecture at 92nd Street Y, in New York, April 1983, that *The Good Terrorist* was 'about a girl—rather loosely based on something I've seen—who drifts into becoming a terrorist out of sheer stupidity or lack of imagination'. The idea for the novel began 'in 1979 when Lord Mountbatten was killed and Lessing, in Ireland at the time, saw disaffected kids running around

cheering.' Virginia Tiger, 'Candid Shot: Lessing in New York City, April 1 and 2', 1984, *Doris Lessing Newsletter* 8 (Fall 1984): 5–6. Reprinted in Claire Sprague and Virginia Tiger, eds., *Critical Essays on Doris Lessing* (Boston: G.K. Hall & Co, 1986), 221–223.

71. Lessing, *The Good Terrorist,* 353.
72. Louise Yelin, *From the Margins of Empire: Christina Stead, Doris Lessing, Nadine Gordimer* (Ithaca and London: Cornell University Press, 1998), 92.
73. Living and teaching in New Delhi, I have interacted with several Afghan refugee families for neighbours. These are families that fled from Afghanistan in the early 1980s. While young women and men have chosen the option of migrating to the United States, older women live out each day in a haze. Occasional encounters with young Afghan students pursuing an education in Delhi University have yielded horrific accounts of the total denial of any kind of rights to women—from the choice of clothing, access to public spaces, education or employment. Most students also spoke of the impossibility of returning to Afghanistan. Several accounts of the lives of Afghan women, oral and circulated on the Web, document their plight.
74. Yelin, *Margins of Empire*, 97.
75. Rowbotham's account of the women's groups, the YWCA and the League of Women Voters in the United States. Rowbotham, *A Century of Women,* 317–319.
76. For a reading of the emphasis on individualism and the value given to it in patriarchal structures and the fact that relational associations within different groups can be seen as the basis of feminist constructions, see Marilyn Friedman, 'Feminism and Modern Friendship: Dislocating the Community' in *Explorations in Feminist Ethics: Theory and Practice,* eds., Eve Browning Cole and Susan Coultrap-McQuin (Bloomington and Indianapolis: Indiana University Press, 1992), 89–101.
77. Radical feminism's starting point is that women are central and their experiences provide the basis of a woman-centred world. The task of radical feminism is to expose the domination of men in public and private relationships.
78. For discussions on this new development that is more woman-centred and deals with female friendships and work and identifies females as emotional and with better relational capacities and ethical values, see Eve Browning Cole and Susan Coultrap-Mcquin, eds., *Explorations in*

Feminist Ethics: Theory and Practice (Bloomington and Indianapolis: Indiana University Press, 1992). For an analysis of femininity as a space where female socialisation involves responsibility as opposed to male socialisation which focuses on autonomy, see Carol Gilligan, *In a Different Voice: Psychological Theory and Women's Development* (Massachusetts and London: Harvard University Press, 1982).

VI

Women and Ageing: The Body in Time

Janna Somers and Joyce, her co-editor, work for a fashionable women's journal called *Lilith*. They are deeply engrossed in conceptualising a section titled 'Images of Women' for the issue under publication. The journal's name evokes associations with Lilith from ancient myth whose story has been obscured due to the focus on the first woman created by God—namely, Eve. Although mythical Lilith had once defied prescriptive codes, the journal named after her continues to evoke images of conventional women. These images are listed under the following categories:

(a) A girl of twelve or thirteen, and she gave us the most trouble. We discarded a hundred photographs, and finally got Michael to photograph Joyce's niece, aged fifteen actually but rather childish. We got a frank healthy sexuality, not Lolita at all, we were careful to avoid that. Miss Promise.

(b) A girl about seventeen, emphasizing independence and confidence. Still at home but you are ready to leave the nest.

(c) Leading your own life. Mid-twenties. Since in our experience women living their own lives, sharing flats, keeping down jobs, feel as if they are walking a tightrope, we chose something pretty and vulnerable. Needing Mr Right but able to do without.

(d) Young married woman, with a child. Emphasizing the child.

(e) Married woman with part-time job, two children, running home and husband.

And that was that.[1]

'Images of Women' ends with this last category. In some versions of mythology, Lilith is represented as an unconventional figure, a woman who chooses to chart out independent territory. In the myth, she is supposed to have been created as Adam's equal—a detail he is unable to accept. When Lilith rejects Adam's authority and leaves, Eve is supposedly carved out of Adam's rib to replace her. Lilith is subsequently associated with wanton sexuality—often bordering on, if not actually, evil.[2]

It is a trifle unsettling that in a journal named after Lilith, despite her potential as a firebrand role model, the images only highlight limited facets of women's lives. These facets, recognisable and saleable, are in a sense sanctioned by the patriarchal societies that continue to endorse them.

Janna and Joyce connive and comply with the media in reinforcing popular perceptions of women. As readers, the questions that we need to ask at this juncture are: Where do we find the real Lilith—for whom the journal has been named? Does she exist at all in our world? Is her experience ever recorded? How do we view the older woman then, who is writing and recording *The Diaries of Jane Somers* and enabling us to enter her experiences? Is this experience, outside of the conventionally listed images, giving us a prototype that we have not seen before? Is this old woman's story unchartered, like Lilith's was?

To go back to the images themselves—these are recognisable identities. The visualising team works hard to present a fifteen-year-old as 'twelve or thirteen' and ensure that such portrayal does not evoke adult paedophilic interest. Given the context of the MeToo movements in 2018, delayed hindsight channelled in by these protests allowed us to recognise how a culture of prurience, over decades, had been nursed and fed through visuals and films that crassly objectified women. The spotlight then shifts to a girl in her late teens—on the threshold of momentous choices—establishing herself economically and professionally, getting married and then getting ensconced into years of demanding child-nurture, punctuated only by the juggling and balancing of work outside the home, along with the demands of housework and family. These images delineate what 'becoming a woman' entails in cultural practice. They also demarcate and highlight the productive years during which women are subjects of discussion or interest. They reiterate the fact that popular perceptions of women are closely linked to notions of their incipient sexuality.

Janna and Joyce reinforce older, and by now familiar, roles for women by circulating certain notions of womanhood that legitimise stereotypes through which women can be understood, or as in this case, visualised. Another pertinent question at this juncture is to enquire whether there is a possibility of creating images of women outside of the categories that are listed in *Lilith*. If the fact of being a woman falls only within these brackets, what do we do with the surplus? Does this universal basis for defining women—one that focuses largely on female physiology, sexuality and reproduction—need to be the only dimension in which women are to be understood?

Neither Janna nor Joyce falls into any of these easily recognisable sets numbered from (a) to (e). As older women, they form part of a new category—ironically, one that they as editors of *Lilith* do not recognise. Widowed and economically independent, Janna leads a secure life as a well-paid professional with a flat of her own. Joyce successfully balances a full-time career with grown-up children and is reconciled to a husband with emotional attachments directed elsewhere. What category do Janna and Joyce inhabit and what exactly is its defining or qualifying feature?

This is a question that Lessing raises in *The Diaries of Jane Somers* (1984) where the narrator gives us an inside view of older women's lives. A similar preoccupation can also be seen in an earlier novel—namely, *The Summer Before the Dark*[3] (1973). Written even more specifically from the woman's point of view, the novel marks a shift from the usual representation—making for an uncommon narrative.

Summer begins by presenting to us the dilemma of Kate Brown, wife to a neurologist and mother to four grown-up children—the youngest of whom is nineteen years old. Kate had abandoned the fast track to career advancement in order to raise the children and support her husband's professional ascent. At the opening of the novel, Kate finds herself at a loose end as 'this was the first time in her life that she was not wanted. She was unnecessary.'[4] A sense of redundancy characterises her life. The flexibility she has cultivated for 'over nearly a quarter of a century,'[5] adapting to the requirements of others, is no longer of consequence. Despite her unwillingness, she is pushed into the category of the more than middle-aged. Kate Brown, approaching her fiftieth year, is grappling with the processes of ageing—like Janna and Joyce.

What is the significance of looking at the lives of these older women? Does an understanding of their lives as old people or old women contribute to our understanding of human possibilities or enable us to re-evaluate human potential? Does this reading of the lives of older women enable us to rethink, de-essentialise and reformulate concepts regarding womanhood? Erica Jong is emphatic in her denial of any such possibility being offered within Lessing's novel. 'For all her occasional polemicism, Doris Lessing has no program for womankind nor for civilization', she declares at the end of her reading of *Summer*.[6]

Despite conceding uneasily that 'feminists have crucial insights to bring to bear on other struggles', feminist Toril Moi warns emphatically of the dangers in feminists' universalising of women's problems. 'For all its virtues, feminism is not a global discourse addressing all possible forms of oppression and exploitation.'[7]

However, studies in social anthropology express a different opinion by drawing attention to ageing. The processes of ageing, as Lamb points out, 'cut across all of our bodies and lives; they play a central role in how we construct gender identities, power relations, and the wider social and material worlds we inhabit'.[8]

Taking a cue from anthropological studies of this kind, Barbara Macdonald also sees ageing as a problem with universal relevance and she accuses women's studies and feminist theorists of having made invisible the lives of women over sixty.[9]

She warns that ignoring 'the meaning and the politics of the lives of women beyond' their 'reproductive years' is evidence of 'male thinking' and she emphasises that 'ageism is a central feminist issue'.[10]

Lessing's documentation of the old in *Summer* and *Diaries* provides valuable insights for theorising about the ways in which men and women are constituted as gendered beings. Both novels echo concerns along the lines first voiced by feminist anthropologist Sherry Ortner in the 1970s.[11] Ortner states unequivocally that the subordination of women is universal and that this condition is not because of biological reasons but due to culturally defined value systems in most societies, which follow the logic of prioritising 'culture' over 'nature'. Women's procreative functions thus become the basis for the formulation of their social roles. Based on the emphasis on their bodily functions, women become invariably associated with nature while men are located in the realm of culture. Challenging this binary division as one that is ideologically constructed, Ortner argues that women participate in culture as much as men do and that this needs to be recognised.

Lessing's observation that women in Western culture remain 'usually tucked away, generally in a subordinate position' within 'dominantly male structures'[12] seems acquiescent with the arguments put forward within anthropological studies in the 1970s and the early 1980s. Coincidentally, Lessing's novels around the 1970s deal with the subject of old age at a time when interest in ageing and geriatrics began gaining visibility.[13]

This chapter examines Lessing's exploration of the processes of ageing in the light of anthropological studies, drawing from their analysis that ageing is not merely a biological process but one that is socially constructed. Providing a close reading of her novels as the starting point for discussing the cultural construction of gender, I will trace how an understanding of ageing enables a critique of prevalent social practice and aligns itself to feminist dialectics of relationships, association and transcendence.

Gerontology and Geriatrics: Body Politics within Medical and Sociological Studies

The word 'geriatrics' actually came into use in medical parlance in 1909, when it was coined by Nascher[14] to refer to the study of ailments afflicting old people. Geriatrics comes from *geras* and *iatrikos,* referring to old age and physician respectively. Paralleling a discipline such as 'paediatrics', this new term announced the presence of the old and the necessity of considering senility and other associated diseases within a separate place in medicine. Geriatric study has become an area of interest only in recent decades, and this perhaps has to do with the fact that it is only in the twentieth century that the benefits of medicine and better standards of nutrition and living for a larger number of people have been so widespread.[15] There were, in terms of actual statistics, more old people alive and well in the world over the decades around the end of the 1960s than at any other point in history.[16]

The use of the term geriatrics, however, has contributed to a false notion about ailments that old people are subject to—these are often considered as specifically designated to the lot of the aged. In fact, it has been pointed out that attribution of such diseases primarily to old age is erroneous as physiological ageing manifests much earlier—in 'the 25th year of life'.[17] Also, most ailments originate in one's middle age and simply get aggravated in old age or are sometimes present in multiple-form within the same body. Geriatrics has thus unintentionally contributed towards making the normal pathological. This has resulted in the creation of the old and ageing as a separate category and has also had the effect of isolating them, heightening their sense of distance from the mainstream—comprising the young, the able-bodied, the mobile and the economically independent. The blinkered perspective with which the old are identified within medical care systems in the West has been further complicated by policy debates in the United States in the 1990s, regarding the extent of medical care a society should provide its very old.[18] As a medical category, the classification 'geriatric' often results in dehumanising and humiliating older persons.

In *Diaries,* we are shown the reduction of Maudie Fowler's self-worth and a diminishing of her selfhood on occasions when she visits doctors, or when experts on cancer or geriatric medicine attend to her. While she lies on a hospital bed, a doctor practising geriatric medicine arrives with a large group of students to diagnose and discuss her problem. Her rights as an older woman are not under consideration; instead, she has been objectified as a case study in the final stages of cancer. He holds forth on the typical and atypical aspects of her case and in effect dehumanises her. He pronounces that she has moved into a coma when in fact Maudie can hear him, despite being in great pain.[19] This process of depersonalisation that Maudie is subjected to is not an isolated instance. Lessing provides a similar account of her experience in a hospital, in her autobiography *Walking in the Shade.*[20]

Referring to attitudes reflected in social policy concerning ageing in Britain, Frank Glendenning draws attention to the growing sense of alarm with which Britain's ageing population is greeted.[21] Ageing, it becomes clear, is treated as a pathological condition not only within the field of medicine and medical care. The negative stereotyping of the elderly is also socially structured. Glendenning goes on to show that in Britain, the Conservative government rolled back the welfare state and cut the social security budget by 7,000 million pounds between 1979 and 1984 while the defence budget recorded an increase of around 9,500 million pounds over the same period.[22] Parallels could be drawn to similar budgetary quotas allotted in many countries around the world.

Peter Townsend draws attention to the role played by the state in structuring a condition of dependency among the elderly by creating a retirement age; thus, virtually introducing forced unemployment.[23] The viewing of an elderly population as an economic burden and as a social embarrassment is paradoxical, given that the yardstick of a developed nation has been characterised by a fall in the death rate. Yet, as Townsend makes clear:

> [s]ociety creates the framework of institutions and rules within which the general problems of the elderly emerge and, indeed, are manufactured. Decisions are being taken everyday, in the management of the economy and in the maintenance and development of social institutions, which govern the position which the elderly occupy in national life, and these also contribute powerfully to the public consciousness of different meanings of ageing and old age.[24]

The old are seen as a burden by the state; adequate funds are not directed to their maintenance and the care and support extended to them in terms of facilities like Home Helps, Good Neighbours and Meals on Wheels, as *Diaries* highlights, does not contribute to the emotional quotient of their lives in the way that extended families and friends may have done. Maudie Fowler, Eliza Bates and Annie Reeves—three women we meet in *Diaries*—testify to the neglect, decrepitude and poverty that an estimated six million elderly people in Britain are reported to be living in, reduced once again to dreary statistics.

Maudie, Annie and Eliza led productive lives in their younger days. Maudie worked as a house help when her father remarried after her biological mother's death. Next, she was apprenticed to a hatmaker and went on to make a bad marriage. Her son from this marriage was stolen by her husband. Annie was a waitress from 'fourteen to seventy, when she was retired against her will.'[25] Eliza was in service, worked as a cook and was married to a man who predeceased her. All three women survived great odds with very little support from the powerful vectors in their life, the husband, the father, the employer and then the state. Now, in their old age, they were left with little money and very few emotional bonds. Consequently, their advancing years show them as suffering from economic as well as emotional deterioration. 'Every street has in it several, perhaps a dozen, old women, old men, who can only just cope, or suddenly can't cope; who dream of absent daughters and sons and granddaughters'.[26] How then do these old men and women survive? They subsist because of the interaction provided by other humans, albeit on a reduced scale.

The header 'A Day in the Life of a Home Help' in the *Diaries* highlights the harried lives of employees who are on the payroll of the council.

> She may be . . . any nationality, but she is unqualified and has a dependant of some kind or children, so that she needs a job she can fit in around her family. She is young, or at least not elderly, for you need strength for this work. She has bad legs/a bad back/chronic indigestion/womb trouble.[27]

Packing in a long day tending to the requirements of her family of three children and a husband—fixing their meals and getting them ready for their schools—Bridget shops for four old people, checking to see what provisions they need. She also buys their medicines, supervises maintenance work, puts away all the groceries, fetches the doctor etc., and is also supposed to provide them with company. Often Bridget does more than she is required to, having developed an attachment to Eliza Bates or to paralysed Hilda Brent's little daughter Rosie. Once, in a crisis, she babysits the little girl till eight in the evening instead of dropping her off at three in the afternoon as usual, since her mother had to be rushed to the hospital. Such situations occur quite often in Bridget's life.

The narrative voice draws attention to the wearying and never-ending nature of daily chores in Bridget's life: '[t]here is a lot of cleaning she should be doing, but she seldom has time for her own place in the week. Bridget does not work at weekends. That is, she does not work as a Home Help.'[28] Maureen, another of the Home Helps, whom Janna dislikes and suspects of stealing money from the old people allocated to her 'presents herself always as very busy (true), kind-hearted, overworked (true), devoted to her charges.'[29] While along with Janna one may suspect Maureen's devotion to her charges or her dedication to the work allocated to her, the narrative clearly indicates that the nature of work required of her is both physically strenuous and inadequately remunerative. Bridget's genuine kindness, which makes her volunteer for additional work whenever the occasion demands it, has less to do with the money she makes and springs altogether from her own generous, magnanimous spirit.

The Audit Commission of 1986 on community care highlights the uneven nature of services provided to the elderly and the absence of a national policy on care.[30] The cutback on welfare, the erratic nature of the services provided to the old and the absence of well-qualified and well-paid staff testify to what feminist economists identify as a feminisation of work.[31] It becomes important to remember that the caregivers to whom the aged are entrusted in most societies provide voluntary care.[32] Care thus tends to be classified as 'work' that is essentially non-productive in economic terms and thereby accorded low priority. There is perhaps a need to re-evaluate the significance of 'care', which is an essential prerequisite and marker of human value.

Other than providing sociological details of the lives of the elderly, *Diaries* is also a fictional narrative dealing with the interiority of old women. Such enquiry into the lives of old women has remained largely outside the ambit of fictional representation. Ageing as a condition has occupied a social space that has several parallels with women's lives. It has been seen as a condition that exists but belongs to the private, personal realm of experience. The silence that surrounds women's lives once they move past category '(e)' extends to the lives of the old.

Ageing has also been one of the more carefully concealed aspects of human existence, one whose presence is silently acknowledged but whose concerns are constantly shelved or shifted to the peripheries of social preoccupation. Since the old tend to be economically unproductive they are viewed as a liability. They thus tend to remain invisible, and their lives rarely attract interest.

As Janna confesses:

> [b]efore a few weeks ago, I did not see old people at all. My eyes were pulled towards, and I *saw*, the young, the attractive, the well-dressed and handsome. And now it is as if a transparency has been drawn across that former picture and there, all at once, are the old, the infirm.[33]

When Janna points out to Joyce that there were no old women among the images of women in *Lilith*, and that this lacuna must be rectified, her observation elicits a vague response from Joyce: '[o]h, but why? It's not our age group.'[34] When confronted with the fact that all women have mothers and grandmothers, Joyce sidesteps it with the possibility of including the old in a later issue—in a feature that could be entitled 'Elderly Relations'[35]—and silently gesticulates for an end to this discussion. Joyce is unwilling to include ageing and elderly women in the current issue of Lilith which is going to press. Her seeing them as irrelevant echoes her internalisation of patriarchal practice and is not too far off from the laws in practice in Margaret Atwood's chilling fiction *The Handmaid's Tale* (1985) where women are valued only if they can provide heirs or do substantive menial work. The women who did not fit into any of those two categories were simply destroyed.

Recognising that Joyce's reluctance stems from her unwillingness to think about ageing as an eventuality in her life, Janna observes: '[h]ow afraid we are of age: how we avert our eyes.'[36] This horror of old age and a refusal to broach the subject, Janna acknowledges, was her response too until her recent revelatory learning experience with the world of the old. Joyce's automatic, unthinking response echoes the fact that ageing in the literary, cultural and social imagination has remained a clinical, pathological term. Referring to a phase of bodily existence outside the norms of productivity, means of employment or exchange as well as aesthetics and associated with loss of power and control, ageing seldom strikes the powerful and the youthful as a subject of sustainable interest.

On the other hand, increasing material progress and the multifaceted nature of contemporary existence has continued to contribute to a preoccupation with the pursuits of the young and the able-bodied. This has been the visible trajectory followed by fiction as well—whether it is the *bildungsroman* narratives or the portraits of artists as young men, all of them conclude at a moment in the protagonist's life when he/she is at his/her best thinking and acting self and in the prime of his/her life. Fiction thus has more often than not imitated or furthered the direction of contemporary society in its strident celebration of youth, the development of egos, *eros* and identities. Literature and ideology have repeatedly celebrated, propelled and propitiated the energies and aspirations of being young, able-bodied and productive. Such a context would hold for any cosmopolitan metropolis anywhere in the world and this has consequently allowed us to turn ageing into 'the great unmentionable', to borrow a phrase from Martha Quest's father.[37] Old age has also invariably been represented as a site of terror. In the ancient Hindu epic the Mahabharata, old King Yayati is shown as yearning for the pleasures of youth now irrevocably lost to him as a result of a curse. Yayati pleads with each of his five sons to take on the mantle of advanced age and grey hair, in exchange for sole heirship of his kingdom. The older sons refuse. Eventually, Yayati manages to persuade his youngest son who agrees, one might surmise, out of a sense of duty to an eccentric parent and possibly because he possessed little understanding of what ageing entailed, being furthest from the nature of old age. In the instance of King Lear—an old man who occupies centre stage as a king in a position of power—his travails begin once he cedes power and control to two of his daughters. Lear's madness and eventual death are played out as a loss of power, seen as inevitable with age.

Another instance is that of the struldbrugs—decrepit and eccentric, in the third book of *Gulliver's Travels*. Swift's imaginative rendering of the struldbrugs is a horrifying picture of what prolonged age can mean. Yet another case in point is Tennyson's 'Tithonus'. Having asked for immortality and received cruel, consuming age instead, he can only bewail his fate. The old woman sighted in Virginia Woolf's

Mrs Dalloway (1925) quickly draws the curtains across her window so that we cannot glimpse anything more of her life. The closure is also indicated by the demands of life and literary convention, wherein old women are required to be scarcely seen or heard. Iris Murdoch's *Bruno's Dream* (1969) is a more recent variant of the loss of power and mobility that the old face. Across cultures, old age is invariably reviled and viewed as constituting an unpleasant phase of life.

The phenomenon of ageing is usually represented in fiction as a terrible experience, one to be avoided at all costs. The old in fiction are also placed outside the structures of power and public life, in the shadowy grey areas of personal, private narratives. Lear's moment of reprieve comes with Cordelia's arrival and the love and care she extends. No such reprieve exists for the struldbrugs since mortality eludes them altogether. Bruno's peaceful journey into the night comes at the end of a long illness that his once unknown daughter-in-law and sister support him through.

The loss of power and control that is so often attributed to old age needs to be viewed as part of a social and political structure that requires urgent re-examination. Why does the institution of the state the world over retire people, relieving them of their positions of responsibility once they attain a certain chronological age? Is this arbitrary decision part of an inbuilt system of selection practised by patriarchal ideologies everywhere? If this is the case, then despite having equal rights and opportunities on paper, the aged invariably get short shrift. Such an ideology is unequivocally entrenched in merely ensuring the 'survival of the fittest' in the long run. The old fall outside the categories of interest and investment.

New Journeys and Discoveries: Kate Brown and Janna Somers

Kate Brown and Janna Somers's perceptions of old age at the beginning of *Summer* and *Diaries* are not very singular. Yeats would have declared the world that they inhabited and lived in was 'no country for old men'—or old women, for that matter. Like everyone else, Kate and Janna are shown as engrossed in their lives, preoccupied with their bodies, their clothes, their domestic arrangements and their routines.

Kate Brown re-enters the corporate world when she is hired by Global Foods at a time of crisis management. A visitor to their house—observing her early training in languages and her skill at organising her home and family—recommends her for this job. Having managed a family for years, Kate demonstrates her flair for interpersonal relationships by successfully attending to all the assembled delegates at the seminar. All of this happens at a time when she has distanced herself mentally from both the pleasures of a high-flying career and playing a pivotal role within her family. She has begun to understand that she has allowed herself and her identity to be worn away completely: '[i]f life had to be looked at in terms of high moments, or peaks, then nothing had "happened" to her for a long time; and she could look forward to nothing much but a dwindling away from full household activity into getting old.'[38]

Janna Somers in *Diaries* is an independent woman—owning a flat, with a substantial work experience that reveals her remarkable professional capabilities. Moving up the rungs in an up-market magazine, she has spent her productive years learning the right rules to success, style and specialisation in a very individualistic, corporate, male world. Having internalised essentially masculine axioms of discipline and hard work and pared-down everything outside of her work, Janna is professionally in the top bracket. She leads a public life where she is feted and admired. Measured by any conventional yardstick, her high-flying and glamorous lifestyle—with its quality of work, travel, food and leisure—is a mark of her success in a First World metropolitan city. It is at this point in her career that we meet Janna. Janna is a role model worth emulating—especially in these days of media blitzkrieg, where beautiful women with fabulous careers tumble out of magazines, television and the cinema at the turn of a page or the touch of a knob.

Janna, like Kate, is initially wrapped up in her synchronised and orderly life. The death of her husband is closely followed by the death of her mother, and these events could have easily been recorded by her in terse sentences such as Meursault's 'Mother died today. Or maybe yesterday; I can't be sure.'[39] Their illness, their pain and suffering do not impinge themselves upon her at all. She is not touched or altered by the experience of the deaths of two people very close to her. Her response to their illness is to bury herself in her work. She responds to their deaths by carrying on with her professional life and shutting away all her emotions. There is nothing very extraordinary about her unfeeling state. Camus' protagonist also shocks the reader by the matter-of-fact announcement of his mother's death. Janna's response to suffering and death is insulated effectively by the glamorous world of London. Lessing records her reactions as symptomatic of the times Janna lives in. Janna, at this stage in the narrative, represents the heights that successful and self-centred individuality can reach—given the impetus of free enterprise and opportunity. Yet Janna's achievements shut out the entire real world around her, cushioned as she is by the paraphernalia of her life as a wealthy achiever.

What is new in the narrative is that Janna is playing out a role that traditionally would be attributed to the male of the species, both in the literary text and outside of it. Instead, here we have a woman embodying all the stock-in-trade characteristics of the man, whose control of history, ideas, culture and public space has allowed him to project an unfeeling façade and get away with it. Janna, at the beginning of her narrative, is a woman whose achievements are at par with men having been garnered by internalising and accepting all the rules of the patriarchal game.

At the beginning of their narratives, the lives of Kate and Janna provide a study in contrast. Yet, both Kate and Janna are made to rethink their lives. Kate is pushed into a job and onto a subsequent journey which sets off the process of discovery. Kate, we are told, was trying to catch hold of something, or lay it bare so that she could make sense of what was troubling her:

> for some time now she had been 'trying on' ideas like so many dresses off a rack. . . . The truth was, she was becoming more and more uncomfortably conscious not only that the things she said, and a good many of the things she thought, had been takendown off a rack and put on, but that what she really felt was something else again.[40]

Janna, on the other hand, moves in the opposite direction—from a full-time job to one that is more flexible and part-time. Speaking of the minimal time she spends in her flat, Janna observes that when she is at home, she thinks a lot.

> This way of thinking . . . it is not so much thinking as holding things in your mind and letting them sort themselves out. If you really do that, slowly, surprisingly results emerge. For instance, that your ideas are different from what you had believed they were. There are things I need to *think* out, which I haven't got around to yet.[41]

Kate's journey into Istanbul, and then further into Spain with Jeffrey does not work out as both of them had planned it. Jeffrey falls very ill in a remote village and waiting for him to recover, Kate catches the virus. She decides to leave for London, checks into a hotel in Bloomsbury and surrenders herself to a long period of illness. When she recovers, she has lost her hair colour and fifteen pounds in weight and her clothes hang on her frame like a sack. When she musters the energy to make a trip to her old home that has been let out for the summer, in this condition, she finds that neither her neighbour Mr Hatch nor her friend Mary recognises her. Suddenly it dawns on Kate that not only has she outlived her central role within the family despite abiding by all the rules, but her external identity has also been chiefly determined by a system of codes that she has followed. Her identity now seems to be constructed entirely around how she has projected herself through clothes and accessories.

> Her closest friend had not known her: a loss of weight, a hat put on any how, probably a walk that dragged, the fact that Mary imagined her somewhere on the shores of the Mediterranean—these small things had been enough for Mary not to recognize a woman she had seen every day of her life for years; all that had been needed was that Kate should play a very slightly different role from the usual one.[42]

The discovery that one's external identity is carefully constructed and directed along certain fixed parameters is reiterated for her when she watches a production of Turgenev's *A Month in the Country*. She had seen the play a few years ago with Michael and identified very strongly with the central character Natalya Petrovna who, in the process of growing old, becomes 'the mirror of every woman in the audience who has been the centre of attention and now sees her power slip away from her.'[43] Distanced from the play now—since she is examining the process of growing old for herself, instead of merely internalising it—Kate becomes very critical of such projections of women desirous of holding on their youth and beauty. This desperation—presented as the only alternative available to women to counter the ravages of time and age—irks Kate.

Recognising that she had also confined herself to similarly limited dimensions, Kate asks herself incredulously:

> had she really spent so many years of her life—it would almost certainly add up to years!—In front of a looking glass? Just like all women. Years spent asleep, or tranced. . . . And now the image had rolled itself up and thrown itself into a corner, leaving behind the face of a sick monkey.[44]

Lolita, Madame Bovary and Natalya Petrovna—three fictional characters referred to in *Summer*—continue to function primarily as the only available literary prototypes for older women.

The fact that they are only literary representations and that their lives need not be emulated as the only choices available for women is an understanding that Kate arrives at eventually. She supplements this understanding with a new self-discovery. Kate begins to recognise that the choices she makes in projecting herself contribute to how people perceive her. By dressing down, she can deflect attention away from herself. Kate learns a lot from the little charades that she enacts while at Global Foods. 'Soon she discovered that if she wanted to be alone, she should sit badly, in a huddled or discouraged posture, and allow her legs to angle themselves unbecomingly. If she did this, men did not see her. She could swear they did not.'[45]

Away from her job and convalescing in a small room off the canal in London, she finds that in public space—whether she is awaiting service at a restaurant or walking up and down the street—her clothes and body language make all the difference. As an unkempt, carelessly dressed woman, nobody pays her any attention. 'She received indifferent glances, which turned off her at once, in search of stimulus. Again, she might have been invisible'.[46] To her surprise, this invisibility more than disconcerts her. Clamouring for attention that she feels should have been hers by right, Kate suppresses

> impulses so far from anything she had ever had, or could have imagined as hers, that she was shocked by them as if reading about them in a newspaper. She knew that if she were not careful, she would march up to one of these groups of lolling men and lift up her skirts to expose herself: *There*, look at that, I'm here, can't you see? Why don't you look at me?[47]

At this juncture, she finds it necessary to assert her female identity and have it validated by the public gaze. Her next step is to attire herself in a close-fitting shift and register the satisfaction of once again 'drawing glances and needs after her with every step.'[48] Kate's analysis of this situation exposes the code that might explain the reasons for this pattern of behaviour.

> A woman walking in a sagging dress, with a heavy walk, and her hair—this, above all—not conforming to the prints made by fashion, is not 'set' to attract men's sex. The same woman in a dress cut in this or that way, walking with her inner thermostat set just so—and click, she's fitting the pattern.
>
> Men's attention is stimulated by signals no more complicated than what leads the gosling; and for all of her adult life, her sexual life, let's say from twelve onwards, she had been conforming, twitching like a puppet to those strings. . . .[49]

This is a crucial moment in *Summer* and must be read carefully. Kate's repetitive enactment of her ritual preparation to meet the quintessential male gaze[50] is one that modulates women's lives; not only within the cinema screen but also outside of it. Her decision to step out of it must be seen as the beginnings of an expansive selfhood, where she will no longer be bound by convention. The change that is seen in Kate is neither drastic nor dramatic. It is a quiet decision that becomes transformative for her.

> Her experiences of the last months—her discoveries, her self-definition, what she hoped were now strengths—were concentrated here: here she would walk into her home with her hair undressed, with her hair tied straight back for utility; rough and streaky, and the widening grey band showing like a statement of intent.[51]

Externally, all that changes is her hairstyle. Yet, it becomes a statement of the new declaration that she has made to herself. Unlike the birds displayed in the zoo who have been confined to a cage for about fifty years, Kate has been able to step out and see her life as part of a larger continuum—framed against the lives of people other than her immediate family. How do we read this decision of Kate's?

As Gayle Greene points out 'Kate's progress consists mainly of repudiations of the conventions that have defined her . . . socialization as a sex object, mother, wife and woman in love.'[52] The nature of her experience could be seen as liberating. Kate's new-found convictions come from inner resources. She develops a new dimension of perception wherein she no longer evaluates herself or her life based on 'highs and lows' but understands it in the context of a larger experience of which she is a part. Growing old offers revelatory freedoms for Kate.

Is this personal freedom enough? Elaine Showalter does not think so. Attributing the belief in the power base found within the individual to Woolf and her generation, Showalter opines that such 'feminine consciousness'—while it asserted its 'superiority to the public, rationalist masculine world' and promised an alternative source of experience and self-esteem—only resulted in legitimising old stereotypes. Dismissing Woolf and her disciples as having 'elevated passivity into a creed', Showalter goes on to announce that the arrival of novelists who are women continues 'a phase of female self-discovery and self-scrutiny in forms and vocabularies very different from those employed by Woolf.'[53] What precisely is this different phase of 'female self-discovery and self-scrutiny'?

Showalter's reply to this is in concurrence with Sheila Rowbotham's analysis that 'the fortunes of new feminism will depend on our capacity to relate to the working class and the action of working-class women in transforming women's liberation according to their needs.'[54] Showalter declares the presence of 'a female voice that has rarely spoken for itself in the English novel—the voice of the shop girl and the charwoman, the housewife and the barmaid. . . . As the women's movement turns to these silent women, they may find their voice at last.'[55]

Ordinary women also make their presence felt in *Summer* and *Diaries*. Kate Brown's voice, one must remember, is also that of the housewife who discovers plural spaces outside of the conventional space of youth, sexuality and power that she has resided within. The extra dimension of age is added to her experience. Her journey—which is personal, and perhaps private—is of little significance when examined in any other context. Kate Brown's experience in London and the relationship she builds up with the younger Maureen articulates aspects of women's lives that usually remain unheard. Kate's protective and thoughtful treatment of a younger woman—reminiscent of Martha Quest's relationship with the next generation in *The Four Gated City*—is part of an altogether new perspective incorporated by Lessing in her fiction. In the context of public discourse, women seldom connect since they are usually competing with each other over men. This is what conventional narratives have led us to believe time and again. Along with the extra dimension of age, mature friendships between women is an experience that is reiterated through each of Lessing's novels, from the 1960s onwards.

Diaries offers a similar account of the personal experiences of old women. Lessing's women in *Diaries* belong to the social spaces from which Showalter and Rowbotham see new life being instilled into the women's movements. These voices, despite being those of women on the threshold of old age, are the new figures that Showalter hopes will take charge and make the tradition of the English novel worthwhile. Yet these voices in Lessing's novels do not speak in the fiery language of revolution that Showalter prophesies but hint at subtle possibilities and shifts in perspective that seem to offer a richer and more textured understanding of life's nuances.

In *Summer*, a young man dreams of revolutions that will stem the rot. Philip is a product of the indoctrination of a right-wing political group referred to as 'the fascists'.[56] The group's brand of politics veers towards jingoism, a readiness to dirty one's hands and an insistence on discipline and order that is offset by the aggressive pragmatism that 'you can't make an omelette without breaking eggs.'[57] Kate's reflection that increasingly 'political attitudes seemed like the behaviour of marionettes, or little clockwork figures wound up and continuing to display their little gestures while they were being knocked about and around and blown in all directions in a typhoon'[58] shows how political groups motivated by a particular ideology or its opposite would be a recurring pattern in the lives of each generation. Meanwhile, social change is recorded through the increasing presence of conglomerates such as Global Food, with vast resources and international delegates, that set up seminars all over the world. These conglomerates seem poised to set in motion new structures of dominance and control that would require new strategies of negotiation and resistance. It is in the face of such change that the vulnerability of the old becomes even more poignant.

From Liberal Feminism to New Feminisms

In the 1960s, women in the West protested against the dominant culture in which they saw themselves incorporated as second-class participants. They rallied around demands that focused on equal rights and access to knowledge and power, as well as legal and political rights. This was feminism's agenda: a 'specific kind of political discourse: a theoretical and political practice committed to the struggle against patriarchy and sexism'.[59] This was a vital phase in the incipient stages of the women's movements in the West and the most viable stance to take in the context of the disadvantaged position of women.

Feminism's initial struggle for a foothold within patriarchal structures has, however, resulted in the equating of the experience of privileged women with that of privileged men. Most of liberal feminism's battles have been fought from this plank. There seem to be two possibilities available here—the idea of a woman who emerges from a state of victimhood and subsequently triumphs over odds, becoming equal to man. In connection to this, valuable inputs are provided by the popular song 'Why can't a woman be more like a man?'[60] This song is a fascinating reminder of how women's demands for rights withheld by patriarchal cultures saw a slow but perceptible shift—to a position where demands for equality resulted in the complete erasure of differences between men and women and in the reiteration of extant hierarchies. As the song suggests, if women were more like men, there would be very few problems.

The important question to ask—while accepting that the feminist agenda calls for rectification in patriarchal hierarchies—is whether feminism at the end of the twentieth century must continue to operate as a reaction against existing systems of oppression? Can feminism also express itself in more proactive ways? It is in this light that the articulation of new feminist ethics provides valuable insights. Lessing's novels, which have been coterminous with several decades of the women's movements, seem to concur with these insights.

A significant feature of Lessing's narratives is the presence of increasingly older protagonists. Other than the adolescent Martha Quest, middle-aged or older women have been part of Lessing's narrative strategies from the early 1960s. Martha Quest eventually grows into middle age and beyond. Lessing's incorporation of old age as an aspect of women's lives and her detailing of the waning years must be read as an indicator of proactive feminism because her narratives extend women's lives as never before.

Janna's jet-setting lifestyle—displaying a self-absorbed individualism and a complete surrender to the demands of her work—has consequences. Her relationship with her husband and her natal family—comprising of her mother, sister, sister's husband and children—remains skewed. Her almost non-existent personal life, juxtaposed with her high-profile public life, is presented as a challenge to patriarchal prescriptions for men. This situation, perfect in the context of liberal feminism, has a female Janna successfully living out a stereotypical male existence.

This is our point of entry into the *Diaries*. At the end of the first section entitled *The Diary of a Good Neighbour,* there is a perceptible change in Janna's way of looking at life and people. By the time we get to *If the Old Could. . .*, the sequel, Janna speaks from a different perspective and has a whole new set of priorities. Both narratives—purporting to be part of an occasional, private diary—look closely at spaces inhabited primarily by women. In doing so, Lessing seeks to reassess and even rewrite earlier societal assumptions about the achievement of individualistic goals which are meant to constitute meaning in life.

It is pertinent to draw attention to the publication details of *The Diaries of Jane Somers* at this juncture. Lessing sent in this manuscript for publication under an anonymous pseudonym, that of an unknown 'Jane Somers'.[61] Lessing takes on a new persona to write this narrative in yet another literary form, that of the diary, which pre-dates the novel form itself. It would be useful to see Lessing's pseudonymous identity and use of the diary format as a deliberate attempt to bring attention to new directions in her work. We are supposed to be looking at an anonymous story, a story about an inner life, which does not even merit the artifice of the novel form. Freed from the too solid authority of being Doris Lessing, Jane Somers—an unknown author—tentatively offers her experiences and insights. Jane's early insights, one may recall, were rather discordant and not in keeping with what should have been elicited by following the codes and rules governing her life.

It is relevant that Lessing uses the form of the *Diaries* to deal with personal and subjective jottings and observations, often providing material that reveals a single person's insights into events or ideas. This material again is inchoate; it exists outside the formal structures of narrative that constitute the novel. What does Lessing hope to project or communicate through the use of this particular form? The reader's attention is once again drawn into an essentially personal world. This world has existed but has seldom been the subject of dissemination.

This is something Janna discovers in the course of the *Diaries*. Lessing focuses on Janna as she comes to terms with the ageing of her body and the possibility of sustaining friendships in old age. Her relationships with Maudie, Annie and Eliza, as well as Joyce and Richard, and her acceptance of the continuum of life and the shifting roles that it entails are described at length.

Janna Somers' life in London is a possible reworking of Woolf's *Mrs Dalloway*. The differences are striking because the two books were published around sixty years apart. Clarissa in *Mrs Dalloway* continues to be safely cushioned from the war, poverty, illness and insanity that exists in the world. Although the novel acknowledges the presence of this grim scenario, it remains peripheral to the interests of the privileged society that gathers at the dinner party hosted by the Dalloways. Janna, on the other hand, is no longer allowed to lead a sheltered life. From a place of privilege, she plunges into the lives of the disadvantaged by choice.

In *Diaries*, Lessing highlights and pinpoints the tensions inherent in public, essentially masculine roles when they are juxtaposed with private spaces. The earlier divide between the public world and the private realm that was once so distinguishable is now shown as contested space. By privileging Janna's personal life over that of her public life, the narrative of the *Diaries* inverts older hierarchies. Janna's *Diaries* become a record of all that is erased in order to achieve success. Like the notebooks that Anna Wulf maintains in *The Golden Notebook*, Janna's diaries draw attention to what is often overlooked.

The *Diaries* thus provide the format through which this loss is recorded and eventually remedied. Janna concedes this in the opening lines of *Diaries*: '[t]he first part is a summing-up of about four years. I was not keeping a diary. I wish I had. All I know is that I see everything differently now from how I did while I was living through it.'[62] Janna's *Diaries* are a record of private experience. The nature of this experience is not only very personal and important but also unfinished and unprocessed. Lessing uses this mode of narration to mediate between two entirely different sets of expectations.

Janna has lived a full and successful life within a patriarchal structure and she has done rather well for herself, even in terms of the limited patriarchal assumptions by which success is measured. Unlike the angry and bewildered Martha Quest, hers is not an existential quest for the self, but an attempt to understand the rules by which she has lived so far. In both diary narratives, a questioning and a re-evaluation are taking place. What is achieved in terms of space or alteration, on the face of it, seems rather minimal.

In the elite, suave and sophisticated world of London, Janna discovers the existence of other kinds of people through a chance encounter with an old crone. Her use of the words 'crone' and 'witch' to describe Maudie in the initial encounters are rather derogatory and dismissive. Robbing Maudie of all the vestiges of humanity that she possesses, Janna uses words that are in keeping with 'sexist attitudes' 'embedded in language' which display 'contempt for old women.'[63]

However, Janna's face-to-face encounter with Maudie Fowler is one of the most powerful juxtapositions that the text provides. This meeting of opposites could have been the basis for a mystical experience in an Eastern text, and the beginnings of a quest culminating in the establishment of a new faith.[64] In this narrative, it becomes the starting point for yet another journey that feminism must make—namely, address the questions of ageing and geriatrics in a society that has always had its pulse on the throbbing vitality of youth. Janna's middle age and Maudie Fowler's ninety years are disquieting in a world of youth culture and courtship.

As readers, we are drawn into viewing women's lives as they are lived—variously in the marketplace, in important jobs, in interpersonal relationships, and also in terms of societal expectations. The individual narratives of Janna and Maudie offer a sociological account of London from the beginning of the 1940s. Focusing on the lives of Maudie and other old women like her who depend on care sanctioned by the state but provided by harried women, Lessing also takes a long, hard look at the workings of the so-called welfare state.

In the first section of the *Diaries,* Lessing—through Janna—takes a close look at the fact of ageing and the spaces provided for such phenomena. Institutional care administered to the elderly has been the traditional responsibility of women in both pre-capitalist and post-industrial societies and continues to be so. The *Diaries* highlight the short shrift such activity receives in the world view of a patriarchal state.

Lessing's first five-volume anthology was called Children of Violence, and her work, in general, has chronicled the world wars. The old women in *Diaries* have also lived through a long history of wars and parliamentary processes. Maudie's story indicates that neither the passing of time nor the enactment of wars has been particularly transformative for the old. Despite the personal betrayal that Maudie faces due to her father's second marriage, her vagrant husband's desertion and subsequent abduction of her only child and the uncertainty of finances, she manages to survive. Maudie's doughty and feisty existence belies conventional assumptions.

One must also remember that as Maudie does not belong to the same social class as Janna, the possibility that the vicissitudes of her life will be addressed is remote. What then is the basis for the fascination that Maudie holds for both Janna and the reader—considering that the old and infirm are rarely the subject of either the imagination or the cynosure of the media? In terms of linear progression, they do not represent promise, erotica, challenge or power. This is the reason that they are rendered invisible.

In response to young Jim's unspoken question about the old, '*Why aren't they in a Home? Get them out of the way, out of sight, where young healthy people can't see them, can't have them on their minds!*' Janna wonders, 'How do we value ourselves? By what? Work?'[65] She concludes that the yardsticks available to her are of little help. Searching for an answer to this question, Janna is forced to look for meaning outside of identities constructed by the workplace and social value systems. For Janna, like Kate, the solution lies not in revolutionary change but in recognising and learning from new engagements and experiences.

Through Maudie—an old and angry woman with a tremendous passion for life—Janna learns to see beyond the perfectibility of the body and the enjoyment of material pleasure. She recognises how associations and relationships feed into the patterns of life. Here again, Lessing does not nostalgically celebrate the good times offered by the edifice of the extended family. Maudie and her sister do not get on, Annie's relatives do not visit her, Janna and her sister Georgie lead very different lives from each other and are as alike as chalk and cheese. Yet what we are offered in *Diaries* is a sense of how women's memories, associations and interactions tend to be rooted in interpersonal exchange. These moments of interaction are prioritised and made significant in the novel. Take, for instance, Janna's thoughts at a point of crisis in Joyce's life.

> Joyce *is* going to America. She will give up a wonderful job. Very few women ever get a job like this one. She will give up family, friends, home. Her children are nearly grown up. She will be in a country that she will have to learn to like, alone with a man who would have been happy to go with another, younger girl. *She has no choice.*
>
> Well, women's lib, well, Phyllis, what do you have to say to that?
>
> What, in your little manifestoes, your slamming of doors in men's faces, your rhetoric, have you ever said that touches this? As far as I am concerned, nothing.[66]

Gayle Greene points out that 'women's relations to work and to other women through work' is 'the locus of emotional intensity' in the novel. She is, however, troubled by 'Jane's denigration of "women's lib"' and finds Jane's reaction 'perversely obtuse' since '"women's lib" "manifestoes" are centrally concerned with "the power men have"'.[67] While *Diaries* does deal with women's work, 'the locus of emotional intensity' comes through women's relationships with one another, outside of the professional structures of work. Work is not the only space which the novel validates—even while the former provides for interaction and activity, possibly even allowing for the sparking of reciprocal interest.

It is not a lack of understanding of what 'women's lib manifestoes' offer that provokes Janna's outburst. Despite being aware of women's lib and the projected empowerment through retaliation—'slamming of doors in men's faces'[68]—Joyce decides to follow her husband. She is aware of limiting her options. Joyce's social and financial status is also very different from Maudie's. What is it that propels Joyce, then? Is it her commitment to her children and her recognition that they need both parents; because two people can parent better than one? Or is she unwilling to hold on to a job at the cost of family life? The suggestion being offered here is that while the financial and legal technicalities are written in black and white, the ways of reading and interpreting them may be vastly different.

This shift can be observed in Phyllis' case as well. Phyllis, an ardent campaigner for women's rights, falls in love with Charlie—a father of two children from an earlier marriage. After her marriage to Charlie, when a baby is born, Phyllis is loath to get back to work.

How do we interpret this act of hers? It would be easy to see both Joyce and Phyllis as women who were never compelled to struggle for their rights. Having gained access to rights too easily, were they only too willing to relinquish them? Since they cannot be classified as belonging to either the socialist or the working class, it would be easy to label them as reactionary and as having betrayed the women's cause. Yet, *Diaries* does not push towards such a reading. It presents choices as being far more complex.

Significantly, Joyce's marriage does not improve. On the other hand, Janna falls in love and it is reciprocated. Yet, Janna chooses to stay back in London instead of furthering her relationship with Richard by shifting to Canada. Such portrayal is a reminder that Lessing is not pushing for women's return to older stereotypes of being bound by love for a man. Again, while heterosexuality is the norm for most people we meet in the *Diaries*, male–female relationships in the novel continue to be only one important facet among many others. Female bonding is an equally serious aspect. Janna's niece is eventually adopted by a lesbian commune.

Another way of looking at the decisions made by Joyce, Phyllis and Janna would be to see the plurality of roles demanded of women in the course of a lifetime and to recognise that identities are not fixed, but shifting and fluid. This calls for new ways of perceiving, instead of being entangled in the rigidity of binary formulas. In such a context, the shifting contours of the body gain significance in time. In the world of feminist theory, the awareness that there is no escape from the human condition has led to an emphasis on the centrality of the body as a conduit for approximating human experience. This has resulted in a displacing of the Cartesian world view that proclaimed the superiority of the transcendental mind over the vagaries of the body.

What feminist theory has begun to reclaim is the primacy of the body over that of the mind. The unitary and universal self, posited by Cartesian reason, has been replaced by the multiplicity of situated bodies. This prioritisation of the body also indicates the possibility for conceptualising alternate ideologies that can allow for a dismantling of the binary and hierarchical oppositions of mind/matter and reason/emotion.[69] Such a dismantling allows for newer interpretations—in particular, the formulation of new feminist ethics. It also enables women to understand the life of the body as an ongoing process encountering the experiences of ageing, instead of being caught in a time warp between adolescence and early adulthood.

By locating herself along the graph of mortality and incorporating the plurality of existence and experiences within, Janna invests meaning and value in the relationships that she shares with various people—ranging from her delinquent niece Katherine, her promising niece Jill, Hannah, Phyllis, Joyce, Vera and Maudie to Annie and Elsa. While Janna gives us glimpses into the lives of other characters or accounts of them, it is her life whose interiority is expressed to the fullest. The narrative ends with her return home after having said goodbye to Richard.

> I look around at this quiet, white, cool, orderly room where soon, I know, into the emptiness will steal one by one, at first lacklustre and inconsiderable, but then familiar and loved, all the little innumerable pleasures and consolations of my solitude.
>
> I can see through the open door of my bedroom into my big living room. There is the grey linen sofa, immaculate now, and the two yellow chairs. Beyond are the windows where in black panes blur and blend the lights from the street.
>
> A stage set! House lights down . . . the sudden hush . . . the curtain goes up. . . .[70]

Janna's thoughts, which really constitute the whole of the *Diaries,* celebrate being alive in London amid a network of relationships and activities that have formed over the years. An earlier system of values that tended to disparage the personal and relational aspects of individual experience is looked at afresh, through Janna's narration.

The curtains that open at the end of *Diaries* announce the staging of a new chapter in feminism. Both parts of *Diaries* can be seen as an exploration in feminist ethics. Through the life and experience of Janna, Lessing asks some important questions with social and philosophical implications. What is it that Lessing directs our attention to? Evelyn Pezzulich refers to the emergence of a new literary genre—the '*reifungsroman*' or novel of ripening.[71] This new genre that Pezzulich identifies as an extension of a *bildungsroman* offers an entirely new framework wherein a long experiential phase of adult life can be examined. Extending its study to the full scope of human experience, Lessing's use of the *reifungsroman* in *Summer* and *Diaries* allows us as readers to discover a whole new perspective on growing old. The *reifungsroman* as a literary device could be appropriated as a significant narrative technique for showcasing women's writing. This technique demonstrates how feminist perspectives are structured around a whole host of issues that are very different from issues that have preoccupied patriarchy.

It is possible to see the *reifungsroman* as opening the doors for a re-examination of a whole range of post-Enlightenment philosophies. Questions of collective bonding, interpersonal relations, the gradual growing into age and the celebration of an ethics of care and interconnectivity occupy centre stage. These are given primary significance and are seen as more viable and of enduring value. Prioritising issues that preoccupy women both within the private and the public world, the *reifungsroman* opens up the discussion on women's contextual relationships. The narrative technique also seems to provide autonomy to women as moral agents.

This is a world where being at the top is not a priority. Similarly, little significance is attached to being in control and nobody is in a hurry to get anywhere. There is the pleasure of discovering the sights and sounds of a large city and responding to the pulsating pleasures of society in peacetime. Under the circumstances, the *reifungsroman* moves along slowly, capturing the textures and striations of a multiplicity of moments. In *Summer* and *Diaries,* we are repeatedly asked to consider the operation of individuals in a complex and heterogeneous world which cannot be summed up satisfactorily by any one kind of perspective. This insight enables a critique of extant hegemonic structures and a questioning of earlier assumptions. With this relocation of perspective, feminism is pushing towards a new philosophy.

While the impetus for feminism has come from the recognition that women do not need to be moulded into the formats that patriarchy, custom and ceremony have planned for them, attempts to circumvent such identities were often deflected by the recognition that the rewards at the end of the struggle were still distributed by patriarchal societies.

The need for a different way of interpreting lives and experience, then, becomes of paramount significance. Historically and sociologically, the time is ripe for feminism to evolve theoretical frameworks of its own. The raw materials of this will come out of women's experience. Stress has been laid on discovering new spaces, articulating them and perhaps moving on to different perceptions and conclusions. These seem to be the trends and directions in Western feminism. The stage is set for a shift from a male-centred universe to one of female plurality, where the articulation and celebration of similarity and difference could be enabling—both politically and philosophically. Alongside the recognition of the role of patriarchal structures in the oppression of women, the rise of new feminist ethics allows feminism in its protean forms to move in various directions and evolve its own systems of value. The novels that Lessing writes, particularly after the mid-1980s, resonate with this belief.

Endnotes

1. Doris Lessing, *The Diaries of Jane Somers* (Great Britain: Michael Joseph, 1984; Harmondsworth: Penguin Books, 1985), 29. Further references to the book are from the 1985 edition. The abbreviation *Diaries* will be used to refer to the book
2. For more information on this less-discussed female identity in ancient myth, see Christopher L.C.E. Witcombe, 'Eve and the Identity of Women,' last modified 2 October 2020, http://witcombe.sbc.edu/eve-women/.
3. Doris Lessing, *The Summer Before the Dark* (Great Britain: Jonathan Cape, 1973; Harmondsworth: Penguin Books, 1975). Further references to this book are from the 1975 edition. The abbreviation *Summer* will be used to refer to the book.
4. Lessing, *Summer*, 21.
5. Lessing, *Summer*, 21.
6. Erica Jong, '*The Summer Before the Dark*: Everywoman out of Love?' in *Critical Essays on Doris Lessing,* eds. Claire Sprague and Virginia Tiger (Boston: G.K. Hall & Co., 1986), 197.
7. Toril Moi in her essay 'Men Against Patriarchy', in *Gender and Theory*, ed. Linda Kauffman (Oxford and Massachusetts: Basil Blackwell, 1989), 182–185. Moi's clarification comes at a time when, historically, the Black women's movements and movements by women from other cultures such as Africa, Asia and the Middle East have articulated their dissonance with mainstream white feminism.
8. See the introduction of Sarah Lamb, *White Saris and Sweet Mangoes: Aging, Gender, and Body in North India* (Berkeley and London: University of California Press, 2000), 9.
9. Sarah Lamb cites Barbara Macdonald's words from her plenary session speech at the National Women's Studies Association in Seattle, 1985 in Lamb, *White Saris,* 9.
10. Barbara Macdonald, 'Outside the Sisterhood: Ageism in Women's Studies,' in *Women and Aging: An Anthology by Women*, eds. Jo Alexander et al. (Corvallis: Calyx Books, 1986), 20.

11. Sherry B. Ortner's influential essay 'Is Female to Male as Nature is to Culture?' (1974) argues that while the meaning, shape and value of being a woman was profoundly variable, it was the cultural and social value attached to universal features like domesticity and nature that tended to devalue women. Thus, an understanding of this logic made it possible to identify the basis for the universal devaluation of women wherein culture was associated with the male world and women were associated with nature by virtue of their physiological contributions to social life. The rest of the paragraph is a paraphrasing of Ortner's argument reproduced in Carol C. Gould, ed., *Key Concepts in Critical Theory: Gender* (New Jersey: Humanities Press, 1997), 16–24.
12. Doris Lessing in an interview in 1980 as cited by Claire Sprague, 'Galactic Orthodoxies,' in *Critical Essays on Doris Lessing,* eds. Claire Sprague and Virginia Tiger (Boston: G.K. Hall & Co., 1986), 211. Lessing's observation also holds true of women in cultures that are non-Western. Given the advancing globalisation that is a part of our lives today, cultures that have not been impacted by Western influence are few and far between.
13. Anthropologist Sarah Lamb dates the 1980s as the years that saw the beginnings of interest in a study of ageing. Lamb, *White Saris,* 8.
14. Dr Ignatz Nascher (1863), born in Vienna and brought up in New York, pioneered the study of geriatrics in the United States while Marjory Warren (1897) made her mark in the UK during the Second World War by single-handedly founding British hospitals for geriatrics.
15. Malini Karkal points out that this is a subject that still needs research and understanding. As an issue, ageing was first debated in the international community at the United Nations in 1948, next in 1969 and subsequently in 1982, which was when the United Nations held the first World Assembly on Ageing and adopted an International Plan of Action on Ageing. 1999 was declared the International Year of Older Persons. Malini Karkal, 'Ageing and Women in India,' *The Economic and Political Weekly* 34, no. 44 (October 30, 1999): 54–56.
16. Miriam Bernard, 'Older People in Britain: Demographic Trends and Social Circumstances,' in *The Elderly Population in Developed and Developing World: Policies, Problems and Perspectives*, eds. P. Krishnan and K. Mahadevan (New Delhi: B.R. Publishing Corporation, 1992), 185–189.
17. See in the special issue on Ageing, Dr M.S. Venkataraman, 'The Age-Old Problem,' *The Hindu Folio*, October 18, 1998, 13.

18. On this subject, see Lawrence Cohen in *No Aging in India: Alzheimer's, the Bad Family, and Other Modern Things* (Berkeley and London: University of California Press, 1998), 71. Cohen discusses the debate between ethicists like Daniel Callahan and American gerontologists on the issue of political incentives to cut Medicare and Medicaid facilities to the frail elderly.
19. Lessing, *Diaries*, 250.
20. Doris Lessing, *Walking in the Shade: Volume Two of My Autobiography, 1949 to 1962* (New York: HarperCollins, 1997), 326–327.
21. See Frank Glendenning, 'Some Issues of Social Policy in Britain's Ageing Society', in *The Elderly Population in Developed and Developing World: Policies, Problems and Perspectives*, eds. P. Krishnan and K. Mahadevan (New Delhi: B.R. Publishing House, 1992), 29–50.
22. Frank Glendenning, 'Some Issues of Social Policy,' 33.
23. Peter Townsend, 'The structured dependency of the elderly,' in *The Peter Townsend Reader*, ed. The Policy Press (Bristol: The Policy Press, 2010), 449–464.
24. Peter Townsend, 'The structured dependency of the elderly,' 452.
25. Lessing, *Diaries*, 176.
26. Lessing, *Diaries*, 154.
27. Lessing, *Diaries*, 189.
28. Lessing, *Diaries*, 202.
29. Lessing, *Diaries*, 366.
30. Frank Glendenning provides these statistics and cites the report of the Audit Commission in Glendenning, 'Some Issues of Social Policy,' 37–40.
31. Linda Nicholson argues that the social relations of women's paid jobs often replicate the social relations of the homes they have left. She describes this transference of gender roles from the home to the workplace as 'public patriarchy' in her essay. Linda Nicholson, 'Feminist Theory: The Private and the Public,' in *Feminism: Critical Concepts in Literary and Cultural Studies*, vol. 3, *Feminist Responses to Industrial Society*, ed. Mary Evans (London and New York: Routledge, 2001), 1–10.
32. The General Household Survey published in 1988 tabulates the following figures: Britain has a total of 6,000,000 carers out of which 4,500,000 care for elderly people. Four out of five carers look after parents or in-laws and the monetary value of this voluntary care works out between 15,000,000 to 24,000,000 pounds a year.
33. Lessing, *Diaries*, 29.

34. Lessing, *Diaries*, 28.
35. Lessing, *Diaries*, 28.
36. Lessing, *Diaries*, 28.
37. Lessing's father uses this phrase to describe the First World War in Lessing's account of her father's life in Doris Lessing, 'My Father,' *A Small Personal Voice: Essays, Reviews, Interviews,* ed. Paul Schlueter (United States: Alfred A. Knopf, 1974; New York: Vintage Books, 1975), 89. The reference corresponds to the 1975 edition.
38. Lessing, *Summer*, 9.
39. Albert Camus, *The Stranger*, trans. Stuart Gilbert (New York: Vintage Books, 1946), 4.
40. Lessing, *Summer*, 5–6.
41. Lessing, *Diaries*, 18. Ellipsis in original.
42. Lessing, *Summer*, 144–145.
43. Lessing, *Summer*, 147.
44. Lessing, *Summer*, 153.
45. Lessing, *Summer*, 44.
46. Lessing, *Summer*, 170.
47. Lessing, *Summer*, 170.
48. Lessing, *Summer*, 176.
49. Lessing, *Summer*, 176–177.
50. See Laura Mulvey, 'Visual Pleasure and Narrative Cinema,' *Screen* 16, no. 3 (Autumn 1975): 6–18.
51. Lessing, *Summer*, 230.
52. Gayle Greene, *Doris Lessing: The Poetics of Change* (Ann Arbor: University of Michigan Press, 1994), 128.
53. Elaine Showalter, *A Literature of Their Own: British Women Novelists from Brontë to Lessing* (New Jersey: Princeton University Press, 1977), 298. The rest of this paragraph is a reproduction of her argument.
54. Sheila Rowbotham, *Hidden from History: Rediscovering Women in History from the 17th Century to the Present* (London: Pluto Press, 1973), 169.
55. Elaine Showalter, *A Literature of Their Own,* 314.
56. Lessing, *Summer*, 179.
57. Lessing, *Summer*, 185.
58. Lessing, *Summer*, 185.
59. Toril Moi, *Sexual/Textual Politics: Feminist Literary Theory* (London and New York: Methuen, 1985), 19.

60. The lyrics of the song are by Allan Jay Lerner and the CD was produced by Stanley Holloway for recording by Goddard Lieberson, Sony and Music Entertainment, 1994. 'Why Can't A Woman Be More Like A Man,' Songfacts, last modified 2 October 2020, https://www.songfacts.com/facts/cast-of-my-fair-lady/why-cant-a-woman-be-more-like-a-man.
61. The manuscript was turned down by Jonathan Cape and Granada, her publishers in London. Michel Joseph, an American publisher who published her first novel, accepted the work as that by a new writer at face value, yet wrote to say that the book reminded them of Doris Lessing. See Lessing, preface to *The Diaries of Jane Somers,* 5–10. Lessing's name charade also draws attention to the business of publishing and the hierarchies that were in place in the 1980s.
62. Lessing, *Diaries,* 13.
63. See Florence Keyworth, 'Invisible Struggles: The Politics of Ageing,' in *Feminism, Culture and Politics,* eds. Rosalind Brunt and Caroline Rowan (London: Lawrence and Wishart, 1982), 131–142.
64. This, incidentally, is the story of Prince Siddhartha who suddenly encountered the aged, the diseased and the dead—an unplanned event in his princely life. Overwhelmed by the discovery of illness and ageing as part of the human condition, he renounced the world. After a spiritual revelation he became the Buddha, the founder of Buddhism. Oddly, the Buddha's abandonment of his wife and infant son for the purpose of seeking spiritual direction is never commented upon unfavourably.
65. Lessing, *Diaries,* 32–33.
66. Lessing, *Diaries,* 77.
67. Greene, *The Poetics of Change,* 201–204.
68. Lessing, *Diaries,* 77.
69. See Susan Bordo, 'Feminism, Postmodernism, and Gender-Skepticism,' in *Feminism/Postmodernism,* ed. Linda J. Nicholson (New York: Routledge, 1990), 133–56.
70. Lessing, *Diaries,* 510. Ellipses in original.
71. Evelyn Pezzulich, 'Coming of Age: The Emergence of the Aging Female Protagonist in Literature,' *Doris Lessing Studies* 24, no. 1–2 (Summer/Fall 2004), 7.

Conclusion

The entire world is battling the Covid-19 virus, which is our most recent pandemic. Many of us can only hope that we will tide over this highly infectious virus that seems to have spread its tentacles all over the planet. This is not the first pandemic that has led to large-scale deaths. In Europe, the plague or Black Death took its toll of lives in the fourteenth century between 1347 and 1351 and by 1610, the transmission of the smallpox virus wiped out Latin American populations.[1] Humans have won protracted battles against smallpox and septicaemia, typhoid and diphtheria in the subsequent centuries. In the twentieth century, after WWI, millions of lives were claimed by the Spanish flu, and closer to living memory, malaria, polio, mad-cow disease, dengue, and in recent times, swine flu, SARS flu and Ebola have ravaged lives. Pandemics, we must remember, have only increased suffering in an inequitable world. To make things worse, race, class, caste and religion have reared their ugly heads all over the world, turning hard-won changes in the previous centuries to nought.

Despite ominous portents and horrendous incidents, humans continue to pride themselves on being the supreme species—controlling the environment and manipulating the natural world and other species with the help of empirical science and its enabling technologies, with scant respect for codes. Yet, as the last forty years have begun to show us, we are a beleaguered civilisation and we seem to be running out of time; our efforts at control and domination with impunity have pushed the planet, its innumerable species and varied natural resources to the brink.

Although modern democracies have travelled long distances from the feudal hierarchies of power and domination, a small elite, more privileged than the rest, has replaced the singular power brokers of the previous centuries all over the world. Today, social distancing exists all over the world and the same elite has access to the sanctuary of lockdown and social distancing. Food, shelter, medical care and money are still not available in these democratic times to large segments of the population. This is a problem affecting lives everywhere in the world. It is becoming increasingly difficult to ignore the fact that at all times in the history of our world, the powerful and the privileged have led cushioned and comfortable lives in peacetime, and during crises and wars.

There cannot be two opinions about the fact that the powerful and the wealthy are responsible for the crisis that continues to engulf our lives and that the victims of this crisis, the poor, the disempowered, the ill and the old remain the most vulnerable.

This is a time as good as any for us to understand why some of the impulses that pushed humans to control and dominate our environment need to be re-examined as also the structures that allowed us to adopt certain patterns of living over others. For a lot of us, this space of the lockdown has involved going on several inner-space journeys and trying to read and think.

Old and new books from the bookshelf are brought down and leafed through to recollect, or gather newer insights in an effort to make sense of the world we live in. In previous centuries, when the word was with God, religious texts were mined for understanding. In our century, having escaped the penumbra of religion, we fall back quite often on the abundant literatures available to us which continue to inspire, inform, prophecy, admonish and sometimes provide sanctuary. At the start of the third decade of the twenty-first century, our world continues to be global in connectivity. Literature, poetry and music continue to be produced, despite being fragmented and splintered by all the battles of previous centuries, which are yet to cease. In fact, the battles of yore have morphed, slid away, resurfaced and taken on protean shapes and identities. The new science, new democracies, new knowledge and technologies, part and parcel of the world we live in, have become our driving impetus, significantly impacting lives all over the world.

This is a complex world, where all manner of specialisations and secondary occupations exist, and yet thankfully this world despite all the change has not outgrown the worlds of writing and reading. Even today, books serve as sentinels to exploration and understanding, in the way they have done for a very long time, keeping a record of things as they were, providing valuable inputs and analysis and also hinting at dystopian and utopian possibilities that could emerge. Despite prophetic warnings and dystopian projections, humans have continued to denude the world and refused to be accountable for their depredations upon each other, other life forms and natural resources.

In *The Theory of the Novel* (1916) George Lukacs speaks of the genre of the novel, as the representative art form of our age. This genre, that reached its apex in the nineteenth century, continues to occupy significant space well after a hundred years. Lessing herself, despite a lifetime of engagement with the writing of novels during the twentieth and the twenty-first century, identified cinema as the most important medium of the twentieth century. In many ways she was right. Film became an important medium, from the experimental talkies to sophisticated televised worlds that are now beamed down to us by a network of cables via satellites. It is becoming increasingly difficult to escape this compelling medium that both hyponotises and deadens as it intensifies in shrillness and graphic detail. However, Lessing's resistance to the idea of her books being turned into films explains clearly where her deeper affections lay. It also recalls for us the power invested in the written word that continues to be retained by the writer of poetry, fiction, history, philosophy and science.

As an academic, teacher and an avid reader, to my mind, the telling of a tale continues to be not only the oldest means of communication but also one of the most powerful. The skills of speech and writing, used to communicate based on a complex system of signs, are specific to the human species and it is from story, myth, history and detail that we draw sustenance. As humans evolved further, across cultures, religion and statecraft laid down codes that humans began to follow. While the control of religion and state shifted and altered with the advent of modernity, Literature continued to hold its ground and the genre of the novel with its ability to reflect, create, imitate and prophecy entire worlds, continued to provide insights and perceptions.

This capacity to spin words and build a world thereby is the special gift that writers bring to the world. Craftspeople par excellence, they weave the fabric of life and imbue it with meaning through their fiction. Doris Lessing was one such extraordinary craftsperson and I would like to conclude by looking closely at the questions that she raised for us and the directions she nudged her readers towards, during the journeys that she provided through the complex and vibrant genre of the novel. Lessing's novels question the strident humanism and optimism that have characterised the progress of the human race over the last few centuries. Lessing felt very strongly that only through an examination of the stories of the system's failures and misfits could answers be found to how, why and where humans have gone wrong. Replacing unbridled humanism with a probing and questioning feminism, Lessing's novels search for solutions in a world where individual achievements have been the benchmark for success for a very long time.

Conclusions are rather difficult to arrive at, especially if one is dealing with a prolific author of Lessing's stature, with eclectic interests and the ability to straddle different genres with ease. Previous sections of this book have closely examined novels written by Lessing between the decades of the 1950s and the 1990s. Lessing began writing as a young woman and was less than thirty years old when she signed her first contract for a manuscript before she set sail for London in 1948. There, she found a new publisher for the manuscript of *The Grass is Singing* by 1950. *The Grass is Singing* dislocates Mary Turner from the fictional tradition of white middle-class feminists who fought for freedom within the fictional worlds of innumerable narratives and real life.

Instead of a conventional narrative where the central protagonist would sail off into the sunset with the hero, having braved a lot of hostility from the environment that fostered her, Mary Turner is scythed to death. Moses, who kills her, is one of the many Black men hired to work on a white farm in colonial Southern Rhodesia. The narrative suggests that Moses could have been a powerful man in the Mashona or Matabele tribe and that the opening up of Africa to white men by selling them vast tracts of land, disrupted regular Black lives, forcing the original inhabitants towards lives of subservience and employment as cheap labour. Lessing's first novel looks unflinchingly at race and unhesitatingly points out the enormous class and race differences that exist in this hitherto unexplored territory, and examines white middle-class women's roles in the colonial enterprise with great rigour.

Mary Turner is not allowed to become the conventional heroine of this narrative but is shown as a victim of the personal and the political. Resisting a world in which women married early, Mary escaped the poverty that dogged her childhood and her youth by becoming economically independent. In England, after the Second World War, an economically independent woman would be a great role model, although the pressures of raising large families and homemaking were then being emphasised upon as stellar identities for women, to recoup the loss of lives during the war.

Mary Turner's economic independence does not free her from the cultural pressure of finding a man to settle down with. Terrified of being seen as odd and strange, Mary accepts Dick's offer of marriage and moves to live on a farm in the veldt, away from the city lights that she was far more comfortable with. Dick Turner, Mary's husband, is another oddball and unsuited for the life on the veldt. Through Dick's breakdown and Mary's death, Lessing makes us aware of the ruthlessness with which the colonial system dispenses not only with the colonised subject but with its own people who do not conform. The colonial overlords are men invested in running the system efficiently, reaping profits on land that was never theirs and willing to humiliate and pulverise people of different skin colour.

Mary and Dick are viewed as having let the white side down. Dick is pitied, for being eccentric, but the disgust and contempt are reserved for Mary, who is sacrificed to perhaps lighten the white man's burden. Lessing's offering up of Mary as a pawn is not sociologically incorrect because, in public and personal myths and histories, women have been allowed little choice and have usually been foot soldiers in both peacetime and in times of war. The extraordinary denouement in this first novel is the starting point of Lessing's discomfort with the *status quo*—one that she sets out to question relentlessly.

In the delineation of Martha Quest, the central figure in the Children of Violence series, Lessing gives us a female protagonist modelled very closely on her own life, who comes of age in colonial Africa and travels to England. Martha Quest is truly Lessing's new woman, economically independent, sexually vibrant, able to chart her own destiny, and extends the idea of the modern young woman for whom the personal involves political choices. On the eve of the Second World War, Martha marries a civil servant, has two children and instead of contenting herself with raising them and running a household, leaves all this behind to join the CPSA, desirous of participating in the public sphere. At this juncture, Lessing's narrative becomes a *bildungsroman* providing insights into the political world of the mid-twentieth-century and women's lives therein. Martha's personal story moves out of the parlour and boudoir, away from the boundaries of the domestic novel, and plunges both Martha and the reader into the maelstrom of the outside world.

Lessing's fiction enables a sighting of female protagonists who grow from strength to strength in their ability to stretch the dimensions of the worlds they occupy. Women characters in Lessing's fiction follow their author's development from an unconventional young woman into an older adult with an entirely new perspective on life and minimal hesitation about sharing it. Lessing's fiction has been mined regularly for autobiographical references and it is possible to see that the fictional Martha Quest parallels Lessing's attitudinal change from youth to age. *Under My Skin* (1994) and *Walking in the Shade* (1997), the two volumes of Lessing's autobiography, provide substantial evidence corroborating this and make for nuanced reading.

Lessing's fictional women travel a long way from the first generations of women who fought for equal spaces in patriarchal societies in the fin de siècle of the nineteenth century. Lessing's early protagonists' search for economic independence and personal freedom contests older, oppressive structures of family, marriage, and motherhood. By locating her protagonists within the interstices of race and class, Lessing demonstrates that white middle-class women's understanding of feminism needs urgent interrogation. The interrogation of this understanding, along with a questioning of Eurocentric empiricism and a critical examination of the key tenets of the Occidental world view commence from Lessing's very first book.

By the time Lessing moves into the third decade of her writing career, her female protagonists are neither young nor in search of husbands. By the 1960s, Lessing's women protagonists are middle-aged or older women and no longer conform to the standard typecast of the promising young woman in search of personal freedom. Through these older female characters, Lessing raises several important issues, providing a window that allows us to see an entire range of experiences uniquely 'from a woman's point of view'. The world that her women characters inhabit is one in which women's lives are lived out in fullness and not in the small portions that were doled out to them, previously.

At the start of the nineteenth century, Jane Austen's fiction—published posthumously—attempted to make heroines witty and pretty by turns while Charlotte Brontë decided that for Jane Eyre, the prototype of several hundred romance narratives of the twentieth century, she would eschew beauty, thereby highlighting Jane's intelligent spirit by drawing serious attention to it. This provided the cue for the binary of plain Janes versus dumb blondes that continues to remain embedded in the cultural imagination.

Lessing's female characters arrive in a world with a dearth of assertive female role models, particularly in literature, and perforce find their footing in complex public spaces, unlike their predecessors. None of these women accept the shrinkage of their lives into that of private individuals in the domestic realm.

Lessing's novels not only offer valuable inputs for the understanding of social and political developments that altered women's lives in the twentieth century but also provide insight into the lives of women who resist all manner of *status quo*. Relocating themselves after being raised in coercive, patriarchal and colonial societies, the road to freedom and self-discovery for Lessing's women protagonists has been long and arduous.

Lessing's generation engaged with racial discrimination and the possibility of a cataclysmic social change through the advent of the socialist revolution, and Lessing's fiction emphatically recorded a generational shift from her mother's time. With greater access to the public sphere and more political and legal rights than her mother's generation, Lessing's fiction documents greater indices of change. Her preferred distancing from the popular endorsements of the progressive twentieth century is evident in her fictional formulations.

Lessing's dissatisfaction with notions of scientific progress and economic prosperity as indicators of human development and her disillusionment with the crumbling of the revolutionary utopias promised by communism led to her persistent examination of systems of belief and practice, pushing her to rethink the question of human life and value. The women characters in her novels, more often than not, enable such rethinking.

My reading of Lessing's novels has drawn attention to how her narratives have intersected, absorbed and explored the prevalent *zeitgeist* of the twentieth century. My analysis of her novels has also broadly surmised the directions that her more recent work is headed towards. Lessing's last novels, namely, *The Fifth Child* (1988) and its sequel *Ben, in the World* (2000), *Love, Again* (1996), *Mara and Dann* (1999), *The Sweetest Dream* (2001) and *The Cleft* (2007) reiterate the philosophic dimensions implicit in her work yet again. Each one of these works underwrites Lessing's belief in the small but possible alternatives in the relational world of ethics and community lives largely lived by women. In these later novels, Lessing reiteratively examines the making of women in traditional patriarchies. Questioning the assumptions implicit in traditional patriarchal world views, Lessing engages in highlighting alternate ways of being, positing these as viable.

Although these novels have not been discussed previously, they draw from Lessing's earlier corpus and continue Lessing's explorations in feminist ethics. By highlighting the relational processes between individuals and focusing on the matrix of interpersonal relationships and their significance in human life, Lessing's last novels serve as beacons.

The centrality of care in dealing with children, friendships and at work, shown as significant in Lessing's novels, has been historically demarcated as an intrinsic part of women's experience. Do Lessing's novels see these activities, traditionally associated with women and devalued by 'masculinist' perspectives, as a liberating political and ethical stance with global ramifications? Does such a reading run the risk of 'biological essentialism'? The possibility of feminist ethics being hijacked by agendas of biological essentialism remains a real danger. How does Lessing address this?

I will discuss briefly, for purposes of illustration, one significant episode from *Mara and Dann*[2] that draws attention to a core concern in Lessing's fiction. Lessing's rewriting of feminism, from her earliest novel, has been about recognising not only the absence of real role models for women but also the coercive practices in place within households, religious structures and received literary traditions.

In Chelops, among the Mahondis, Larissa—the official instructor—gave lessons to young women 'which were tales from long ago, from a medical textbook found in ancient records.'[3] This 'medical textbook' contains accounts of unhappy young women in several cultures ranging from Western Europe to Russia. The common link between all these cultures is the hostility directed at hapless young girls who grow up under oppressive rules, overbearing fathers or tyrannical husbands. These young women fall in love, unsuitably most of the time, and eventually resort to killing themselves as a result of social or personal betrayal.

Collating narratives that document women as victims of patriarchal systems and presenting them as details from a medical textbook, Lessing presents a brilliant spoof on the background of women's lives within cultures. She offers up the literary history of women's lives as diagnostic evidence about the malaise of civilisation. 'Jula' (Juliet), 'Mam Bova' (Madame Bovary) and 'Ankrena' (Anna Karenina), among a pantheon of women evoked from the past, have played a prominent role—first in fashioning women's notions of themselves in a patriarchal culture and then as valuable case studies of patriarchal oppression in feminist readings.

These women were imagined and created by male authors. Their identities are deliberately corrupted in the world of Chelops and significantly, they are no longer salutary role models. The younger women listening to these stories can neither conceive of the oppressive nature of the characters' worlds nor comprehend their reasons for self-annihilation. Lessing is very firmly stating that new roles and contexts must be sought.

In *Mara and Dann,* Lessing's critique of a literary tradition that engages with women only to freeze all possibilities in their lives must be read as feminist stocktaking. Surveying women's unhappiness through this brief capsule, Lessing identifies patriarchal oppression across cultures as the malaise. The deliberate distortion of the names of familiar fictional characters is suggestive of a shift in feminist strategy. In the world of *Mara and Dann*, the old tales cease to be relevant to the lives of Mara, Kira and Leta, three young women who form part of a small community at the end of the novel. Lessing's reader is nudged towards the recognition that the concept of woman as victim or woman as a specifically constructed entity, which rightly fuelled the demand for women's rights in historic movements, must now be jettisoned in favour of sustainable new icons.

In other words, Lessing calls for a shift from 'reactive feminism' towards what Elizabeth Gross terms 'a politics of autonomy'.[4] This does not imply a reneging on feminism's stand against patriarchal practice. As Gayatri Spivak emphasises: 'feminism must negotiate with the structures of phallocentrism, because in fact that is what enables us.'[5] The conclusion of *Mara and Dann* shows Mara, Kira and Leta exercising options that are fraught with difficulties and indicate a clean break with older prescriptions. Mara abandons her calling as a princess to live as an ordinary person. Leta leaves behind her life at the brothel, while Kira, who had escaped to security and luxury from the hardships at Chelops, abandons this choice for the uncertainties of a partnership with Dann. Effectively, all three of them rewrite possibilities by refusing to follow conventional or prescriptive options unthinkingly. Alongside this interrogation of patriarchy in each of her novels, Lessing's appropriation of feminist ethics allows her to create new standards of value.

Lessing achieves this by refusing to confine feminist ethics to women's experiences alone. In doing so, she effectively sidesteps the danger of pushing women back into the primary roles of care and nurture that they invariably undertook in phallocentric societies in earlier times. Instead of reiterating biological essentialism, both men and women in her narratives create a new order. At the end of *Mara and Dann,* a small group of people—seven in number—settle down to a life of agrarian pursuits in a cottage. The rules outlining their lives are fairly simple; all kinds of work are to be shared between men and women, spelling an end to servants, hierarchies or consolidation of power among a few. Lessing's conclusion of this novel emphasises her belief in the ethics of care, which she retrieves from biological essentialism by taking it out of gendered female space and presenting it as a new community space. Could this be seen as a distillation of both feminist and Marxist agendas?

Lessing highlights the significance of relationships and exchanges set up by the characters in her novels and in doing so creates a shift in focus, from the publicly won battles to a sharp look at the finer details that make up human lives. Lessing pushes the reader to recognise that the central signifiers of individual lives must be structured around relationships and people. *Love, Again* reveals Sarah Durham's emotional vulnerability, one that is shared by other men and women in a world where heterosexuality no longer occupies centre stage.

Lessing's novels indict colonial exploitation and attempt to end women's oppression. She was once fuelled by the belief that communism would be transformative, making the world a better place, and that both psychoanalysis and Marxism would change things altogether. Her science fiction, and its dystopic vision of the world, issued ominous warnings about what the arrogant human race was doing to the planet, to water and land and air and drew attention to hapless victims, species and environmental degradation worldwide, at that time. Today, this is no longer a dystopic projection; this, and worse, is the condition of our world.

The Sweetest Dream provides a stocktaking of over five decades of the twentieth century, examining closely the great ideas in ferment during this time.

The Sweetest Dream is Lessing's literary conversation with John Osborne's *Look Back in Anger.* Lessing responds in this novel to the issues raised by Osborne's play, thereby providing commentary on the shortcomings of the post-Second World War years, the rise of ravaged postcolonial nations, the Cold War, years of counterculture, women's movements and a new world politics, where guerrilla warfare, extremism, terrorism and an ascending arsenal of weapons became new transactional currencies. Lessing reinvents Osborne's central protagonist—the Left revolutionary and his wife—and changes the narrative altogether, pushing it in directions that Osborne's play does not anticipate.[6]

When Lessing arrived in London in 1949 from Southern Rhodesia—fleeing the claustrophobia of suburban life there—she was already an active member of the CPSA, drawing succour from the idea of an extraordinary revolution that would transform lives all over the world. Communism, inspired by Marxist thought, provided utopian hope for people who believed in equal spaces and were deeply desirous of casting off the crippling inequalities of class and race forever.

In the third decade of her life, Lessing found herself in ugly, insular London, recovering from the wars and the bombings while the rest of Britain was compulsorily weaning itself off from the colonial excesses that it had commandeered over the centuries. Despite Labour being voted to power in 1945, the amalgamation of the welfare state was a slow and laborious process; continued shortages and rationing soon led to disenchantment. The ongoing erosion of religious faith, a social levelling of class disparity and liberalisation of sexual mores went alongside the economic recovery of the 1950s.[7] Although England's colonial power was on the wane, exciting ideas of personal, sexual and political freedoms were the order of the day in a society with an aspirational class.

Around this time, a new generation described as 'the angry young men' orbited into literary visibility because of novels such as John Wain's *Hurry On Down* (1953) and Kingsley Amis's *Lucky Jim* (1954). Lessing was mistakenly identified as part of the 'angry young men' club, although her writing already focused on a world imbricated by race and class, over and above war and displacement. Lessing brought to her work the perspective of gender that was missing from Osborne's play *Look Back in Anger*. Gender has remained an afterthought, outside of the triptych, in representations of life, class and race in Osborne's play.

Look Back in Anger, written during May and June 1955, was part of the literature of protest—wherein 'characters with a working-class background' poured 'out invectives against the society, its codes and institutions in seething and vitriolic rhetoric.'[8] Revisiting the play after long years of teaching it to undergraduates and also viewing the film version, the hindsight of history enables us to understand why Jimmy Porter will forever be nothing other than an angry young man.

Jimmy Porter, from the working class, is married to the more privileged Alison. Despite his not so *pucca* university education, Jimmy works at Hugh Tanner's sweet stall. Isolated and alienated, an irate Jimmy grapples with larger political and social structures. He assails the ruling conservative party—the Tories, condemns the bomb, attacks the church and the upper classes. Jimmy's iconoclasm seems to be contained by a vitriolic attack on everything and everyone around him and there is no real direction that his anger can be channelised towards.[9]

Jimmy lists the terrible wrongs in the political and economic situation which has damaged people's lives, and violent rage is all he can bring to the table to sort out the ugly scenarios around him. He rants at his friend and directs the bulk of his rage at his wife Alison, displays intense grief at his father's death—wounded in the Spanish civil war, 1936–1939—but extends little charity to Alison's parents. Except for Hugh Tanner's mother, who helped him set up the sweet stall, Jimmy Porter's treatment of all other women leaves much to be desired.[10]

In Act I, Jimmy jostles Alison when she is ironing clothes and she is badly scalded. This is part of his rough love, alongside rummaging through her handbag and discussing with Cliff his assessment of Alison's written correspondence to her natal family.[11]

Jimmy declares in Lawrentian manner that Alison has 'the passion of a python' and 'devours' him 'whole', echoing the accusation levelled at Miriam in *Sons and Lovers* (1913) about sucking out Paul's soul. Nothing seems to have changed about the way women continue to be portrayed, although forty-odd years have now given them the right to work, the vote, welfare and greater access to education.

Jimmy remains unconcerned about a pregnant Alison's trauma and remains convinced that her departure with her father is a slighting of the dying Mrs Tanner. Act II ends with the strange morphing of Alison's friend Helena into a pliable sexual object, from an independent woman. The play positions women reductively,[12] and expects them as subservient to men at all times. Act III concludes with the return of Alison, who tearfully reconciles with Jimmy and befriends Helena again.[13]

This conclusion is bizarre since nothing has changed for Alison. Is her grovelling before Jimmy the only way to portray her as someone who has suffered? Is miscarriage the solution for the world's ills? Can selective auto-abortions of the womb, predicted by men of vicious words, be the new praxis? The play closes on a disturbing note, not really moving away from the quagmire generated by crumbling value systems and ineffectual male tyranny.

Helena observes that Jimmy was born out of his time and that 'he doesn't know where he is, or where he is going. He will never do anything, and he will never amount to anything.'[14] These are important pointers. Arguably, Johnny Lennox's persona in *The Sweetest Dream* is structured around such insight. Frances Lennox and her husband Johnny Lennox, possibly remodelled from Jimmy Porter and his wife Alison, are introduced to us under similar historical circumstances in England.

The Sweetest Dream examines at close quarters the lives of successive generations of women and is a hard-hitting spoof directed at Marxist ideologue Johnny Lennox, whose bid to transform the world leads him to abandon all duties and responsibilities in his personal life. The novel's emotional centre has little to do with Johnny's political acumen. It focuses instead, on the lives of Johnny Lennox's mother, wife, their sons and their daughter from another marriage.

Significantly, *The Sweetest Dream* does not explain away this terrible period and the state of England after the Second World War by blaming it on women. Lessing's *Golden Notebook*, which speaks of the 1950s in London, reveals a world that takes on a different hue since it is viewed through the filter of a woman's perspective. Here too, Lessing applies what Sheila Rowbotham calls the 'gender lens'[15] to a whole range of issues and retrieves women's lives, documenting women's significant contributions that have been subsumed due to patriarchal cultural practice.

Moving away from the stranglehold of Osborne's play, Lessing's novel relocates its action to a period that stretches well before and beyond the 1960s, documenting the fissures and seismic shifts of the twentieth century. Replacing the chauvinistic vision of Johnny Lennox—who is modelled on the prototype of Jimmy Porter—with a woman's perspective, Lessing's novel makes the reader recognise that Frances Lennox, unlike Alison, is no pushover. Johnny Lennox is Jimmy Porter all over again except for the fact that Johnny's parents belong to the privileged middle class. Johnny disowns them to set himself up as a revolutionary figure. He, like Jimmy, wages a struggle against the state, sacrificing family ties and obligations altogether.

Frances and Johnny meet during the Second World War, which recruits their services. They marry and have two children by 1945. Johnny pretends to be in Spain fighting the civil war, but hides out in a section of London and fecklessly turns down jobs offered by the capitalist system after the war, remaining preoccupied with notions of revolution.

Frances' refusal to join the party adds more pressure to the marriage, pushing her into a life of 'squalor and hardship'[16] with her two young sons. Johnny falls in love with another comrade and moves out. Johnny subsequently returns to his wife but moves out once more with another comrade. When he returns yet again, Frances chooses not to debase herself any further and shows him the door. Although the novel documents the existence of the sexual double standard, nowhere is this endorsed at any point in the narrative. Frances struggles to raise her kids, putting her erotic life on hold. Unlike Alison who is cursed with miscarriage and made to grovel, Lessing ends misogynist perspectives instead of furthering them in *The Sweetest Dream*.

Frances has a difficult time making ends meet with two small children and little contribution from Johnny. Eventually, when Frances accepts Julia's continued offer of a house to live in, both women sort out the economies of payment and run the house by themselves. Through the portrayal of generations of strong women characters, Lessing pries out solutions to the crisis that engulfs Jimmy Porter. Lessing also sets up a new archetype—namely, that of the large-hearted and caring mother-in-law who stands by her son's wife, countering stereotypes of the controlling mother-in-law figure that dominates both the cartoon strip and the soap opera, reinforcing cultural perception.

In the 1960s, Frances's freelance journalism and minor theatre roles put food on the table, pay for gas and electricity and feed and lodge a large number of angry young people—who are 'screwed up' as Julia and Frances put it, as they are children born after the wars. All the young people who bunk down at Julia's house, wherein Frances runs an open kitchen, have dysfunctional family lives and a strong sense of what is owed to them but little sense of duty or obligation.

The ironing table which occupies centre space in the Porter household and binds both Alison and Helena to labour has been iconised as a symbol of female oppression by women writers, such as Marge Piercy in her poem 'Breaking Out' (1984) and Jeanette Winterson when she expresses outrage regarding a shift in women's roles. In *The Sweetest Dream*, the kitchen table replaces the ironing table. The kitchen table, now in everyday use, becomes the new symbolic centre of the household. Frances regularly cooks up a storm and around the table sit innumerable people, members of the family, and outsiders, who partake of this nurturing. 'The life of the house', we are told 'went on in the kitchen.'

The history of this table dates back to the fact that it was first laden with food by Julia, a diplomat's daughter and wife who hosted very important parties for important people. Earlier traditions of formal and fine dining invariably involved an almost invisible workforce that made such opulent lifestyles possible. *The Sweetest Dream* records the democratic reduction in the gap between the preparers of food and its consumers, setting in play new perspectives of social formation and an emphasis on the centrality of food in human life. Even in peacetime, Lessing suggests, armies of people can march only on their stomachs, concurring with Frances who cooks and feeds a large household. Frances Lennox prepares food for the angry, disconnected young people who sleep in her basement and eat huge meals around her dining table. This is the new community that Julia enables Frances to raise, even as she takes on the responsibility for paying for Frances's sons and Phyllida's daughter Sylvia. Johnny, the biological father of Andrew and Colin and stepfather to Sylvia, abdicates his responsibilities and frees Phyllida from the responsibility of raising her biological daughter by dropping the child off at the house where his wife and sons live, without any discussion.

Sylvia's biological father, Alan—whom Sylvia does not want to meet at all—is yet another communist hero. He abandons his wife and child with little compunction, fights in the Spanish civil war and is all for the revolution. Lessing indicates in no uncertain terms that such versions of heroism and the time for them is now over. Johnny Lennox, moves from one cause and one woman to other causes and other women well into the 1980s but remains ineffective in creating any productive change.

By contrast, Julia and Frances—Johnny's mother and wife respectively—shoulder a lot of responsibilities. The white woman's burden that Jimmy Porter accuses Alison of not being able to understand is shouldered by the older women in *The Sweetest Dream*.

We must recall that Mrs Redfern, Mrs Drury and Mrs Tanner, older women characters in *Look Back in Anger*, play minimal roles offstage and are not central to the action of the play. By comparison, all the women in *The Sweetest Dream* lead significant lives, free of Johnny's overarching presence. He may hate his parents and do little for his wives and children but despite his prolonged absences, Julia and Frances, being strong-willed women, move on with their lives and manage admirably. Lessing sets up nurture and food and the world of the kitchen as significant options in this brave new world. We are also told that what Frances is doing at Hampstead is being replicated in different parts of the world by other women. Frances discovers through letters and overseas visitors that in North Carolina. California, Scotland, Ireland, France and in Spain, other earth mothers like her exist, providing open house to waifs and strays, warped by their circumstances—in a world that has been allowed to spin out of control. Lessing's narrative promotes an interdependent and nurturing community life and a sharing of spaces as the new normal.

Somewhere in this attempt on the part of small individuals to provide succour to the young, in the replacement of the insular, nuclear family with the possibility of a connected space and an extended family formed by associations, Lessing is suggesting new modes of interaction and probably newer possibilities. The struggling heroic individual—predominantly male—who must abandon home and all connections in order to begin life afresh as an adult, who was the familiar icon of the twentieth century, has been rendered inconsequential. The novel concludes with more young people from privileged backgrounds outgrowing their sense of entitlement, recognising that the world is an unequal space, and are willing to harness their collective energies towards the greater welfare of the world.

By comparison, *Look Back in Anger* comprises a vitiated world of friends and family and little redemptive options. Jimmy Porter banters with the friend who lives with him and often engages in friendly fisticuffs but their camaraderie constantly reverts to Jimmy's early revolutionary days and the tribe that existed then, as the point of reference. Juxtaposed with the memories of those early days, everything else pales in significance, becoming inconsequential. Osborne's quintessentially masculine arena has lost all its glory and will not proceed any further from the shadowy past in which it is anchored. Lessing's novels challenge such masculine, patriarchal perspectives by showing them up to be part of a regressive world view.

Johnny Lennox's flamboyance ensures him a large coterie of friends to hang out with. His friends change over the years, as his political interests shift from Europe to Africa. In the interim, while Johnny flirts with causes, his mother and his wife take on the nurture of several people who require it. These angry young people, usually white, are very often shown as suffering a total disconnect with the homes and families they were raised in.

Their decrepit lives signal the complete failure of the nuclear family as an idea. Often enough, their idea of attacking the establishment consists of shoplifting on Oxford Street. There are visitors from Africa, who also get co-opted into the Lennox commune. Rose refers to the house as Freedom Hall. Lessing does not valorise the nuclear family which has, in any case, withered away. What is now under construction in the Lennox home and in several such homes all over the world is the possibility of a new tribe or a nascent community that learns to connect and bond and is provided as a more stable response to the problems of the 1960s and the 1970s. This is in place of the egomaniacal singular male, espousing revolution and doing very little other than running down the establishment and contributing very little to the upkeep of the family in terms of emotional or financial support, and the disjunctive nuclear family, caving in upon itself.

Frances and Julia rewrite their choices, economic, emotional, social and sexual. Sexual mores in *The Sweetest Dream* are extended to accommodate women's desire unlike in *Look Back in Anger*, where women's sexual desire remains irrelevant. Alison holds on to a notion of faithfulness not adhered to either by her husband or by her friend. Helena enters into a relationship with Jimmy and is altogether inconsiderate of Alison. Helena serves neither as a friend to Alison nor as an intelligent combatant to Jimmy. Her moral ambiguity and her unreliability are also projected as an aspect of her gender. In the world of the play, Helena and Alison serve merely as props to the male protagonist Jimmy. Osborne does not explore any real or emotional connection between the two women. They do not connect with each other or with other people. They are also not involved with any significant issues outside of their sexual roles in the domestic sphere.

Johnny in *The Sweetest Dream* is polygamous and takes three wives, to say nothing of various comrades he lives with from time to time. Julia learns to live alongside a motley community in her old age, very different from the elite life that she lived as a young woman with her husband. Frances, who switches off her sexual life because of her responsibility as a nurturer, finds time for a weekend jaunt and eventually manages to take time off from parenting to nurture a new relationship. The man she settles down with, Rupert Bolan, has a wife and two children and the women in the novel are shown as far better equipped at handling partners and family life in comparison to the men. This portrayal of women as complex and not simply unidimensional figures viewed through a masculine gaze challenges the sexist and reductive portrayal of women in *Look Back in Anger*.

Human companionship, Lessing suggests, is important and enriching, irrespective of the politics one chooses. What one makes of it, seems to depend on the dominant DNA men and women choose to follow. Again, in the course of the novel, Jimmy's father, Julia's friend Wilhelm Stein and a host of ordinary men lead fulfilling lives as husbands and fathers.

It is true that the youngsters nurtured and looked after by Julia and then Frances, in particular, are fairly dysfunctional but eventually all or most of them grow up and display greater concern and charity towards their less privileged fellow humans than either Johnny or Jimmy ever display in their lifetimes.

In *The Sweetest Dream*, the large home run by Frances Lennox—which is owned by her mother-in-law Julia—becomes a microcosmic world. Frances's kitchen is the centre of social, emotional and political life for her children and their friends. While Julia—a diplomat's daughter in Germany—married Philip Lennox during the Second World War and shifted to London, eventually owning a house in Hampstead, Frances, her daughter-in-law, shifts away from her early communist leanings to eventually set up residence in Julia's Hampstead house after a protracted attempt at roughing it out with young children. The ground floor and basement of what began as a private home for a nuclear family becomes a commune of sorts, and Frances takes on the mantle of a community mother for all practical purposes. Mothering a group of young people is a significant role that Lessing endorses over single-parenting. The first time this idea was explored was in Lessing's science fiction, *The Marriages between Zones Three, Four and Five*, when Al • Ith—ruler of the realm—speaks about the mind fathers of her child. The idea that children need more nurture and interaction than their biological parents can offer is a valuable blueprint on offer in Lessing's fiction.

Instead of setting up traditional rivalries between mothers-in-law and daughters-in-law, Lessing unravels the intricacies of support and friendship shared by the two women in this very complex relationship. Julia and Frances' raising of Sylvia, Lennox's step-daughter by his marriage to Phyllida, is one of the success stories of the novel. The sharing of space and infrastructure to accommodate more people is another compelling idea.

Focusing on the sustenance provided by lodging and feeding a large number of youngsters, Lessing reaffirms the nucleus of the female realm and its significance in all dimensions of existence that one could term human. Her last novels, by unequivocally shifting focus from grandly lived public lives such as those of Johnny Lennox to the otherwise invisible lives of women who nurture entire communities, provide new insights and understanding. For Lessing and her readers, this is not a return to convention but an upturning of it. The home and the world change position, merge and are reconfigured. Women and their work emerge as the locus of a brave new world.

Three generations of women from their position as caregivers and nurturers are made to play a far more significant and substantial role. Lessing's narrative is sharply critical of Johnny Lennox while stating unequivocally that no possibilities will be forthcoming from revolution. Yet she makes more visible the quieter, but insistent and resilient lives of the individual figures that allow the world and our hope in it to be sustained by the sheer doggedness with which they go about their work. This is a new history of doing. In place of the larger quests and revolutions that have fuelled the dreams and imagination of both lived and imagined lives, Lessing's women characters draw attention to the minutiae of living.

In *The Sweetest Dream*, at the end of two world wars, we are given a glimpse of how the privileged in London dealt with their lives. The protests of the 1950s are replaced by those of the 1960s, followed by the decades of the 1970s and the 1980s in which the issues of colonialism, race, class and gender do not simply fade away, but multiply and interweave into complicated patterns that run through the novel.

Sylvia trains to be a doctor and opts to work in fictionalised Africa, bringing two young boys home with her when violence breaks out. When Sylvia dies unexpectedly of a heart attack, the onus of raising the two Black boys falls upon Frances, her new partner Rupert and her son, Andrew. They all soldier on and along with Colin, his wife and little daughter form one large rambling group, representing possibilities. Andrew and Franklin work to empower the global poor. Colin becomes a successful novelist.

The Sweetest Dream does not valorise flawed unequal personal relationships as the only bulwark against the ugliness of the world, unlike *Look Back in Anger*. Nor does it advocate a schism between the personal and the political. It also looks closely at the responsibility of parenting, throwing out of the window stereotypes about step-mothers, stepfathers and foster parents and draws attention to the frailties and foibles of real parents.

The novel's conclusion pushes towards an ideal world, where innumerable survivors from bad marriages, childhood traumas, sexism, class, racism and colonialism are incorporated into the fabric of a new community. Responsibility is taken, older debts are repaid, and compassion and nurture seem to be operating metaphors in place of older analogies of control and exploitation. These are the suggestions that *The Sweetest Dream*, Lessing's last full-length realist novel, nudges its readers towards. In my opinion, this novel is meant to be read as a testament to Lessing's deepest hopes and convictions. The novel is ground-breaking in its highlighting of the nature of the new challenges that feminism must address or shoulder so that an earlier phallocentric humanism can be completely overhauled and a more expansive, plural and nurturing feminist universe be fostered in its stead.

Six months after the first outbreak of Covid-19, the familiar world around us has slowly ground to a halt. The air, the oceans, and the earth, freed from human onslaughts seem to have recovered. Flora and fauna, the world over have welcomed new spaces suddenly available to them. Yet, on the human front, despite the raging virus and the mounting death toll, schisms and hostilities between groups continue world-wide. America and Russia, despite the ending of the cold war, continue hostilities. Iraq has been hobbled, and Iran remains under the scanner. Syria has been wrecked beyond belief and embroiled in a civil war with international players for nine long years. The Middle East remains troubled and Israel continues its unprecedented attack on Palestine. Afghanistan is a ravaged country. China and Nepal are scaling up border disputes with India, resulting in sporadic attacks on Indian citizens from the North-Eastern states. ethnic North Korea and South Korea remain at a stand-off. Ostensibly in a time of world peace, the whole world is on the boil.

Meanwhile, hatred percolates down to the grassroots all over the world. Hatred against Black communities and other migrant communities and Islamophobia is rampant in America. Anti-minority sentiment in India and Myanmar, hatred against the Arabs, by Israeli Zionists is now systemic and shows little signs of abatement. Policemen brutalise and kill people they undertook to protect in Minneapolis and Tuticorin respectively because of different skin colours or religious affiliation. Powerful democracies such as America and India refuse to discharge their sovereign responsibilities towards their poorest and most vulnerable citizens. Medical care and support in times of Covid-19 has been abysmal, especially for affected people with inadequate support systems. Also, women continue to be second-class citizens all over the world, subject to all manner of attacks and violence that cuts across class and race. This moment of collective failure and a total disregard for the sanctity of human lives or rights is how things stand today. In a post-Covid world, our sorry predicament must make us heed the words of poets and writers who had forecast this grim harvest. Perhaps it will finally be the turn of literature to direct us towards a humane world, in the aftermath of the failure of religion, science, technology and political and legal processes to chalk up victories.

Endnotes

1. Chandra Bhushan, 'Opinion: The clean environment we're enjoying currently will only be short term, without fundamental changes,' TOI Edit Page, *Times of India*, April 25, 2020.
2. Doris Lessing, *Mara and Dann: An Adventure* (London: Flamingo, 1999). All further references to the novel are from this edition.
3. Lessing, *Mara and Dann*, 166.
4. Gross speaks of what she sees as a shift from a 'politics of equality to a politics of autonomy' in her essay. Elizabeth Gross, 'What is Feminist Theory?' in *Feminist Challenges: Social and Political Theory*, eds. Carole Pateman and Elizabeth Gross (Sydney, London and Boston: Allen & Unwin, 1986), 193.
5. Gayatri Chakravorty Spivak, *The Post-Colonial Critic: Interviews, Strategies, Dialogues*, ed. Sarah Harasym (New York and London: Routledge, 1990), 147.
6. *Look Back in Anger* also provides for a great deal of cross referencing, introducing literary and fictional personas, bits of poems and sentences etc. For further references see citations in Prashant K. Sinha, introduction to *Look Back in Anger*, by John Osborne (London: Faber & Faber, 1957; New Delhi: Oxford University Press, 2001), 40–41.
7. Sinha, introduction, 20–21.
8. Sinha, introduction, 21.
9. Osborne's observation, at the beginning of Act I, that Jimmy Porter 'is a disconcerting mixture of sincerity and cheerful malice, of tenderness and

freebooting cruelty, restless, importunate, full of pride, a combination which alienates the sensitive and the insensitive alike', remains the defining tone for Jimmy's persona throughout the play. In John Osborne, *Look Back in Anger* (London: Faber & Faber, 1957; New Delhi: Oxford University Press, 2001), 1.1. References are to act and scene.

10. Apparently, Alison jumps into bed like 'someone launching a battleship'. Noisy women sit at their dressing tables 'dropping their weapons' while women in front of their bedroom mirrors are a refined sort of butchers. Osborne, *Look Back in Anger*, 1.1.68. References are to act, scene and page number.
11. Act I concludes with a vituperative and misogynistic Jimmy objecting to Helena's intended visit. He tells Alison, 'If only something would happen to you and wake you out of your beauty sleep . . . if you could have a child and it would die.' Osborne, *Look Back in Anger*, 1.1.82. References are to act, scene and page number.
12. Jimmy is overwhelmed by the formidable nature of female sexuality and must, therefore, both objectify and abuse women. He refers to Alison as some sort of pet—a squirrel with big eyes and a sleek, bushy tail—and declares that all women love caveman tactics. Brutalising and abusing women apparently whets sexual appetite. This is reinforced by Helena who finds the hatred in Jimmy's eyes '[h]orrifying . . . and oddly exciting'. Osborne, *Look Back in Anger*, 2.1.86. References are to act, scene and page number.
13. Act III opens with Helena taking on Alison's ironing and laundering duties. Jimmy is now reduced to mouthing banalities:

    > There aren't any good, brave causes left. If the big bang does come, and we all get killed off, it won't be in aid of the old-fashioned grand design. It'll just be for the Brave New-nothing-very-much-thank-you. About as pointless and inglorious as stepping in front of a bus. No, there is nothing left for it, me boy, but to let yourself be butchered by the women.

    See Osborne, *Look Back in Anger*, 3.1.131. References are to act, scene and page number. Act III shows a revival of Alison and Helena's friendship, after the former's return. Helena declares that it was wrong and evil of her to believe that one could throw away the book of rules and have sex resolve everything. Jimmy hands Helena her clothes as she leaves. Alison cowers and weeps. She has lost her baby and is grovelling, 'I am in the mud at last!' See Osborne, *Look Back in Anger*, 3.2.142. References are to act, scene and page number. Jimmy and she fall into each other's arms and the play ends with a disquieting resolution in which both of them are shown as reverting to playing their pretend bear and squirrel game, all over again.

14. Doris Lessing, *The Sweetest Dream* (Great Britain: Flamingo, 2001; New York: HarperCollins, 2002), 136. All references to the book are from the 2002 edition.
15. Sheila Rowbotham, *A Century of Women: The History of Women in Britain and the United States* (London and New York: Viking Books, 1997; London and New York: Penguin Books, 1999), 3. The reference is from the 1999 edition.
16. Lessing, *The Sweetest Dream*, 9.

Bibliography

Primary Readings: Works by Doris Lessing

Fiction, Non-Fiction and Articles

Lessing, Doris. *The Grass is Singing*. London: Grafton Books, 1980. Reprint, Paladin/Grafton Books, 1989. First published 1950 by Michael Joseph (Great Britain).

———. *Martha Quest. Children of Violence*. London and New York: Granada, 1966. Reprint, London and New York: Granada, 1982. First published 1952 by Michael Joseph (Great Britain).

———. *A Proper Marriage. Children of Violence*. London and New York: Granada, 1966. First published 1954 by Michael Joseph (London).

———. *Retreat to Innocence*. London: Michael Joseph, 1956.

———. *Going Home*. London: Panther Books, 1968. Reprint, London: Grafton Books, 1989. First published 1957 by Michael Joseph (Great Britain).

———. *A Ripple from the Storm. Children of Violence*. London and New York: Granada, 1966. First published 1958 by Michael Joseph (Great Britain).

———. *Fourteen Poems*. Middlesex: Scorpion Press, 1959.

———. *The Golden Notebook*. London: Flamingo, 1993. First published 1962 by Simon & Schuster (New York).

———. *The Black Madonna*. London: Panther Books, 1966.

———. *Landlocked. Children of Violence*. London and New York: Granada, 1967. First published 1965 by MacGibbon & Kee (Great Britain).

———. *The Four-Gated City. Children of Violence*. London and New York: Granada, 1972. First published 1969 by MacGibbon & Kee Ltd (Great Britain).

———. *Briefing for a Descent into Hell*. London: Grafton Books, 1972. First published 1971 by Jonathan Cape (Great Britain).

———. *The Summer Before the Dark*. Harmondsworth: Penguin Books, 1975. First published 1973 by Jonathan Cape (Great Britain) and Alfred A. Knopf (United States).

———. *This Was the Old Chief's Country*. Vol. 1 of *Collected African Stories*. London: Triad/Granada, 1979. First published 1973 by Michael Joseph (Great Britain).

———. *The Sun Between Their Feet*. Vol. 2 of *Collected African Stories*. London: Triad/Granada, 1979. First published 1973 by Michael Joseph (Great Britain).

Lessing, Doris. *A Small Personal Voice: Essays, Reviews, Interviews.* Edited by Paul Schlueter. New York: Vintage Books, 1975. First published 1974 by Alfred A. Knopf (United States).

———. *The Memoirs of a Survivor.* London: Picador/Pan Books, 1976. First published 1974 by Octagon (Great Britain).

———. *To Room Nineteen.* Vol. 1 of *Collected Stories.* London: Triad/Panther Books, 1979. First published 1978 by Jonathan Cape (Great Britain).

———. *The Temptation of Jack Orkney.* Vol. 2 of *Collected Stories.* London: Triad/Panther Books, 1979. First published 1978 by Jonathan Cape (Great Britain).

———. *Re: Colonised Planet 5, Shikasta.* Canopus in Argos: Archives. New York: Alfred A. Knopf, 1979.

———. *The Marriages between Zones Three, Four, and Five, Canopus in Argos: Archives.* New York: Vintage International, 1992. First published 1980 by Jonathon Cape (Great Britain) and Alfred A. Knopf (United States).

———. *In Pursuit of the English.* London: Granada, 1980. First published 1960 by MacGibbon & Kee Ltd (Great Britain).

———. *The Sirian Experiments: The Report by Ambien II, of the Five.* Canopus in Argos: Archives. New York: Alfred A. Knopf, 1981. First published 1980 by Jonathon Cape (Great Britain) and Alfred A. Knopf (United States).

———. *The Making of the Representative for Planet 8.* Canopus in Argos: Archives. New York: Alfred A. Knopf, 1982.

———. *Documents Relating to The Sentimental Agents in the Volyen Empire.* Canopus in Argos: Archives. New York: Alfred A. Knopf, 1983.

———. *The Diaries of Jane Somers.* Harmondsworth: Penguin Books, 1985. First published 1984 by Michael Joseph (Great Britain).

———. *The Good Terrorist.* London: Grafton Books, 1986 First published 1985 by Jonathan Cape (Great Britain) and Alfred A. Knopf (United States).

———. *Prisons We Choose to Live Inside.* New York: Harper and Row, 1987.

———. *The Wind Blows Away Our Words.* London: Picador/Pan Books, 1987.

———. *The Fifth Child.* London: Grafton Books, 1989. First published 1988 by Jonathan Cape (Great Britain).

———. *The Doris Lessing Reader.* London and Toronto: Paladin/Grafton Books, 1991. First published 1989 by Jonathan Cape (Great Britain) and Alfred A. Knopf (United States).

———. *Particularly Cats . . . And Rufus.* New York: Alfred A. Knopf, 1991.

———. *African Laughter: Four Visits to Zimbabwe.* New York: HarperCollins, 1992.

———. *London Observed: Stories and Sketches.* London: Flamingo, 1993. First published 1992 by HarperCollins (Great Britain).

———. *Under My Skin: Volume One of My Autobiography, to 1949.* New York: HarperCollins, 1994.

Lessing, Doris. *Playing the Game*. London: HarperCollins, 1995.

———. *Play with a Tiger and Other Plays*. London: Flamingo, 1996.

———. *Love, Again*. New York: HarperCollins, 1996.

———. *Walking in the Shade: Volume Two of My Autobiography, 1949 to 1962*. New York: HarperCollins, 1997.

———. *Mara and Dann: An Adventure*. London: Flamingo, 1999.

———. *Ben, in the World*. London: Flamingo, 2000.

———. *The Sweetest Dream*. New York: HarperCollins, 2002. First published 2001 by Flamingo (Great Britain).

———. *The Grandmothers: Four Short Novels*. United Kingdom: Flamingo, 2003.

———. *Time Bites: Views and Reviews*. New York: Harper Perennial, 2006. First published 2004 by Fourth Estate (Great Britain).

———. *The Story of General Dann and Mara's Daughter, Griot and the Snow Dog*. New York: Harper Perennial, 2006. First published 2005 by Fourth Estate (Great Britain).

———. *The Cleft*. London: Fourth Estate, 2007.

———. *Alfred and Emily*. London: Fourth Estate, 2008.

Articles

Lessing, Doris. 'A Small Personal Voice.' In *Declaration*, edited by Tom Maschler, 12–27. London: MacGibbon & Kee, 1957.

———. 'Unexamined Mental Attitudes Left Behind by Communism'. In *Our Country, Our Culture: The Politics of Political Correctness*, edited by Edith Kurzweil and William Philips. New York: Partisan Review Press, 1994.

———. 'In fact, only a minority of journalists are any good.' *British Journalism Review*, January 29, 1990.

———. 'Between the fax and the fiction'. *The Guardian*, December 13, 1991.

———. '*On the Commanding Self* by Idries Shah: A Tribute to a Great Exponent of Sufism'. *The London Times*, May 5, 1994.

Related Readings

Books

Acheson, James, ed. *The British and Irish Novel since 1960*. New York: St. Martin's Press. 1991.

Adam, Roberts. *Science Fiction*. London and New York: Routledge, 2000.

Agonito, Rosemary. *History of Ideas on Women: A Source Book.* New York: Perigee Books, 1977.

Ardis, Ann L. *New Women, New Novels: Feminism and Early Modernism.* New Brunswick and London: Rutgers University Press, 1990.

Arendt, Hannah. *Crises of the Republic.* New York: Harcourt Brace Jovanovich, 1972.

Armstrong, Nancy. *Desire and Domestic Fiction: A Political History of the Novel.* New York: Oxford University Press, 1987.

Arnstein, Walter L. *Britain Yesterday and Today: 1830 to the Present.* Toronto and Massachusetts: D.C. Heath, 1988.

Arora, Neena. *Nayantara Saghal and Doris Lessing: A Feminist Study in Comparison.* New Delhi: Prestige Books, 1991.

Astrow, André. *Zimbabwe: A Revolution That Lost Its Way?* London: Zed Press, 1983.

Atwood, Margaret. *Alias Grace.* Random House: Toronto, 1996.

———. *The Blind Assassin.* Random House: Toronto, 2000.

———. *Cat's Eye.* Random House: Toronto, 1988.

———. *The Handmaid's Tale.* Random House: Toronto, 1985.

———. *Robber Bride.* Random House: Toronto, 1993.

Austen, Jane. *Emma.* 1815. Penguin Books: Harmondsworth, 1966.

———. *Mansfield Park.* 1814. Penguin Books: Harmondsworth, 1972.

———. *Northanger Abbey.* 1817. Penguin Books: Harmondsworth, 1968.

———. *Persuasion.* 1817. Penguin Classics: Harmondsworth, 1965.

Balandier, Georges. *The Sociology of Black Africa: Social Dynamics in Central Africa.* Translated by Douglas Garman. London: Andre Deutsch, 1970.

Banks, Olive. *Faces of Feminism: A Study of Feminism as a Social Movement.* New York: St. Martin's Press, 1981.

Bardwick, Judith M. *Women in Transition: How Feminism, Sexual Liberation, and the Search for Self-fulfillment Have Altered Our Lives.* Sussex: Harvester Press, 1980.

Benhabib, Seyla and Drucilla Cornell, eds. *Feminism as Critique: Essays on the Politics of Gender in Late-Capitalist Societies.* Cambridge: Polity Press, 1987.

Blackburn, Helen. *Women's Suffrage: A Record of the Women's Suffrage Movement in the British Isles, With Biographical Sketches of Miss Becker.* London and Oxford: Williams & Norgate, 1902.

Blixen, Karen. *Out of Africa—and—Shadows on the Grass.* Harmondsworth: Penguin Books, 1986. This compiled edition with both books first published 1985 by Penguin Books (United Kingdom).

Bloom, Harold, ed. *Bloom's Modern Critical Views: Doris Lessing.* New York: Chelsea House, 1986.

Bordo, Susan. 'Feminism, Postmodernism, and Gender-Skepticism,' In *Feminism/Postmodernism*, edited by Linda J. Nicholson, 133–56, New York: Routledge, 1990.

Bouchier, David. *The Feminist Challenge: The Movement for Women's Liberation in Britain and the USA*. New York: Schocken Books, 1984.

Bowman, Larry W. *Politics in Rhodesia: White Power in an African State.* Cambridge, Massachusetts: Harvard University Press, 1973.

Bridenthal, Renate and Claudia Koonz, eds. *Becoming Visible: Women in European History*. Boston and London: Houghton Mifflin Company, 1977.

Bristow, Joseph. *Sexuality.* London: Routledge, 2000.

Brontë, Charlotte. *Jane Eyre*. 1847. Edited by Jane Jack and Margaret Smith. Oxford: Oxford University Press, 1969. Reprint, 1975.

Brotz, Howard. *The Politics of South Africa: Democracy and Racial Diversity*. London: Oxford University Press, 1977.

Budhos, Shirley. *The Theme of Enclosure in Selected Works of Doris Lessing.* New York: Whitston Publishing House, 1987.

Bulbeck, Chilla. *Reorienting Western Feminists.* United Kingdom: Cambridge University Press, 1998.

Byatt, A.S. *Angels and Insects*. London: Chatto and Windus, 1992.

———. *Possession*. London: Chatto and Windus, 1990.

Caldicott, Helen. *Nuclear Madness: What You Can Do!* Toronto: Bantam Books, 1980.

Callinicos, Alex. *Southern Africa: After Zimbabwe.* London: Pluto Press, 1981.

Cameron, Deborah, ed. *The Feminist Critique of Language: A Reader*. London and New York: Routledge, 1991.

Camus, Albert. *The Myth of Sisyphus*. Translated by Justin O'Brien. Harmondsworth: Penguin Books, 1975. First published 1942 by Gallimard.

———. *The Stranger*. Translated by Stuart Gilbert. New York: Vintage Books, 1946.

Carter, Angela. *Black Venus*. London: Pan Books, 1986.

———. *The Passion of New Eve*. London: Virago, 1982.

Cederstrom, Lorelei. *Fine-Tuning the Feminine Psyche: Jungian patterns in the Novels of Doris Lessing*. American University Studies Series IV. New York: Peter Lang, 1990.

Chodorow, Nancy. *The Reproduction of Mothering: Psychoanalysis and the Sociology of Gender.* Berkeley: University of California Press, 1978.

Chown, Linda Eileen. *Narrative Authority and Homeostasis in the Novels of Doris Lessing and Carmen Martin Gaite*. New York and London: Garland, 1990.

Cohen, Lawrence. *No Aging in India: Alzheimer's, The Bad Family, and Other Modern Things.* Berkeley and London: University of California Press, 1998.

Cole, Eve Browning and Susan Coultrap-McQuin, eds. *Explorations in Feminist Ethics: Theory and Practice.* Bloomington and Indianapolis: Indiana University Press, 1992.

Cott, Nancy F. *The Grounding of Modern Feminism.* New Haven and London: Yale University Press, 1987.

Cunningham, Gail. *The New Woman and the Victorian Novel.* London and Basingstoke: Macmillan, 1978.

Daley, Caroline and Melanie Nolan, eds. *Suffrage and Beyond: International Feminist Perspectives.* Auckland: Auckland University Press, 1994.

Darwin, John. *Britain and Decolonisation: The Retreat from Empire in the Post-War World.* London: Macmillan, 1988.

Davidoff, Leonore, Keith McClleland, and Eleni Varikas, eds. *Gender and History: Retrospect and Prospect.* Oxford and Massachusetts: Blackwell Publishers, 1999.

Davis, Angela Y. *Women, Race & Class.* New York: Random House, 1981.

De Beauvoir, Simone. *The Second Sex.* 1949. Translated by H.M. Parshley. Harmondsworth: Penguin Books, 1972.

Deegan, Heather. *South Africa Reborn: Building a New Democracy.* London: UCL Press, 1999.

De Lauretis, Teresa. *Alice Doesn't: Feminism, Semiotics, Cinema.* Bloomington: Indiana University Press, 1984.

———. *Feminist Studies/Critical Studies.* Bloomington: Indiana University Press, 1986.

DeShazer, Mary K., ed. *The Longman Anthology of Women's Literature.* New York, London and Montreal: Longman, 2001.

Dinesen, Isak. *Letters from Africa, 1914–1931.* Translated by Anne Born and edited by Frans Lasson. London: Weidenfeld & Nicolson, 1978.

Drabble, Margaret. *The Gates of Ivory.* London: Viking, 1991.

———. *The Millstone.* Harmondsworth: Penguin Books, 1965.

———. *The Middle Ground.* London: Weidenfeld & Nicolson, 1980.

Draine, Betsy. *Substance under Pressure: Artistic Coherence and Evolving Form in the Novels of Doris Lessing.* Wisconsin: University of Wisconsin Press, 1983.

DuPlessis, Rachel Blau. *Writing Beyond the Ending: Narrative Strategies of Twentieth-Century Women Writers.* Bloomington: University of Indiana Press, 1985.

Dyhouse, Carol. *Feminism and the Family in England, 1880–1939.* Oxford: Basil Blackwell, 1989.

Eagleton, Terry. *The English Novel: An Introduction.* Malden, Oxford and Carlton: Blackwell Publishing, 2005.

Eagleton, Terry. *The Function of Criticism*. London: Verso, 1984.

El Guindi, Fadwa. *Veil: Modesty, Privacy and Resistance*. New York and Oxford: Berg Publishers, 1999.

Essed, Philomena, David Theo Goldberg, and Audrey Kobashi, eds. *A Companion to Gender Studies*. Malden, Oxford and Carlton: Blackwell Publishing, 2005.

Evans, Mary, ed. *Feminism: Critical Concepts in Literary and Cultural Studies*. 4 vols. London and New York: Routledge, 2001.

———. *Introducing Contemporary Feminist Thought*. Oxford, Cambridge and Malden: Polity Press, 1997.

Fahim, Shadia S. *Doris Lessing and Sufi Equilibrium: The Evolving Form of the Novel*. New York: St. Martin's Press, 1994.

Faludi, Susan. *Backlash: The Undeclared War Against American Women*. New York and London: Anchor Books Doubleday, 1991.

Fanon, Frantz. *Black Skin, White Masks*. Translated by Charles Lam Markmann. New York: Grove Press, 1967.

Felski, Rita. *The Gender of Modernity*. Cambridge, Massachusetts and London, England: Harvard University Press, 1995.

Fishburn, Katherine. *The Unexpected Universe of Doris Lessing: A Study in Narrative Technique*. Westport: Greenwood Press, 1985.

Flaubert, Gustave. *Madame Bovary*. 1856. New York: W.W. Norton & Company, 2005.

Ford, Boris, ed. *The Modern Age*. Vol. 7 of *The Pelican Guide to English Literature*. Harmondsworth: Penguin Books, 1961.

Forster, E.M. *A Passage to India*. Harmondsworth: Penguin Books, 1936.

French, Marilyn. *Beyond Power: On Women, Men, and Morals*. New York: Ballantine Books, 1985.

Friedan, Betty. *The Feminine Mystique*. New York: W.W. Norton & Company, 1963.

———. *The Fountain of Age*. London: Vintage, 1994.

Fullbrook, Kate. *Free Women: Ethics and Aesthetics in Twentieth-Century Women's Fiction*. New York and London: Harvester Wheatsheaf, 1990.

Galin, Muge. *Between East and West: Sufism in the Novels of Doris Lessing*. Albany, New York: State University of New York Press, 1997.

Gamble, Sarah, ed. *The Routledge Companion to Feminism and Postfeminism*. New York and London: Routledge, 2001.

Gardiner, Judith Kegan. *Rhys, Stead, Lessing, and the Politics of Empathy*. Bloomington: Indiana University Press, 1989.

Gilligan, Carol. *In a Different Voice: Psychological Theory and Women's Development*. Massachusetts and London: Harvard University Press, 1982.

Gindin, James. *Postwar British Fiction: New Accents and Attitudes*. Connecticut: Greenwood Press, 1962.

Gordon, Lewis R., T. Denean Sharpley-Whiting, and Renée T. White, eds. *Fanon: A Critical Reader*. Oxford and Cambridge, Massachusetts: Blackwell Publishers, 1996.

Green, Martin. *The English Novel in the Twentieth Century: The Doom of Empire*. London: Routledge & Kegan Paul, 1984.

Greene, Gayle. *Doris Lessing: The Poetics of Change*. Ann Arbor: University of Michigan Press, 1994.

Greene, Gayle and Kahn Coppelia, eds. *Making a Difference: Feminist Literary Criticism*. London and New York: Methuen, 1985.

Grimshaw, Jean. *Feminist Philosophers: Women's Perspectives on Philosophical Traditions*. London: Wheatsheaf Books, 1986.

Gould, Carol C., ed. *Key Concepts in Critical Theory: Gender*. New Jersey: Humanities Press, 1997.

Gramsci, Antonio. *Selections from the Prison Notebooks*. 1947. Translated and edited by Quintin Hoare and Geoffrey Nowell Smith. New York: International Publishers, 1971.

Grosz, Elizabeth. *Sexual Subversions: Three French Feminists*. St. Leonards, Australia: Allen & Unwin, 1989.

Gunew, Sneja, ed. *A Reader in Feminist Knowledge*. London and New York: Routledge, 1991.

Hampson, Norman. *A Social History of the French Revolution*. London: Routledge & Kegan Paul, 1963.

Haraway, Donna J. *Simians, Cyborgs, and Women: The Reinvention of Nature*. London and New York: Routledge, 1991.

Hayward, Susan. *Cinema Studies: The Key Concepts*. London and New York: Routledge, 2000.

Hetherington, Penelope. *British Paternalism and Africa, 1920–1940*. London: Frank Cass, 1978.

Higonnet, Margaret R., ed. *Borderwork: Feminist Engagements with Comparative Literature*. Cornell: Cornell University Press, 1994.

Hite, Molly. *The Other Side of the Story: Structures and Strategies of Contemporary Feminist Narratives*. Ithaca: Cornell University Press, 1989.

Hobsbawm, Eric. *The Age of Empire, 1875–1914*. London: Cardinal Books, 1987.

———. *The Age of Extremes: The Short Twentieth Century, 1914–1991*. London: Michael Joseph, 1994.

Holton, Sandra Stanley. *Feminism and Democracy: Women's Suffrage and Reform Politics in Britain, 1900–1918*. Cambridge and New York: Cambridge University Press, 1986.

Hooks, Bell. *Ain't I a Woman: Black Women and Feminism*. Boston: South End Press, 1981.

———. *Talking Back: Thinking Feminist, Thinking Black*. Boston: South End Press, 1989.

Horner, Avril and Angela Keane, eds. *Body Matters: Feminism, Textuality, Corporeality*. Manchester and New York: Manchester University Press, 2000.

Huntington, John. *Rationalizing Genius: Ideological Strategies in the Classic American Science Fiction Short Story*. New Brunswick: Rutgers University Press, 1989.

Jackson, Stevi and Sue Scott, eds. *Feminism and Sexuality: A Reader*. Edinburgh: Edinburgh University Press, 1996.

Jaggar, Alison M. and Iris Marion Young. *A Companion to Feminist Philosophy*. Massachusetts and Oxford: Blackwell Publishers, 2000.

Johnson, Paul, ed. *20th Century Britain: Economic, Cultural and Social Change*. Harlow: Longman, 1994.

Jouve, Nicole Ward. *White Woman Speaks with Forked Tongue: Criticism as Autobiography*. London and New York: Routledge, 1991.

Joyce, James. Dubliners. London: Grant Richards Ltd, 1914. Reprint, Harmondsworth: Penguin Books, 1976.

———. *Portrait of the Artist as a Young Man*. London: Guild Publishing, 1979. First published 1916 in book format by B.W. Huebsch (New York). First British edition published 1917 by the Egoist Press.

———. *Ulysses*. 1922. Harmondsworth: Penguin Books, 1960.

Kaplan, Carey and Ellen Cronan Rose. *The Canon and the Common Reader*. Knoxville: University of Tennessee Press, 1990.

———, eds. *Doris Lessing: The Alchemy of Survival*. Ohio: Ohio University Press, 1988.

Kaplan, Sydney Janet. *Feminine Consciousness in the Modern British Novel*. Urbana: University of Illinois Press, 1975.

Kapungu, Leonard T. *Rhodesia: The Struggle for Freedom*. Maryknoll, New York: Orbis Books, 1974.

Karl, Frederick R. *A Reader's Guide to The Contemporary English Novel*. London: Thames and Hudson, 1963.

Kelly, Linda. *Women of the French Revolution*. London: Hamish Hamilton, 1987.

Kemp, Sandra and Judith Squires, eds. *Feminisms*. Oxford and New York: Oxford University Press, 1997.

Kennedy, Ellen and Susan Mendus, eds. *Women in Western Political Philosophy: Kant to Nietzsche*. Sussex: Wheatsheaf Books, 1987.

Keohane, Nannerl O., Michelle Z. Rosaldo, and Barbara C. Gelpi, eds. *Feminist Theory: A Critique of Ideology*. Sussex: Harvester Press, 1982.

King, Jeannette. *Doris Lessing*. London and New York: Edward Arnold, 1989.

King, Peter. *Twentieth-Century British History Made Simple*. London: W.H. Allen, 1980.

Kirkup, Gill and Laurie S. Keller, eds. *Inventing Women: Science, Technology and Gender*. Oxford: Polity Press, 1992.

Knapp, Mona. *Doris Lessing*. New York: Ungar, 1984.

Krishnan, P. and K. Mahadevan, eds. *The Elderly Population in Developed and Developing World: Policies, Problems and Perspectives*. New Delhi: B.R. Publishing Corporation, 1992.

Kumar, Alka. *Doris Lessing: Journey in Evolution*. New Delhi: Books Plus, 2001.

Lamb, Sarah. *White Saris and Sweet Mangoes: Aging, Gender, and Body in North India*. Berkeley and London: University of California Press, 2000.

Landes, Joan B. *Women and the Public Sphere in the Age of the French Revolution*. Ithaca and London: Cornell University Press, 1988.

Landry, Donna and Gerald Maclean, eds. *Materialist Feminisms*. Massachusetts: Blackwell Publishers, 1993.

Latifa. *My Forbidden Face: Growing Up Under the Taliban; A Young Woman's Story*. 2001. Translated by Lisa Appignanesi. London: Virago, 2002.

Lederman, Muriel and Ingrid Bartsch, eds. *The Gender and Science Reader*. London and New York: Routledge, 2001.

Lenin, Vladimir. *Philosophical Notebooks*. Translated by Clemens Dutt. Vol. 38. Moscow: Progress Publishers, 1961.

Loomba, Ania. *Colonialism/Postcolonialism*. New York: Routledge, 1998.

MacKinnon, Catharine A. *Feminism Unmodified: Discourses on Life and Law*. Massachusetts and London: Harvard University Press, 1987.

Malson, Micheline R., Jean F. O'Barr, Sarah Westphal-Wihl, and Mary Wyer, eds. *Feminist Theory in Practice and Process*. Chicago and London: University of Chicago Press, 1989.

Mama, Amina. *Beyond the Masks: Race, Gender and Subjectivity*. London: Routledge, 1995.

Mamdani, Mahmood. *Citizen and Subject: Contemporary Africa and the Legacy of Late Colonialism*. New Jersey: Princeton University Press, 1996.

Marks, Elaine and Isabella De Courtivron, eds. *New French Feminisms: An Anthology*. London: Harvester Press, 1981.

Martens, Lorna. *The Diary Novel*. London: Cambridge University Press, 1985.

Maslen, Elizabeth. *Doris Lessing*. Plymouth: Northcote House in association with the British Council, 1994.

McClintock, Anne. *Imperial Leather: Race, Gender and Sexuality in the Colonial Contest*. New York and London: Routledge, 1995.

Mernissi, Fatima. *Beyond the Veil: Male–Female Dynamics in Muslim Society*. Cambridge, Massachusetts: Schenkman Publishing Company, 1975. Revised edition, London: Al Saqi Books, 1985.

Meyers, Diana Tietjens. *Feminist Social Thought: A Reader*. New York and London: Routledge, 1997.

Midgley, Claire, ed. *Gender and Imperialism*. Manchester and New York: Manchester University Press, 1998.

Millet, Kate. *Sexual Politics*. London: Abacus Press, 1972. First published 1970 by Doubleday (United States). First British edition published 1971 by Rupert Hart-Davis.

Minogue, Sally, ed. *Problems for Feminist Criticism*. London and New York: Routledge, 1990.

Mitchell, Juliet and Ann Oakley, eds. *What is Feminism?* Oxford, UK: Basil Blackwell, 1986.

Mitchell, Juliet. *Psychoanalysis and Feminism: Freud, Reich, Laing and Women*. New York: Vintage Books, 1975.

———. *Women: The Longest Revolution*. New York: Pantheon Books, 1966.

Rowe, Margaret Moan. *Doris Lessing*. Basingstoke: Macmillan, 1994.

Moi, Toril. *French Feminist Thought: A Reader*. Oxford: Basil Blackwell, 1987.

———. *Sexual/Textual Politics: Feminist Literary Theory*. London and New York: Methuen, 1985.

———. *What Is a Woman? And Other Essays*. Oxford and New York: Oxford University Press, 1999.

Morgan, Robin. *The Anatomy of Freedom; Feminism, Physics, and Global Politics*. New York: Doubleday/Anchor Press, 1982.

———. *The Demon Lover: On the Sexuality of Terrorism*. New York and London: W.W. Norton & Company, 1989.

Mphahlele, Ezekiel. *The African Image*. London: Faber & Faber, 1962.

Murdoch, Iris. *Bruno's Dream*. London: Chatto and Windus, 1969.

Myerhoff, Barbara. *Number Our Days*. New York: Simon and Schuster, 1978.

Nandy, Ashis, ed. *Science, Hegemony and Violence: A Requiem for Modernity*. Delhi and Bombay: Oxford University Press, 1988.

Narayan, Uma and Sandra Harding, eds. *Decentering the Center: Philosophy for a Multicultural, Postcolonial, and Feminist World*. Bloomington and Indianapolis: Indiana University Press, 2000.

Newton, Judith and Deborah Rosenfelt, eds. *Feminist Criticism and Social Change: Sex, Class and Race in Literature and Culture*. New York and London: Methuen, 1985.

Nicholson, Linda, ed. *Feminist Contentions*. New York and London: Routledge, 1995.

Nyatsumba, Kaiser Mabhilidi. *A Vision of Paradise*. Fordsburg: Cosaw, 1991.

Nye, Andrea. *Feminist Theory and The Philosophies of Man*. London and New York: Croom Helm, 1988.

Oakley, Ann. *Woman's Work: The Housewife, Past and Present*. New York: Vintage Books, 1976.

O'Brien, Mary. *Reproducing the World: Essays in Feminist Theory*. San Francisco and London: Westview Press, 1989.

Offen, Karen. *European Feminisms, 1700–1950: A Political History*. California: Stanford University Press, 2000.

Osborne, John. *Look Back in Anger.* London: Faber & Faber, 1957. Reprinted with an introduction by Prashant K. Sinha. New Delhi: Oxford University Press, 2001.

Pateman, Carole and Elizabeth Gross, eds. *Feminist Challenges: Social and Political Theory.* Sydney, London and Boston: Allen & Unwin, 1986.

Paton, Alan. *Cry, the Beloved Country.* New York/London: Charles Scribner's Sons/Jonathan Cape. Reprint, Harmondsworth: Penguin Books, 1958.

Pearce, Malcolm and Geoffrey Stewart. *British Political History, 1867–1990: Democracy and Decline*. London and New York: Routledge, 1992.

Perham, Margery. *Colonial Sequence, 1930–1949: A Chronological Commentary Upon British Colonial Policy Especially in Africa*. London: Methuen, 1967.

Perrakis, Phyllis Sternberg, ed. *Spiritual Exploration in the Works of Doris Lessing*. Westport, CT: Greenwood Press, 1999.

Pickering, Jean. *Understanding Doris Lessing*. Columbia: University of South Carolina Press, 1990.

Plath, Sylvia. *The Bell Jar.* New York: Harper and Row, 1971. First published 1963 by Heinemann, England, under the name of Victoria Lucas.

Purvis, June and Sandra Stanley Holton, eds. *Votes for Women*. London and New York: Routledge, 2000.

Rajan, Rajeswari Sunder. *Real and Imagined Women: Gender, Culture, and Postcolonialism*. London: Routledge, 1993.

———. *The Scandal of the State: Women, Law and Citizenship in Postcolonial India*. New Delhi: Permanent Black, 2003.

Rich, Adrienne. *Adrienne Rich's Poetry and Prose.* Selected and edited by Barbara C. Gelpi and Albert Gelphi. London and New York: W.W. Norton & Company, 1993.

———. *Collected Early Poems, 1950–1970*. London and New York: W.W. Norton & Company, 1993.

———. *On Lies, Secrets and Silence: Selected Prose, 1966–1978*. New York: W.W. Norton & Company, 1979.

Richards, Janet Radcliffe. *The Sceptical Feminist: A Philosophical Enquiry.* Harmondsworth: Pelican Books, 1982. First published 1980 by Routledge & Kegan Paul (United Kingdom).

Robinson, Sally. *Engendering the Subject: Gender and Self-Representation in Contemporary Women's Fiction.* Albany: State University of New York Press, 1991.

Rogers, Cyril A. and C. Frantz. *Racial Themes in Southern Rhodesia: The Attitudes and Behaviour of the White Population.* New Haven and London: Yale University Press, 1962.

Rossi, Alice S., ed. *The Feminist Papers: From Adams to de Beauvoir.* New York: Columbia University Press, 1973. Reprinted with a new preface by Alice S. Rossi. Boston: Northeastern University Press, 1988.

Rothschild, Joan, ed. *Machina Ex Dea: Feminist Perspectives on Technology.* Athene Series. New York: Pergamon Press, 1983.

Rowbotham, Sheila. *A Century of Women: The History of Women in Britain and the United States.* London and New York: Viking Books, 1997. Paperback edition, London and New York: Penguin Books, 1999.

———. *Women in Movement: Feminism and Social Action.* New York and London: Routledge, 1992.

———. *Hidden from History: Rediscovering Women in History From the 17th Century to the Present.* London: Pluto Press, 1973.

———. *Women, Resistance and Revolution: A History of Women and Revolution in the Modern World.* Harmondsworth: Penguin Books, 1972.

Rowbotham, Sheila, Lynne Segal, and Hilary Wainwright. *Beyond Fragments: Feminism and the Making of Socialism.* London: Merlin Press, 1979.

Rowe, Margaret Moan. *Doris Lessing.* Basingstoke: Macmillan, 1994.

Rubenstein, Roberta. *Home Matters: Longing and Belonging, Nostalgia and Mourning in Women's Fiction.* New York and Basingstoke: Palgrave, 2001.

———. *The Novelistic Vision of Doris Lessing: Breaking the Forms of Consciousness.* Urbana: University of Illinois Press, 1979.

Russ, Joanna. *How to Suppress Women's Writing.* London: The Women's Press, 1984. First published 1983 by University of Texas Press (Austin).

Sage, Lorna. *Doris Lessing.* London and New York: Methuen, 1983.

Said, Edward W. *Orientalism.* London: Routledge & Kegan Paul, 1978.

Sangari, Kumkum and Sudesh Vaid, eds. *Recasting Women: Essays in Colonial History.* New Delhi: Kali for Women, 1989.

Sasson, Jean P. *Mayada, Daughter of Iraq: One Woman's Survival Under Saddam Hussein.* London and Toronto: Bantam Books, 2004.

———. *Princess: A True Story of Life Behind the Veil.* 1992. London and New York: Bantam Books, 1993.

Saxton, Ruth and Jean Tobin, eds. *Woolf and Lessing: Breaking the Mold.* New York: St. Martin's Press, 1994.

Schechter, Ronald, ed. *The French Revolution: The Essential Readings.* Oxford and Massachusetts: Blackwell Publishing, 2001.

Schreiner, Olive. *The Story of An African Farm.* London: Penguin Books, 1939. Reprint, London, New York and Australia: Penguin Classics, 1986. First published 1883 by Chapman & Hall (Great Britain).

Segal, Lynne. *Why Feminism? Gender, Psychology, Politics.* Cambridge: Polity Press, 1999.

Shanley, Mary Lyndon and Carole Pateman, eds. *Feminist Interpretations and Political Theory.* Oxford: Polity Press, 1991.

Sherry, Ruth. *Studying Women's Writing: An Introduction.* London and New York: Edward Arnold, 1988.

Showalter, Elaine. *A Literature of Their Own: British Women Novelists from Brontë to Lessing.* New Jersey: Princeton University Press, 1977.

———, ed. *The New Feminist Criticism: Essays on Women, Literature, and Theory.* London: Virago Press, 1985.

Singer, June. *Androgyny: Toward a New Theory of Sexuality.* 1976. New York: Anchor Press, 1977.

Smith, David. *Socialist Propaganda in the Twentieth-Century British Novel.* London: Macmillan Press, 1978.

Smith, Dorothy E. *Texts, Facts, and Femininity: Exploring the Relations of Ruling.* London and New York: Routledge, 1990.

Spacks, Patricia Meyer, ed. *Contemporary Women Novelists: A Collection of Critical Essays.* London: Prentice-Hall, 1977.

Spark, Muriel, *Curriculum Vitae: A Volume of Autobiography.* Harmondsworth: Penguin Books, 1992.

———. *The Prime of Miss Jean Brodie.* London: Macmillan, 1961.

Spender, Dale. *Women of Ideas: And What Men Have Done to Them.* London: Routledge & Kegan Paul, 1982.

Spivak, Gayatri Chakravorty. *The Post-Colonial Critic: Interviews, Strategies, Dialogues.* Edited by Sarah Harasym. New York and London: Routledge, 1990.

Sprague, Claire and Virginia Tiger, eds. *Critical Essays on Doris Lessing.* Boston: G.K. Hall & Co., 1986.

Sprague, Claire, ed. *In Pursuit of Doris Lessing: Nine Nations Reading.* London: Palgrave Macmillan, 1990.

———. *Rereading Doris Lessing: Narrative Patterns of Doubling and Repetition.* Chapel Hill: University of North Carolina Press, 1987.

Staley, F. Thomas, ed. *Twentieth-Century Women Novelists.* London and Basingstoke: Macmillan, 1982.

Stevenson, Randall. *The British Novel Since the Thirties: An Introduction.* London: Batsford, 1986.

Still, Judith. *Feminine Economies: Thinking Against the Market in the Enlightenment and the Late Twentieth Century.* Manchester and New York: Manchester University Press, 1997.

Stockwell, Peter. *The Poetics of Science Fiction.* Textual Explorations. Harlow: Longman, 2000.

Stoler, Ann Laura. *Race and the Education of Desire: Foucault's History of Sexuality and the Colonial Order of Things.* Durham and London: Duke University Press, 1995.

Stolte-Heiskanen, Veronica, ed. *Women in Science: Token Women or Gender Equality*? New York: St. Martin's Press, 1991.

Swift, Jonathan. *Gulliver's Travels.* 1726. Great Britain: Viking Penguin, 1981.

Swinfen, Ann. *In Defence of Fantasy: A Study of the Genre in English and American Literature Since 1945.* London: Routledge & Kegan Paul, 1984.

Tanner, Leslie B., ed. *Voices from Women's Liberation.* New York: Mentor Books, 1970.

Taylor, D.J. *After the War: The Novel and English Society Since 1945.* London: Flamingo, 1994. First published 1993 in hardcover by Chatto and Windus.

Taylor, Jenny, ed. *Notebooks/Memoirs/Archives: Reading and Rereading Doris Lessing.* London: Routledge & Kegan Paul, 1982.

Thackeray, William Makepeace. *Vanity Fair.* 1847–1878. Great Britain: Penguin Popular Classics, 1994.

Thébaud, Françoise, ed. *Toward a Cultural Identity in the Twentieth Century.* Vol. 5 of *A History of Women in the West,* edited by Georges Duby and Michelle Perrot. 1994. Cambridge, Massachusetts and London: Harvard University Press, 1996.

Thompson, Henry O., Jan Knappert, and Helen Bell Feddema, eds. *Africa: Land and People.* Delhi: ISPCK, 1995.

Thorpe, Michael. *Doris Lessing's Africa.* Modern African Writers. London: Evans Brothers, 1978.

Thurman, Judith. *Isak Dinesen: The Life of Karen Blixen.* London: Weidenfeld & Nicolson, 1982.

Todorov, Tzvetan. *The Fantastic: A Structural Approach to a Literary Genre.* 1970. Translated by Richard Howard. New York: Cornell University Press, 1975. First published 1970 by Editions du Seuil.

Tolstoy, Leo. *Anna Karenina.* 1877. New York: W.W. Norton & Company, 1995.

———. *War and Peace.* 1869. Translated by Anthony Briggs. London and New York: Penguin Classics, 2007.

Visvanathan, Nalini, Lynn Duggan, Nan Wiegersma, and Laurie Nisonoff, eds. *The Women, Gender & Development Reader*. London: Zed Books, 1997.

Wandor, Michelene, ed. *The Body Politic: Writings from the Women's Liberation Movement in Britain, 1969–1972*. London: Stage I, 1972.

Warhol, Robyn R. and Diane Price Herndl, eds. *Feminisms: An Anthology of Literary Theory and Criticism*. New Brunswick and New Jersey: Rutgers University Press, 1991.

Waugh, Patricia. *Feminine Fictions: Revisiting the Postmodern*. London and New York: Routledge, 1989.

———. *Harvest of the Sixties: English Literature and Its Background, 1960–1990*. Oxford and New York: Oxford University Press, 1995.

Weldon, Fay. *The Life and Loves of a She-Devil*. Great Britain: Hodder and Stoughton, 1983.

Whittaker, Ruth. *Doris Lessing*. New York: St. Martin's Press, 1988.

Wilford, Rick and Robert L. Miller, eds. *Women, Ethnicity and Nationalism: The Politics of Transition*. London and New York: Routledge, 1998.

Winterson, Jeanette. *Oranges Are Not the Only Fruit*. London: Pandora, 1985.

Woolf, Virginia. *A Room of One's Own*. London: Panther Books, 1977. First published 1929 by Hogarth Press (London).

———. *Carlyle's House and Other Sketches*. With a foreword by Doris Lessing. London: Hesperus Press, 2003.

———. *The Common Reader*. London: Hogarth Press, 1925. http://gutenberg.net.au/ebooks03/0300031h.html.

———. *The Common Reader: Second Series*. 1932. London: Hogarth Press, 1935. http://gutenberg.net.au/ebooks03/0301251h.html.

———. *The Pargiters: The Novel-Essay Portion of THE YEARS*. Edited by Mitchell A. Leaska. New York: Harcourt Brace Jovanovich, 1978.

———. *Three Guineas*. London: Hogarth Press, 1938.

———. *A Writer's Diary*. London: Hogarth Press, 1953.

———. *Mrs Dalloway*. London: Hogarth Press, 1925.

Yelin, Louise. *From the Margins of Empire: Christina Stead, Doris Lessing, Nadine Gordimer*. Ithaca and London: Cornell University Press, 1998.

Zeigler, Heide and Christopher Bigsby, eds. *The Radical Imagination and the Liberal Tradition: Interviews with English and American Novelists*. London: Junction Books, 1982.

Journals, Periodicals, Articles, Essays and Interviews

Alcoff, Linda. 'Cultural Feminism versus Post-Structuralism: The Identity Crisis in Feminist Theory.' *Signs* 13, no. 3 (Spring 1988): 405–436.

Allen, Orphia Jane. 'Structure and Motif in Doris Lessing's *A Man and Two Women.*' *Modern Fiction Studies* 26, no. 1 (Spring 1980): 63–74.

As, Berit. 'More Power To Women.' In *Sisterhood Is Global: The International Women's Movement Anthology,* edited by Robin Morgan, 509–514. Garden City and New York: Anchor Press/Doubleday, 1984.

Bazin, Nancy Topping. 'The Moment of Revelation in "Martha Quest" and Comparable Moments by Two Modernists.' *Modern Fiction Studies* 26, no. 1 (Spring 1980): 87–98.

Benjamin, Walter. 'Critique of Violence.' In *One-Way Street and Other Writings,* 132–154. Translated by Edmund Jephcott and Kingsley Shorter. Great Britain: NLB, 1979.

Berets, Ralph. 'A Jungian Interpretation of the Dream Sequence in Doris Lessing's *The Summer Before the Dark.*' *Modern Fiction Studies* 26, no. 1 (Spring 1980): 117–129.

Bergner, Gwen. 'Who Is That Masked Woman? Or, The Role of Gender in Fanon's *Black Skin, White Masks.*' *PMLA* 110, no.1, (January 1995): 75–88.

Bertelsen, Eve. 'Veldtanschauung: Doris Lessing's Savage Africa.' *Modern Fiction Studies* 37, no. 4 (Winter 1991): 647–658.

Bhushan, Chandra. 'Opinion: The clean environment we're enjoying currently will only be short term, without fundamental changes.' TOI Edit Page, *Times of India*, April 25, 2020.

Birke, Lynda and Marsha Henry. 'The Black Hole: Women's Studies, Science and Technology.' In *Introducing Women's Studies: Feminist Theory and Practice,* edited by Victoria Robinson and Diane Richardson, 220–238. Basingstoke and London: Macmillan, 1993.

Bush, Barbara. '"Britain's Conscience on Africa": white women, race and imperial politics in inter-war Britain.' In *Gender and Imperialism*, edited by Claire Midgley, 200–223. Manchester and New York: Manchester University Press, 1998.

Butcher, Margaret K. '"Two forks of a Road": Divergence and Convergence in the Short Stories of Doris Lessing.' *Modern Fiction Studies* 26, no. 1 (Spring 1980): 55–61.

Caine, Barbara. 'Feminism and the Woman Citizen in the Interwar Years.' In *English Feminism, 1780–1980,* 173–221. Oxford: Oxford University Press, 1997.

Carby, Hazel V. 'White Woman Listen! Black Feminism and the Boundaries of Sisterhood.' In *Black British Cultural Studies: A Reader*, edited by Houston A. Baker, Jr, Manthia Diawara, and Ruth. H. Lindeborg, 61–106. Chicago and London: University of Chicago Press, 1996.

Cederstrom, Lorelei. 'Doris Lessing's Use of Satire in *The Summer Before the Dark*.' *Modern Fiction Studies* 26, no.1 (Spring 1980): 131–145.

Coetzee, J.M. 'The Autobiography of Doris Lessing.' In *Stranger Shores: Literary Essays, 1986–1999*, 284–303. London: Secker and Warburg, 2001.

Das, Kamala. 'Love is the Only Ritual I Believe in.' Interview by Priya Pathiyan. *The Times of India*, April 1, 2001.

Davis, Angela Y. 'Complexity, Activism, Optimism: An Interview with Angela Y. Davis.' Interview by Kum-Kum Bhavnani. *Feminist Review*, no. 31 (Spring 1989): 66–81.

Drabble, Margaret. 'Doris Lessing: Cassandra in a World Under Siege.' *Ramparts* 10 (February 1972): 50–53.

Draine, Betsy. 'Nostalgia and Irony: The Postmodern Order of "The Golden Notebook".' *Modern Fiction Studies* 26, no. 1 (Spring 1980): 31–48.

Duyfhuizen, Bernard. 'On the Writing of Future History: Beginning the Ending in Doris Lessing's *The Memoirs Of a Survivor*.' *Modern Fiction Studies* 26, no. 1 (Spring 1980): 147–156.

Eliot, T.S. 'Tradition and Individual Talent.' In *Selected Essays 1917–1932*. London: Faber & Faber, 1932.

Fuoroli, Caryn. 'Doris Lessing's "Game": Referential Language and Fictional Form.' *Twentieth Century Literature* 27, no. 2 (Summer 1981): 146–165.

Gibbons, Fiachra. 'Lay off men, Lessing tells feminists.' *The Guardian*, August 14, 2001. https://www.theguardian.com/uk/2001/aug/14/edinburghfestival2001.edinburghbookfestival2001.

Graham, Ruth. 'Loaves and Liberty: Women in the French Revolution.' In *Becoming Visible: Women in European History*, edited by Renate Bridenthal and Claudia Koonz, 236–253. Boston and London: Houghton Mifflin Company, 1977.

Halliday, Fred. 'Revolution in Afghanistan.' *The New Left Review*, no. 112 (November–December 1978): 3–44.

Horwitz, Rainey. 'Barbara Seaman (1935–2008).' *The Embryo Project Encyclopedia*, May 25, 2018. https://embryo.asu.edu/pages/barbara-seaman-1935-2008.

Hull, Keith N. 'What is Human? Ursula Leguin and Science Fiction's Great Theme,' *Modern Fiction Studies* 32, no. 1 (Spring 1986): 69.

Karkal, Malini. 'Ageing and Women in India.' *The Economic and Political Weekly* 34, no. 44 (October 30, 1999): 54–56.

Kaveney, Roz. 'Return to the Ice Deserts.' Review of *The Story of General Dann and Mara's Daughter, Griot and the Snow Dog*. *The Hindu Literary Review*, Sunday, August 7, 2005.

Kermode, Frank. 'The Bliss of the Big City.' *New York Times Archives*, September 14, 1997.

Keyworth, Florence. 'Invisible Struggles: The Politics of Ageing.' In *Feminism, Culture and Politics*, edited by Rosalind Brunt and Caroline Rowan, 131–142. London: Lawrence and Wishart, 1982.

Kymlicka, Will. 'Feminism.' In *Contemporary Political Philosophy: An Introduction*, 377–430. Oxford and New York: Oxford University Press, 2002.

Lerner, Gerda. 'Chapter Eleven.' In *The Creation of Patriarchy*, 212–229. London: Oxford University Press, 1986.

Lessing, Doris. 'Acknowledging a New Frontier.' Interview by Eve Bertelsen. In *Doris Lessing: Conversations*, edited by Earl G. Ingersoll, 120–145. Princeton: Ontario Review Press, 1994.

———. 'A Notorious Life.' Interview by Dwight Garner. *Salon*, November 12, 1997.

———. 'Doris Lessing: Hot Dawns.' Interview by Harvey Blume. *The Boston Book Review*, 1998. http://mural.uv.es/vemivein/dorisinterviews.html.

———. 'Doris Lessing on Feminism, Communism and "Space Fiction".' Interview by Lesley Hazelton. *The New York Times*, July 25, 1982. https://archive.nytimes.com/www.nytimes.com/books/99/01/10/specials/lessing-space.html?_r=1.

———. 'Life is stronger than fiction—at 76, Doris Lessing wants to be alone.' Interview by Helena de Bertodano. *The Daily Telegraph*, April 11, 1996.

———. 'The Progressive Interview.' Interview by Jonah Raskin. *The Progressive*, June 1999. https://progressive.org/dispatches/doris-lessing-progressive-interview/.

Macdonald, Barbara. 'Outside the Sisterhood: Ageism in Women's Studies.' In *Women and Aging: An Anthology by Women*, edited by Jo Alexander, Debi Berrow, Lisa Domitrovich, Margarita Donnelly et al., 20–25. Corvallis: Calyx Books, 1986.

Mama, Amina. 'Violence against Black Women: Gender, Race and State Responses.' *Feminist Review*, no. 32 (Summer 1989): 35.

Marder, Herbert. 'The Paradox of Form in "The Golden Notebook".' *Modern Fiction Studies* 26, no.1 (Spring 1980): 49–54.

McIntosh, Mary. 'The Family in Socialist-Feminist Politics.' In *Feminism, Culture and Politics*, edited by Rosalind Brunt and Caroline Rowan, 109–130. London: Lawrence and Wishart, 1982.

Mohan, Rajeswari. 'Loving Palestine.' *Interventions* 1, no. 1 (1998): 52–80.

Mohanty, Chandra Talpade. 'Under Western Eyes: Feminist Scholarship and Colonial Discourses.' In *Third World Women and the Politics of Feminism*, edited by Chandra Talpade Mohanty, Ann Russo and Lourdes Torres, 51–80. Bloomington and Indianapolis: Indiana University Press, 1991.

Moi, Toril. 'Men Against Patriarchy.' In *Gender and Theory*, edited by Linda Kauffman, 181–190. Oxford and Massachusetts: Basil Blackwell, 1989.

Moore, Henrietta. 'The Cultural Constitution of Gender.' In *The Polity Reader in Gender Studies*, edited by Polity, 14–21. Cambridge: Polity Press, 1994.

Mulvey, Laura. 'Visual Pleasure and Narrative Cinema.' *Screen* 16, no. 3 (Autumn 1975): 6–18.

Oates, Joyce Carol. 'A Visit with Doris Lessing.' *The Southern Review* 9 (Autumn 1973): 873–882.

Parmar, Pratibha. 'Other Kinds of Dreams.' *Feminist Review*, no. 31 (Spring 1989): 55–65.

Peel, Ellen. 'The Self is Always an Other: Going the Long Way Home to Autobiography.' *Twentieth Century Literature* 35, no. 1 (Spring 1989): 1–16.

Pezzulich, Evelyn. 'Coming of Age: The Emergence of the Aging Female Protagonist in Literature.' *Doris Lessing Studies* 24, nos. 1–2 (Summer/Fall 2004): 7–10.

Pickering, Jean. 'Marxism and Madness: The Two Faces of Doris Lessing's Myth.' *Modern Fiction Studies* 26, no. 1 (Spring 1980): 17–30.

Rege, Josna and Ruth Saxton, eds. 'Coming to Age'. Special issue, *Doris Lessing Studies* 24, nos. 1–2 (Summer/Fall 2004).

Rowe, Margaret Moan. 'Review.' *Modern Fiction Studies* 26, no. 1 (Spring 1980): 163–165.

Roy, Arundhati. 'Democracy: Who's she when she's at home?' *Outlook*, May 6, 2002.

Sarvan, Charles and Liebetraut Sarvan. 'D.H. Lawrence and Doris Lessing's *The Grass is Singing*.' *Modern Fiction Studies* 24, no. 4 (Winter 1978–1979): 533–537.

Scanlan, Margaret. 'Memory and Continuity in the Series Novel: The Example of "Children of Violence".' *Modern Fiction Studies* 26, no. 1 (Spring 1980): 75–85.

Schemo, Diana Jean. 'At The Guggenheim With: Doris Lessing; A Portrait Unwinds, As in Life.' *The New York Times Archive*, November 2, 1994. https://movies2.nytimes.com/books/99/01/10/specials/lessing-guggenheim.html.

Schweickart, Patrocinio P. 'Reading a Wordless Statement: The Structure of Doris Lessing's *The Golden Notebook*.' *Modern Fiction Studies* 31, no. 2 (Summer 1985): 263–279.

Scott, Joan W. 'Women's History.' In *New Perspectives on Historical Writing*, edited by Peter Burke, 42–66. Cambridge: Polity Press, 1991.

———. 'Gender: A Useful Category of Historical Analysis.' *The American Historical Review* 91, no. 5 (December 1986): 1053–1075.

Scott, Lynda. 'Similarities Between Virginia Woolf and Doris Lessing.' *Deep South* 3, no. 2 (Winter 1997): 42–66. https://www.otago.ac.nz/deepsouth/vol3no2/scott.html.

———. 'Lessing's Early and Transitional Novels: The Beginnings of a Sense of Selfhood.' *Deep South* 4, no. 1 (Autumn 1998). https://www.otago.ac.nz/deepsouth/0498/0498lynda.htm.

Seligman, Dee. 'The Four Faced Novelist.' *Modern Fiction Studies* 26, no. 1 (Spring 1980): 2–16.

Sharma, Kalpana. 'Egypt's Face of Courage.' *The Hindu Magazine*, Sunday, June 3, 2001.

Sprague, Claire. '"Without Contraries is No Progression": *Lessing's The Four Gated City*.' *Modern Fiction Studies* 26, no. 1 (Spring 1980): 99–116.

Sullivan, Alvin. '*The Memoirs of a Survivor*: Lessing's Notes Toward a Supreme Fiction.' *Modern Fiction Studies* 26, no. 1 (Spring 1980): 157–165.

Suroor, Hasan. 'A Feminist Rallies Behind Men.' *The Hindu*, August 16, 2001.

Taylor, J. Douglas Allen. 'Novelist and short-story writer Octavia Butler defies categories.' *Metro,* January 4–10, 1996. http://www.metroactive.com/papers/metro/01.04.96/books-9601.html.

Tiger, Virginia. '"Taking Hands and Dancing in (Dis)unity": Story to Storied in Doris Lessing's "To Room Nineteen" And "A Room."' *Modern Fiction Studies* 36, no. 3 (Autumn 1990): 421–433.

Townsend, Peter. 'The structured dependency of the elderly.' In *The Peter Townsend Reader*, edited by The Policy Press, 449–464. Bristol: The Policy Press, 2010.

Venkataraman, M.S. 'The Age-Old Problem.' *The Hindu Folio*, October 18, 1998.

Visvanathan, Susan. 'Women and Work: From Houswifisation to Androgyny.' *Economic and Political Weekly* 31, nos. 45–46 (November 1996): 3015–3017 and 3019–3020.

Westfahl, Gary. 'Janeways and Thaneways; the Better Half, and Worse Half, of Science Fiction Television.' *Interzone*, no. 140 (February 1999): 31–33.

Winterson, Jeanette. 'What planet is Doris on?' *The Guardian,* August 15, 2001. https://www.theguardian.com/books/2001/aug/15/edinburghfestival2001.edinburghfestival.

Index

G

Y

Z

Y

Z

About the Author

Ratna Raman is Associate Professor at Sri Venkateswara College, University of Delhi, where she teaches English language and literature to undergraduate and graduate students. A student of Delhi University, she has been teaching for over three and a half decades and remains deeply involved in the pursuit of learning. The joy of classroom interactions with undergraduate students has been central to her life as a university teacher. She has also presented papers at international conferences and seminars.

She has reviewed books and films for Indian newspapers, news magazines, journals, and has published several short stories and articles on subjects ranging from literature, poetry, women's rights, travel, food journeys and significant events in contemporary culture, such as Jallikattu, the opening up of Sabarimala to women, as well as the Me Too Movement of 2018 in *Hardnews*, a newsmagazine with an international presence, also available online.

Her weekly column 'Mind Your Language' for the *Tribune*, Chandigarh, from November 2014 to March 2017, discussed language and grammar through the use of words from everyday contexts, and she provided regular commentary on the sociocultural and political scenario in India and the world. Her own blog at ratnaraman.blogspot.in voices her own opinions on various issues and occasionally features her published articles.

Her areas of academic interest centre around 19th-century literature and 20th-century novels, women's representation and contemporary fiction.

She is convinced that if Indians were to replace the culture of solely growing exotic ornamental plants in private homes and gardens with local species and support the practice of growing fruits and vegetables in kitchen gardens, on walls or terraces for everyday consumption, this ground-level effort will contribute enormously to the general health and well-being and transform local habitat and environment.